BEAT THE HEAT OF SUMMER
WITH A REFRESHING
CURAÇAO COOLER.
UNWIND ON THE NINETEENTH HOLE
WITH A BRACING
MINTED GIN.
TITILLATE YOUR TASTE BUDS
WITH ONE OF TWENTY
MARTINI
VARIATIONS.
INDULGE YOUR SWEET TOOTH
WITH A SINFULLY DELICIOUS
CHOCOLATE BLACK RUSSIAN.
DAZZLE YOUR GUESTS WITH
A FESTIVE, FLAMING
CAFÉ DIABLE.
TREAT YOUR CELEBRATION CROWD
TO A COLD
APPLE GINGER PUNCH
OR A HOT
MULLED CLARET.
TRANQUILIZE YOURSELF
THE MORNING AFTER
WITH A SOOTHING
FRENCH PICK-ME-UP.

PLAYBOY'S
NEW BAR GUIDE

offers you recipes for these
and many, many more drinks
— for any occasion, any mood —
plus all the basic know-how needed
to transform the novice home bartender
into a knowledgeable mixologist.

Most Jove Books are available at special quantity discounts for bulk purchases for sales promotions, premiums, fund raising, or educational use. Special books or book excerpts can also be created to fit specific needs.

For details, write or telephone Special Sales Markets, The Berkley Publishing Group, 200 Madison Avenue, New York, New York 10016; (212) 686-9820.

PLAYBOY'S NEW BAR GUIDE

THOMAS MARIO

A JOVE BOOK

Portions of this book originally appeared in PLAYBOY magazine:
Copyright © 1954, 1955, 1956, 1957, 1958, 1959, 1960, 1961, 1972
by Playboy. Other portions originally appeared in PLAYBOY'S
New Host & Bar Book: Copyright © 1971, 1979 by Thomas Mario.

PLAYBOY'S NEW BAR GUIDE

A Jove Book / published by arrangement with
the author

PRINTING HISTORY
Playboy Paperbacks edition / September 1982
PBJ edition / December 1982
Jove edition / May 1983
Sixth printing / May 1986

All rights reserved.
Copyright © 1982 by Thomas Mario
Cover photo copyright © 1962 by PBJ Books, Inc.,
formerly PEI Books, Inc.
This book may not be reproduced in whole or in part,
by mimeograph or any other means, without permission.
For information address: The Berkley Publishing Group,
200 Madison Avenue, New York, N.Y. 10016.

ISBN: 0-515-08889-7

Jove Books are published by The Berkley Publishing Group,
200 Madison Avenue, New York, N.Y. 10016.
The words "A JOVE BOOK" and the "J" with sunburst
are trademarks belonging to Jove Publications, Inc.

PRINTED IN THE UNITED STATES OF AMERICA

CONTENTS

THE CONTEMPORARY HOST AND HIS HOME BAR 7

Stocking the Bar 12
Understanding Spirits 16
Accessories to Alcohol 25
Glassware 27
Tools for the Bar 30
Barmanship 33
Bar Measurements 39
Party Drinking 42

WINES 47

Exploring Wines 48
Wine Tasting 50
Serving Wine 52
Wine Dictionary 56

COCKTAILS 79

After-Dinner Cocktails 83
Aperitifs 105

    Apple-Brandy Cocktails   *116*
    Brandy Cocktails   *122*
    Champagne Cocktails   *135*
    Gin Cocktails   *139*
    Rum Cocktails   *163*
    Tequila Cocktails   *188*
    Vodka Cocktails   *197*
    Whiskey Cocktails   *205*
    Wine Cocktails   *221*
    Miscellaneous Cocktails   *226*

HIGH SPIRITS   *235*

    Bucks   *239*
    Cobblers   *242*
    Collinses   *246*
    Coolers—Miscellaneous Tall Drinks   *250*
    Daisies   *318*
    Fixes   *321*
    Fizzes   *325*
    Rickeys   *335*
    Sangarees   *339*

ODDBALLS   *343*

    Flips   *345*
    Mists   *349*
    Pick-Me-Ups   *351*

THE BRIMMING BOWL   *355*

HOT CHEER   *371*

INDEX   *389*

THE CONTEMPORARY HOST
AND HIS HOME BAR

The drink oft proclaims the host.

Some hosts are content to offer any swig to their guests, as long as it provides a passing sensation of alcohol in the body. Others know that superb spirits and fine wines, like the best examples of the culinary arts, are carefully chosen, skillfully served, and remembered with vivid pleasure.

Drinking styles change or they wouldn't be styles. Eleven years ago, when *Playboy's Bar Guide* was first published, no host would have thwarted his guests at a business lunch by offering cold white wine instead of the obligatory stiff martini, nor would he have dreamed that one day one of the most popular liqueurs for sipping after the meal would be a nectar from Ireland whose principal flavor was based on fresh dairy cream, of all things, bottled at an incredibly low 34 proof.

Over the centuries, changes in mixed drinks have been radical and never-ending. While Commodus, the Roman emperor, enjoyed his customary red wine mixed with lemon juice and dried adder, compounded by a bartender who, significantly, was also Commodus's physician, today dried adder has obviously lost its esteem as a staple bar ingredient. Sir Walter Raleigh's sack posset, made with sherry, ale, cream, sugar, mace, and nutmeg, sounds plausible for bibulous knights in the dank castles of Elizabethan England, but Sir Walter's famed drink mixture took from two to three hours' simmering on the fire before it was ready for drinking, a delay hardly advised nowadays for an *après-ski* party of thirsty drinkers gathered round a roaring fireplace.

Modern mixed drinks have created what distillerymen call the white-goods era, one in which white or nearly white spirits—vodka, light rum, tequila, and gin—have nosed out, though not demolished by any means, the once-heavy bourbons, Scotches, brandies, and demon rums. As though moved along by the white-spirits blitz, wine drinkers have been happily jugging it up with cold white wines from California Chablis to German Liebfraumilch.

When you consider the stylish spirits of our times, you see in all of them a common element: their fascinating endless mixability. Here and there you may find an isolated guzzler who sneaks in a shot of neat vodka during his morning coffee break, in the misguided notion that vodka is breathless and hopefully undetectable, but anyone who remembers when vodka was first introduced to the United States in the forties will also remember the hordes of people who quickly adopted the new white spirits not because they loved liquor less, but because they loved orange juice more. When hosts and bartenders discovered that vodka could sail beautifully in the same boat with mixers as different as ginger beer and beef bouillon, they began creating, and are still imaginatively creating, drink combinations for those who appreciate the nuances of flavor rather than just a flash of lightning in the mouth.

White or light rum, now in such high esteem, is sometimes described as vodka with a rummy accent, providing just enough of a lightly coaxing rum taste to suggest the accompaniment of limes, mangoes, bananas, papayas, guavas, and other fragrances and flavors of the tropics. Even tequila, which isn't neutral in flavor but is now infinitely more gentle than the skullpopping mescal one used to encounter in rural Mexico, finds its way into countless mixed drinks, from brave bulls to vampiros.

If there are somewhat fewer gin mixed drinks than others in the contemporaneous world of liquid white goods, the reason is obvious. Plain gin as it comes from the bottle is, in effect, an elaborate mixed drink. In making gin, the distilleryman starts with a neutral base of spirits, something similar to vodka, which is then redistilled with a piquant mixture of sometimes a dozen aromatics, the principal one of which is juniper berries supplemented with angelica root, aniseed, cinnamon bark, coriander, orange and lemon peel, and other flavors. Each gin maker guards his own secret formula. The simple combination of ingredients, therefore, that goes into a conventional gin drink such as a martini or a tom collins actually contains an elaborate medley of flavors.

Recently, liqueur sales have been flaring up like rockets in the spirits world. Some liqueurs are enjoyed straight; others, from simple fruit liqueurs such as banana or blackberry to complex specimens made with a dazzling variety of herbs and spices, are often mixed with other spirits, fruit juices, or cream in sumptuous after-dinner cocktails, taking the place of pastries or other desserts at party dinner tables.

All of this isn't an argument to prove that people are no longer sipping bourbons, Scotches, and brandies straight or in highballs. One has only to walk into a liquor shop to see the shelf space occupied by the blended whiskeys, straight bourbons, California brandies, cognacs, and dark rums from the Caribbean to verify that whiskey on the rocks or brandy in a balloon glass is very much alive and appreciated. In recent years, however, most of the dark-brown spirits have been modified in flavor and bottled at lower proofs, taking on a new velvety mien, with the result that they, too, are now eminently mixable.

When Prohibition was ended in the thirties, whiskey drinkers, liberated from bathtub gin, needle beer, and other atrocities of the dry era, would stroll into bars and frequently call for the popular old-fashioned cocktail: whiskey on the rocks, mixed with bitters and sugar, and sometimes garnished with fruit. The whiskey could be any kind of legal firewater as long as it was deep mahogany brown, often made that way with the addition of caramel color. Present-day drinkers are still asking for old-fashioneds, but, unlike the earlier generation, they enjoy their whiskey connoisseurship by ordering the old-fashioned made with this brand of blended whiskey or that brand of bourbon or with the almost rare genuine rye whiskey or with one of the Tennessee, Irish, Scotch, Canadian, or Japanese whiskies—which classifications, by the way, are all described in the "Understanding Spirits" glossary, pages 18–24.

When young men and women plan a get-together, something instinctively tells them that, no matter how much money is spent on the preparations, the one indispensable ingredient from which the party must draw its fun is imagination and that, therefore, as surely as the champagne bubbles follow the drawn cork, the best way of inaugurating a memorable party is to include a new drink recipe.

Imagination can deceive you if you think that just throwing together a hodgepodge of spirits and juices will create a rich, exciting bowl of wassail. When you contemplate serving a new drink, you should try it long before partytime. The ingredients should be precisely measured, made with the best available spirits, carefully stirred, shaken, or brewed, poured into the same glass in which the drink will be served, and made to stand the test of your own eyes, nose, and tastebuds. Invariably when guests are given such an offering, they don't just sniff and sip it like something to be scored from one to ten but, like good trenchermen, hail it as they would a new dish at your buffet or dinner table by asking for more.

Good hosting means knowing how to stock your bar, what tools and glassware you'll need, familiarity with the techniques of professional mixing or barmanship, knowing how to calculate the number of bottles needed for party drinking, and being well grounded both in the main types of important wines and the practical guides for serving wines. Gearing up to those needs and current trends, the sections that follow provide guidance not only for party hosts but for those who enjoy drinking and dining *intime*.

Many of the more than 1000 drinks in this new, enlarged edition appeared in the nation's outstanding festival of youth, PLAYBOY magazine.

Stocking the Bar

Starting from scratch, there are three trustworthy guides in stocking a liquor cabinet. First, you should be able to draw upon your bar for those liquid goods needed for the popular drinks of the day. At one time, any host who kept whiskey, gin, and vermouth on hand could satisfy the great majority of guests, who routinely called for manhattans, martinis, or highballs. Now, faster than you can say either screwdriver, daiquiri, or margarita, you realize that in addition to the old standbys you should have vodka, light rum, and tequila as essential wellsprings for both casual drop-ins and party entertainment. Secondly, you should stock those liquors that may be heavily favored in your neck of the woods. There are bourbon towns, Scotch suburbia, and Pernod purlieus where one liquor or another or even a heavily favored brand has become the darling of the local spirit gods and therefore belongs in your inventory. Finally, as a host, you may have developed certain mixed drinks as specialties of your bar repertoire. You may be renowned, for instance, for your planter's punch, for which you'd need heavy Jamaica rum, or for stingers, for which you'd need white crème de menthe, neither of which is included in the basic list below.

A typical supply, assuming you're planning for the first time to stock a home bar, would include:

3 vodka
2 bourbon
2 blended whiskey, U.S.
2 Scotch
1 Irish whiskey
1 Canadian whisky
2 gin
2 light rum
2 tequila
1 dry vermouth
1 sweet vermouth
1 brandy, U.S.
3 assorted liqueurs (fruit, coffee, Galliano, etc.)

The above list is a reasonable beginning, not a dogmatic roll call. The two vermouths, generally used as mixers, will quickly suggest to many people one or several of the aperitif wines, such as Dubonnet, Lillet, or Punt e Mes. If you savor the prestige Scotches, you'll want to supplement your inventory with a twelve-year-old Scotch or one of the great single-malt Scotches. If you find pleasure in an after-dinner brandy in addition to a brandy for mixed drinks, you'll acquire one of the eminent cognacs.

A special word about liqueurs and the almost bewildering variety now available in this country from all over the world: For hosts who don't have the shelf room to store a wide assortment of liqueurs, the compartmented liqueur bottle containing from two to four assorted liqueurs is a convenient asset. If there's a new domestic or imported liqueur that seems intriguing but whose flavor is unknown to you, buy the miniature 50-milliliter (1.7-ounce) size for taste exploration before you invest in a larger bottle. Often you'll want to keep as a basic bar item a liqueur for use in a mixed drink. A host who frequently serves margaritas, for example, will need a bottle of Triple Sec or some other orange liqueur. If you enjoy orange liqueur straight, you may want to consider one of the prestigious imports such as Cointreau or Grand Marnier. There are vogues in liqueurs, and two that have soared to conspicuous success in recent years are the rich Irish cream liqueurs and the amarettos with their full-bodied almond flavor.

No basic bar can be considered complete these days

without white wine. Like a tidal wave showing no signs of receding, white wine has not only swept aside the businessman's martini at the noontime luncheon but is now at the top of the tree at many a sundown celebration. It needn't be the kind of costly vintage that you'd serve as a conversation piece for wine savants at the dinner table, but it should have the appetite-provoking effect of a wine that's bone-dry or at least on the dry side. If it's a jug wine, it can be stored in the liquor cabinet along with your spirits. If it's a liter bottle or smaller and the closure is a cork, it should be stored on its side in a wine rack. Remember that white wine should be chilled an hour or two before it's poured.

Among California whites, Chablis (the generic type, not to be confused with Chablis from France, a very different wine) seems to be completely on the beam with most of the white-wine crowd at the cocktail hour. If you want to serve a white wine with more character, the California Chenin Blancs, dry Semillons, and dry Sauvignon Blancs are all pleasant, and many of them are distinguished. While dryness is the quality that lures most Americans to preprandial white wines, large numbers are obviously happy with the semi-dry fruity wines made in the German style, such as the generic Rhine wines, Rieslings, Gray Rieslings, and Sylvaners. Finally, for those who prefer a dry white wine with a distinctive mouth-filling flavor, Pinot Chardonnays, especially those from some of the smaller "boutique" wineries in California, may be served either before or with dinner for guests who appreciatively drink the more expensive aged white wines.

Among the reasonably priced imported dry white wines from France for serving at the cocktail hour, Bordeaux Supérieur, Bordeaux Blanc, and Muscadet from the Loire region are usually crisp and lively. If you lean to the Italian whites, Soave and Frascati (the *secco*, or dry, type of the latter) are refreshing.

Having stocked your bar, you may consider whether any of the imposing list of bottled premixed cocktails would be useful. At the end of a long, dusty day, you may not have fresh lemons for your tom-collins thirst. On long boat trips, in cramped galley quarters, at wayside picnics, for tailgate parties at football or ski sites, the premixed party-mates are most welcome, but the fact is that little labor is saved by using them. If you're serving a bottled martini, for example, you still have to prechill the glasses, take ice out of the freezer, stir the makings in a shaker, pour the drinks, and adorn each martini with an olive or a lemon twist. The quality of premixed spirits varies considerably. Bottled manhattans, in which whiskey and vermouth are not only mingled but married by long blending, may be superior to some freshly mixed manhattans; but all those drinks that contain fruit juices can't begin to match the fresh. Be as selective about the premixes you purchase as you are about the appropriate occasions to serve them. For most purposes, and people, it's more fitting (and more fun) to do it yourself.

It's well for hosts to remember when restocking their bar that spirits do *not* improve in flavor *in the bottle,* unlike some expensive table wines that depend upon bottle aging for their flavor development. Once opened, spirits don't spoil quickly. If the opened bottles, however, are kept to the aged-in-the-coffin stage, the contents may deteriorate noticeably. Unlike an old rock collection, your spirits aren't to be preserved like dusty museum pieces. The best thing you can do to keep your spirits up, once they're opened, is to drink them.

Understanding Spirits

Many a man stocking his liquor cabinet finds himself befuddled, not with strong drink, but by the illusory names of the spirits he buys. Hosts looking for the best spirits available learn that the costly Tennessee sour mash whiskey isn't sour at all, that the bottle of elegant *grande champagne* cognac neither is made with nor tastes like champagne, and that the imposing bottle of liqueur Scotch has absolutely none of the identifiable sweetness of a liqueur.

Some of the jumble of liquor terminology is due to the built-in lethargy of language. A word once used, even though its meaning has been changed, goes on being used. An outstanding example: drinkers call for rye and ginger ale in bars or go into a liquor store asking for a bottle of rye, when what they really mean is not the old-fashioned genuine rye whiskey, which has almost disappeared from the market, but U.S. blended whiskey described below. Or they continue to ask bartenders for a very dry martini, meaning, not one that is drier in the correct sense that it's less sweet, but a martini that has more gin and therefore less dry vermouth than might otherwise be used. The stubborn momentum of spirit legends continues to ascribe explosive qualities to certain spirits such as tequila or white corn whiskey, myths that can be instantly dispelled by simply reading the proofs on liquor bottles and understanding that 80-proof tequila carries no more of a jolt than 80-proof vodka or 80-proof slivovitz.

The best way to clarify the names spirits go by as well as to understand the jargon distillerymen and barflies use when they talk about different types of spirits is to draw a brief profile of the steps in making vodka, the most popular spirits in the U.S. Keep in mind that in the land of the free, vodkamen may vary their techniques only in minor details. All must comply with federally mandated regulations that apply to all types of distilled beverage spirits. It's as if a government agent were bending over a chef's shoulder, saying, "Be as creative as you wish with that recipe, as long as you comply strictly with our four pages of fine-print regulations."

Vodka begins with chopped grain and water cooked together, called a mash. The grain is usually corn and not the legendary potatoes, except in some primitive stills in eastern Europe. Malt (sprouted barley) is added, turning the corn's starch to sugar. Yeast ferments it, resulting in a liquid with a small amount of alcohol and a large amount of water. Heat distills it, first vaporizing it and then condensing it, into a liquid with a large amount of alcohol and a small amount of water. The distilled product is called neutral spirits. It's neutral in the sense that it has little color, little flavor, and little aroma but is at least 95 percent alcohol. Instead of 95 percent alcohol, you could say 190 proof, since the term *proof* in this country is always twice the alcoholic content. Before neutral spirits becomes vodka, it's strained through charcoal or other finishing material to reduce vestiges of flavor, color, or aroma. Finally, before vodka is bottled, water is reintroduced to bring it to bottling strength, from a minimum of 80 proof to approximately 100 proof, a range that, incidentally, is the proof spread of most distilled spirits in bottle shops, with the exception of liqueurs.

To throw light on spirits other than vodka, consider these four pointers:

1. If spirits are distilled at proofs somewhat lower than 190, a noticeable amount of flavor remains. It's like a steak that is broiled well done but still retains identifiable beef juices.

2. If they're distilled at proofs lower than 160, still more

flavor—something approaching bourbon—is the result. A steak cooked medium rare.

3. If they're distilled in an old-fashioned pot still, a device that looks like a huge tea kettle with a fire beneath it, in which one batch of mash at a time is distilled, instead of the modern column or continuous still in which a continuous flow of mash is vaporized by steam, the proof is generally still lower, the flavor more rugged and intense. A steak bloody rare, with the juices flowing copiously. Remember the pot still when you think of certain full-flavored spirits such as unblended Scotches, cognacs, and tequila.

4. If distilled spirits are stored in casks of oak or other wood, they eventually pick up flavor, aroma, and color from the wood. New casks that are charred inside produce still more flavor.

With this orientation, the glossary that now follows should help cut through the fog of drink terminology and nail down the meaning of the important terms in today's world of spirits.

Grain spirits. Neutral spirits stored in oak containers. You're not likely to see a bottle labeled "Grain Spirits" in your liquor store. The term, however, is widely used by liquor dealers, distillers, and others. You may run across it on bottle labels listing the contents of certain spirit blends.

Bourbon. Spirits made from a mash containing at least 51 percent corn. Normally about 60 percent corn is used. Balance of the grain consists of rye and barley. Supposedly first made by a Baptist clergyman, the Reverend Elijah Craig, in Bourbon County, Kentucky, in 1789. Must be distilled at 160 proof or less and stored at no more than 125 proof in charred new oak containers.

Straight bourbon. Bourbon stored no less than two years in wood. In actual practice, the well-known straight bourbons are stored from at least four years to six years or more before bottling. Most prestigious of U.S. whiskeys.

Corn whiskey. Whiskey distilled at less than 160 proof from a mash containing at least 80 percent corn. Need not be aged or may be aged in uncharred or new wood containers. Most of it sold for spirit bibbing in the Deep South.

Rye whiskey. Made in the same way as bourbon, except that the mash contains at least 51 percent rye.

Straight rye. Like bourbon, must be aged at least two years. Actual age more likely to be at least four years. Outside of a few illustrious brands such as Old Overholt, rye whiskeys are a small minority in the whiskey hierarchy.

Blends of straight whiskey. Two or more straights united to combine their best features—some for mellowness, some for body, some for aroma.

Bottled-in-bond whiskey. Straight whiskey at least four years old, bottled at 100 proof, produced in a single distillery in one year, kept under "bond," or lock and key, in hands of federal agents. Bottled-in-bond is not necessarily superior to other straight whiskeys of 100 proof. Recognized by green rather than red stamp on bottle neck. Represents small segment of U.S. whiskey sales.

Light whiskey. Whiskey with corn as its principal ingredient, distilled between 161 and 189 proofs, may be aged in used wooden containers with no minimum age requirements. New type of U.S. whiskey, first produced in 1968. Only a few brands have proved popular. May be used as one of the components in U.S. blended whiskey, below.

U.S. blended whiskey. Next to straight bourbon, the most popular and best-selling whiskey. Often misnomered rye. By definition, a blend of at least 20 percent straight whiskey and balance of neutral spirits or whiskey. In actual practice, best blends contain about one-third straight whiskey and balance of neutral spirits, grain spirits, or light whiskeys.

Sour mash whiskey. Almost all U.S. whiskeys include *some* sour mash in their production. You will look in vain for a *sweet mash* whiskey. The term *sour mash* refers to a step in the fermentation process in which some of the fermented (therefore sour) mash from a previous run of whiskey—sometimes up to 25 percent—is used as a portion of the new batch headed for distillation. It's the kind of leftover that up- rather than downgrades flavor, like a baker's using some of a previously made sourdough for his sour rye bread. It doesn't mean that the end product—the whiskey in the bottle—has sour overtones in its flavor. When the term *sour mash* appears on a label, it means that more than the average amount was used. If the label says, "Old-Time Sour Mash," "Old-fashioned Sour Mash," or "Genuine Sour Mash," it indicates that the whiskey contains at least 50 percent mash from a previous run and that the flavor is uniquely heavy.

Tennessee whiskey. Whiskey distilled in Tennessee, usually straight bourbon, famed for mellowness brought about by slow filtering through special charcoal of Tennessee maple.

Canadian whisky. Canadian distillers, unhampered by U.S. federal regulations, which mandate grain requirements, types of wood, age, etc., for U.S. whiskeys, produce whiskies whose famed lightness and delicacy are distinctively Canadian—whiskies that are equally good for sipping straight or for mixing. Principal grains are rye, corn, and barley. Proportions used by each distillery are, naturally, kept under safe cover. Minimum age is three years; actual age, six years or older. Note: Canadians, like Scotsmen, spell their whisky without an *e*.

Scotch whisky. Whisky from Scotland, made in compliance with laws of the United Kingdom. Distinctive flavor depends upon barley rather than American corn.

Scotch single malts. Cream of the Scotch sipping whiskies, made in the Scottish Highlands, produced in old-fashioned pot stills, product of one distillery. Flavor of barley with vivid aftertaste is brought about by smoking barley over peat fires before barley is made into mash. Flavor differences of various single malts due not only to techniques of distillerymen but to waters of local Highland streams upon which each distillery depends.

Scotch blended whisky. By all odds, the greatest number of Scotches coming to the U.S. are blended whisky, that is, mixtures of single malt whiskies and their smoky flavors blended with grain spirits in which corn is the principal ingredient. Produced in column stills. Though many Scotch labels indicate no age, minimum is four years; average, between five and seven years. Prestige Scotches known for flavor and satiny smoothness are twelve years old or older.

Liqueur Scotch whisky. A term distillers use on labels for certain expensive Scotch whiskies of more than average age. The whisky has no resemblance to a sweet liqueur. The term may be a hangover from medieval times when spirits, some of which were sweet, distilled by alchemists, were intended to transmute base metals into gold; hence something very valuable, hence the gilt-edged potation called liqueur Scotch.

Irish whiskey. Like Scotch, the special flavor of Irish whiskey depends upon barley for its principal flavor component. Unlike Scotch, however, its barley is not smoked over peat and, therefore, its distinctive mellowness, sometimes described as regal, makes it especially useful in mixed drinks from icy cocktails to mulled winter libations. Modern Irish whiskeys, unlike their pot-stilled ancestors, are blends of spirits produced in both pot and column stills.

Japanese whisky. Oriental Scotch. Made from peat-smoked barley in huge, modern pot stills and blended with grain spirits from column stills. Youngest age is four years. Balanced flavor, less doughty than Scotch from Scotland. Leaves gentle but vivid aftertaste.

Gin. Unaged spirits made from grain in column stills. Flavored with juniper berries and other aromatics. May be made by immersing juniper berries and aromatics such as orange peel, coriander, bitter almonds, etc., right in the still or by redistilling neutral spirits over a separate chamber with aromatics known as a gin head. The phrase *London Dry* has no geographical significance. Both English and American gins are dry. They vary because of different formulas for aromatics, different waters, etc. Gins higher than the minimum 80 proof have more flavor because they contain more spirits with their aromatic flavors and therefore less water.

Hollands gin. Completely different in flavor from English or American gins, Hollands is made from a mash containing a large proportion of barley malt along with other grains. Hollands is redistilled with juniper berries in pot stills at low proofs, resulting in a deeply pungent flavor.

Rum. Spirits made from fermented juice of sugarcane, sugar syrup, or molasses; produced below 190 proof. Biggest sources of dry, light rums favored by U.S. market are Puerto Rico and Virgin Islands, where they are produced in column stills. Youngest of these light rums are at least a year old; most are older. Flavor is extremely mild and color light. Older, darker rums from Puerto Rico are more flavorful. Still more heavily flavored varieties, made in pot stills or combined as blends of pot- and column-stilled rums, originate in Jamaica, Haiti, Martinique, Barbados, and Trinidad. Some of the latter varieties aged to a delectable smoothness are sipped straight like old brandies.

Tequila. Mexican spirits made principally from fermented mash of blue agave plant called maguey in Mexico. The heart of monster plants, weighing from 80 to 400 pounds, is steam-cooked, chopped, and pressed into a mash, after which it's double-distilled in pot stills at very low proofs, slightly above 100, resulting in spirits with very heavy body. Tequila may be unaged, colorless spirits or aged from several months to four years, during which time it acquires a golden hue and more mellow flavor. Many tequilas shipped to the U.S. are blends of agave and sugarcane, resulting in a lighter flavor. Similar spirits produced in other regions of Mexico are called mescal.

Brandy. Distillate of fermented juice of fruit, usually grapes, produced at less than 190 proof.

Cognac. Most prestigious of all brandies, produced in pot stills near ancient town of Cognac in western France. Cognacs are twice-distilled and aged in special casks of wood from the nearby Limousin forest. Since almost all cognacs are blends of different years, no age is indicated on the bottle labels. Superb cognacs naturally contain more liquid age than youth. The area adjoining the town of Cognac is divided into seven grape-growing sections, of which the two most important, in the center, are called Grande Champagne and Petite Champagne. The word *champagne* in this instance means, literally, an open stretch of land and has no connection with the area of France that produces the famed sparkling wine. To be labeled *fine champagne*, cognac must have been made from grapes of which at least 60 percent came from Grande Champagne. To be labeled *grande fine champagne*, cognac must have been made from grapes 100 percent of which came from Grande Champagne heartland. Stars on cognac labels, as well as initials such as V.O. (very old) or V.S.O.P. (very superior old pale or particular), provide much less guidance than your own nose and taste buds.

Armagnac. Brandy from Gascony, France; produced like cognac with same type of grapes, but grapes having been grown in another area with different soil and weather, the resulting brandy is slightly more pungent than cognac. Remains in pantheon of great brandies.

Non-Cognac European brandies. Best known are from France, Spain, Portugal, Italy, and Germany. All of them lack the complexity, mellow body, and balance of cognac. Some are produced in pot stills, some in column stills, and some are blends of both stills. German brandies have a somewhat flowery aroma and are light- to medium-bodied. Brandies from Spain and Portugal, where sherry and port are respectively produced, tend to be rather heavy and reminiscent of those wines. Italian brandies, of medium body and about four years of age, like California brandies, are known for their mixability.

Marc. Colorless, unaged brandy from France, distilled from stems and skins of grapes. Of little flavor, it leaves a harsh aftertaste.

Grappa. Same type of rough white spirits as marc, produced in Italy. Provides jolt from alcohol and little else.

California brandies. Four out of five bottles of brandy sold in the States are Californian. Most of them are produced in column stills. Small quantities of pot-stilled brandies are used for blending purposes. Although some California brandies contain small amounts of sweet additives, most are of light to medium body, well balanced, and superb in mixed drinks.

White fruit brandies. European spirits produced from fruits other than grapes. Colorless and unaged. Best known are kirsch from cherries, quetsch and mirabelle from plums, Himbeergeist (Germany) and framboise (France) from raspberries, and poire Williams from pears.

Slivovitz. Plum brandy from central European countries. Though aged in wood and dark in color, it generally lacks mellowness.

Apple brandy, U.S. (also known as applejack). Spirits distilled from fermented juice of apples; produced at less than 190 proof. Minimum age in wood is two years. Unlike grape brandies, which retain little original flavor of grapes, apple brandy keeps vivid perfume of apples. Blended apple brandy or applejack is a mixture of at least 20 percent straight apple brandy or applejack and the balance of neutral spirits.

Calvados. Apple brandy most of which is produced in pot stills in France. Aged a minimum of two years. Actual age of calvados coming to U.S. is approximately four to five years. The older the calvados, the less it retains the fresh apple flavor, the more it acquires flavors reminiscent of cognac.

Pisco. Grape brandy from Peru. Aged briefly in paraffin-lined containers rather than wood to keep brandy from acquiring color or flavor of wood. Though brief aging may remove some harshness of spirits, pisco, at 90 proof, remains a rough distillate whose best use is the pisco sour.

Aquavit. Caraway-flavored spirits from Scandinavia. First distilled as neutral spirits, then redistilled with caraway and other aromatics. Aquavit (also spelled akvavit) may be bone-dry or slightly sweetened but is much less sweet than kümmel liqueur, also made from caraway.

Liqueurs or cordials. Both terms, meaning exactly the same thing, are infusions, percolations, or distillations of flavors with a base of brandy or other spirits, sweetened with sugar at least 2½ percent by weight. The term *crème* used by some liqueur makers is designated for liqueurs with a special smoothness and a flavor of pronounced body, such as crème de menthe. Other liqueurs bear proprietary names, such as Cointreau (orange liqueur), Chartreuse (made with approximately 130 herbs and spices by Carthusian monks), Peter Heering (cherry liqueur), etc. Flavors may be complex mixtures of fruits, flowers, herbs, seeds, spices, roots, bark, or kernels gathered from every corner of the world or may be simple and self-explanatory, as in coffee liqueur, peach liqueur, etc. Proofs vary from a low of 34 (Irish cream liqueur) to a high of 110 (green Chartreuse). Though most liqueurs are planned for after-dinner drinking, some are predinner spirits, such as Campari, a bittersweet Italian liqueur, mixed with soda or other spirits; pastis, an anise-flavored, sweet distillate; and crème de cassis, a black-currant liqueur, usually mixed with white wine or vermouth as an aperitif drink.

Flavored brandies. A special U.S. term for a class of liqueurs, not to be confused with cognac, California brandy, and other dry brandies. The term applies to sweet spirits all of which are made with a brandy base, as distinguished from liqueurs, which may be made with other bases such as neutral spirits or whiskey. All must be bottled at no less than 70 proof, which is higher than many liqueurs.

Okolehao. Popularly known as oke. Hawaiian spirits made from a mash of the ti plant. Unaged, it is offered at 80 proof in white or golden versions and may be used in place of rum in mixed drinks.

Accessories to Alcohol

Of course, the applied art of mixing drinks also depends on many things that aren't alcohol. Liquor must be made tart, sweet, rich, bitter, foamy and, in countless other ways, congenial to sophisticated taste buds. Frequently it's garnished in a manner that accents a drink's appearance as well as its flavor and aroma, as with the olive in the martini, the cucumber peel in the Pimm's Cup, or the strawberry in the champagne cocktail.

Although the total number of accessories available for mixing purposes is far too great to be listed here, there are several that deserve mention simply because they're called for so often. Among them are mixers: bitter lemon, club soda, ginger ale, quinine water, Seven-Up, and tomato juice; garnishes, including—but certainly not limited to—cherries, lemons, limes, olives, cocktail onions, and oranges; and various additives, such as bitters, sugar, Rose's lime juice, and bar foam. Whether or not you should stock other, more exotic bar items will depend on your personal preferences. If, for example, you're turned on by banana daiquiris, you'll obviously need bananas; if your crowd has developed a special fondness for Caribbean rum drinks, you might want to sweeten them with guava jelly melted down to a syrup. And so on. Here, as elsewhere in the barkeeper's art, the question preceding all decisions is, what do *you* like to drink?

A couple of points worth remembering when you're laying in supplies are: First, small containers of seasonings such as bitters are less likely to lose their zest than larger bottles that hang around the shelf too long. Large bottles of syrups such as Falernum will lose their bright color and flavor if untouched for months. If this occurs, don't hesitate to discard the old stock and buy fresh replacements. Second, fruits and other perishables should be emphatically fresh. Whenever possible, use real limes, lemons, orange juice, etc., rather than the bottled, canned, or frozen variety.

Glassware

The glass in which you serve a drink is more than just a medium for transferring liquor from bottle to bibber. It frames the contents for the eye, directs the aroma to the nose, and touches the lips before the liquid releases its storehouse of flavor. Small wonder, then, that attractive glasses make drinking all the more pleasurable.

When buying glassware, you may run across the following terms, which are guides to price and quality.

Crystal. Most expensive. Contains a percentage of lead, which gives the glass weight, a bell-like tone, and magnificent luster.

Lime glass. Lacks lead as one of its components and is comparatively inexpensive. Lacks brilliance of crystal. In some cases, may be more durable than crystal and is more practical for big party entertaining.

Hand-blown. Individually crafted glassware by a method wherein the glassmaker picks up a blob of molten glass at one end of his pipe and then, with his lips and breath as tools, blows until a bowl takes shape, after which it is turned, rubbed, and paddled until the glass reaches a perfect curve.

Pressed. Least expensive. Made by pouring molten glass into molds from which it takes its shape.

Cut glass. Glass, usually crystal, cut or engraved and

polished to reflect as much prismatic light as possible. The darling of conservative drinkers.

Bar glassware is available in two basic shapes: tumblers and stemware. (Sometimes the stem is reduced to a squat pedestal and the glass is called footed.) Stemware is more gracious to the eye and easier on furniture, since condensation on the cold glass rarely makes its way down to the base. Tumblers are less formal, more secure, and usually less expensive. The glasses traditionally used for various kinds of drinks are illustrated here. If you want to limit yourself to two kinds, we suggest the old-fashioned or on-the-rocks glass and the all-purpose tulip-shaped wineglass. With them, you'll be able to serve in style anything from ale to zinfandel, from champagne to stout.

Old-fashioned
6 to 15 ozs.

Cocktail
3 to 6 ozs.

All-purpose wine
8 to 11 ozs.

Brandy snifter
2 to 25 ozs.
6-oz. most
widely used

Delmonico or sour
4½ to 7 ozs.

Shot or jigger
1½ ozs.

Deep-saucer
champagne
at least 6 ozs.

Cordial
1 oz.

Cooler
14 to 21 ozs.

**Highball or collins
8 to 11 ozs.**

To avoid breakage and to keep your glassware sparkling, no matter whether you hire a bartender for your party or do your own pouring, the following guides have been found practical.

- Wash glasses in warm water with detergent as soon as possible after each use. Use a dishwasher if glasses are dishwasher-safe, but stack them in the machine with special care. If glasses are expensive crystal, it may be prudent to wash them by hand no matter what the label says.
- Avoid putting glasses in scalding water; temperature extremes may crack them.
- Glasses that may be sticky on the inside bottom after being used for liqueurs should be soaked before washing.
- Cut glass sometimes shows a film on the cut areas and may have to be soaked in warm water with detergent and scrubbed with a small brush in the crevices of the design.
- Do not stack glasses in the sink or on the shelf. If by any chance glasses have been stacked and are locked, place the bottom glass in warm water and fill the top with cold; the resulting expansion and contraction should separate them safely.
- If hand-washed, dry glasses with a lint-free towel; or, better yet, if thirsty guests aren't waiting for another round of drinks, let the glasses air dry on a rack or drainboard.
- Use a paper towel or tissue paper to give added brilliance to crystal.
- Glasses may be stored on the shelf either right side up or upside down, but, in either case, never crowd the glasses; allow a margin of about an inch, if possible, between them.
- If glasses have been stored on the shelf for months and have been unused, they may become covered with a dusty or sticky film caused by cooking fumes; check them before partytime and wash them if necessary.
- Be especially sure all glasses used for wine tasting are immaculate, with no trace of detergent from a previous washing.

Tools for the Bar

Like glassware, bar tools, equipment, and serving accessories should be both attractive and functional. What looks good often works well. Small bar gadgets should be kept in one place for easy access and, if possible, near the sink for quick rinsing and repeated use.

Among the many gadgets and equipment available, the most useful ones are:

Jigger. In two joined sections of 1½ ounces and 1 ounce. Some jiggers are attached to handles for easy pouring into shaker or into lined-up glasses.

Cocktail shaker. May be professional bartender's set of glass mixer and metal mixer that fit compatibly into each other for shaking, plus coil-rimmed strainer; or home-type shaker with metal cap and pouring spout.

Martini pitcher. Glass pitcher with stirrer, used not only for martinis but for manhattans and other drinks that are stirred rather than shaken. (Glass mixer above may be used alone for stirring.)

Corkscrew. One of the most useful is the folding flat waiter's corkscrew with knife for cutting bottle foil and lever that hooks onto rim of bottle for extracting cork. Others are: traditional T-shaped corkscrew with wood handle and clamping ring that removes cork while handle is turned; cork puller with two thin blades that slide alongside cork, useful in removing corks that tend to break or crumble; wing-type corkscrew, requiring less muscle power than traditional corkscrews; wooden corkscrew with counterscrew, also requiring less exertion.

Piercing can opener. Heavy-duty with fang that sinks easily into tops of cans containing tomato juice, pineapple juice, etc.

Bottle-cap opener. For bottled beer; type with long handle provides good leverage.

Jar-cap opener. For stubborn caps of jars containing olives, cherries, etc.

Bar mixing spoon. Long-handled; for measuring and adding sugar to cocktail shaker and for stirring (rather than shaking) certain drinks.

Measuring spoons. In set, from ¼ teaspoon to tablespoon; tablespoon is equal to half-ounce measurement.

Small knife. For slicing fruit and peel.

Cutting board. Heavy type is less likely to warp than thin board.

Lime-juice squeezer. Useful for squeezing fruit and dropping shell into tonic drinks, gin rickeys, etc.

Fruit-juice squeezer. Hand type; for small quantities of lemon juice, lime juice, etc.

Electric juice extractor. For fresh citrus juice when preparing drinks in quantity.

Olive or cherry grabber. With plunger for reaching bottom of tall jars.

Metal grater. For scraping nutmeg into hot drinks.

Ice-cube bucket. Plastic type serviceable for outdoor parties; for indoor drinking, bucket should be of chrome or silver-plated.

Tongs. For snugly gripping ice cubes.

Champagne bucket. For cooling not only champagne but white wine; may be floor type or bucket that rests on table.

Electric blender. For frozen daiquiris, foamy-type drinks, etc.

Electric ice crusher. Large model that holds enough crushed ice for four to six drinks is preferable to smaller types; one of best models is a removable crusher with handle that fits over large bottom section holding crushed ice.

Coasters. Choose type large enough for double old-fashioned glass.

Stirrers or swizzle sticks. May be glass, plastic, or metal; for on-the-rocks drinks, highballs, etc.

Barmanship

Given a choice selection of spirits, fresh and flavorful mixing ingredients, and attractive glassware, the host at home is still several steps away from the professional bartender's finesse, an art that is public property for every drinker astride a barstool to behold. It looks deceptively easy, especially to the eye that's been mellowed by two or three dry martinis. But there are skills, tricks of the trade, and tips in creating and serving drinks—icemanship, mixing, stirring, garnishing, and others—which can be briefly explained in the same way that a pro on the golf course can make a detailed analysis of each of the strokes and positions he's carefully mastered. Familiarize yourself with the basic barman's skills that follow, consult them for special potables, and every time you pour drinks, you'll generate among your guests the mood described superlatively by novelist Henry Fielding as "one universal grin."

ICEMANSHIP

There was a time when rocks were really rocky, when a bartender armed with an ice pick hacked away at his block of ice until it eventually disappeared. On a summer's day you'd ask for a gin rickey, and it would come to you with one or two tottering crags of ice. It looked cool, but it couldn't possibly stand up to a contemporary gin rickey, because of a simple, undisputed fact: ice is now much colder than it once was. Frozen water may be 32° F. or, just as possibly these days, −32° F. Most of the cubes in the present ice age range from 0 to −10° F. Needless to say, for fast cooler-offers, the colder the ice the better. Crushed ice or cracked ice is chillier in a bar glass than the cubed variety, because more cooling ice surface comes into intimate contact with the drink.

The number of muscle-powered as well as plug-in ice crushers seems to have kept pace with the population explosion. There are ice-crusher blender attachments that can reduce a tray of ice cubes to crushed ice or snow ice in twenty to thirty seconds. Even simple ice trays are now designed not only for cubes but for ice slices, thirty-eight to a tray, and, perhaps most useful of all, for cracked ice. Lacking this equipment, a man needn't find the technique for cracking or crushing ice too difficult. Simply place the ice cubes in a canvas bag designed for this purpose or in a large, clean kitchen towel (wrap the towel around the ice so that there is a double thickness of cloth); on a carving board, bang the bag or towel with a mallet or the smooth side of a meat tenderizer. Keep your banging somewhat restrained if you want fair-size pieces of cracked ice; for crushed ice, whack away with abandon.

Every barman—amateur or pro—should insist that his ice be clean, hard, and dry and should make each drink or batch of drinks with fresh ice. Hoard your ice in the freezing section of your refrigerator until you actually need it. Use ice buckets with vacuum sides and lids; plastic-foam ice tubs are convenient for throwaway service. When you empty your ice trays, don't run water over them unless it's absolutely necessary to spring the ice free; the water will cause the cubes to stick together after they're put into the bucket. Most new ice trays, especially those with nonstick surfaces, discharge their cargo with a single swift yank. There are also refrigerators that not only make ice cubes automatically but turn them out and store them night and day—a comforting thought when one is party planning. If the water in your fiefdom is heavily chlorinated, use bottled spring water for ice. Finally, as a host, be the most prodigal of icemen. If you're gambling on the fact that you may just possibly get by with two buckets of ice at a sum-

THE HOST AND HIS BAR

mer fling, don't gamble. Provide at least three or four bucketfuls for supercooling your crowd. If your ice-making equipment is somewhat limited, find out before your rumpus takes place just where you can buy or borrow additional ice.

Here are three icy ideas you might want to try:

Punch-bowl ice. There are still commercial icehouses where you can buy a chunk of ice tailored to fit your punch bowl, but you can make your own ice floe by filling a deep pot or plastic bucket with water—at least a day in advance of the party—and placing it in the freezer. The top of the ice may congeal in a hump as the water expands; when you're ready to use it, run warm water over the sides of the pot and invert it, permitting the round glacier, with its smooth bottom upright, to slide into your bowl.

Aquavit in ice. At smorgasbord parties, it's a delightful custom to serve a bottle of aquavit (or sometimes straight vodka) encased in a block of ice. The job's simple: Place the bottle of liquor in an empty two-quart paper milk container with the top removed; fill the container with water; then set it in the freezer. The alcohol will keep the liquor from solidifying as the surrounding water freezes. Finally, tear off the paper or remove it with a knife. The long robe of ice with its rectangular sides should be partly covered with a napkin for serving and then returned to the freezer to preserve it for second skoals.

Frappéed ice cap. After-dinner frappés—refreshing alternatives to cloying desserts—are made by drizzling a liqueur or liqueurs over finely crushed ice in a saucer champagne glass. A cool and convenient variation is to make them beforehand and store them a few hours or even overnight in the freezer. In time the liqueur settles to the bottom and the ice forms a solid cap on top; after you remove the glass from the freezer, the cap will loosen slightly, allowing the icy liqueur to be sipped from the rim of the glass sans straw.

GLASS PREPARATION

There are three basic ways to prepare glasses beforehand: chilling, frosting, and sugar-frosting.

Chilling glasses. Every cocktail glass should be chilled before it's filled. There are three ways: (1) Before drinking time, store glasses in the refrigerator or freezer until they're cold; (2) bury the glasses completely in cracked ice; (3) fill them with cracked ice and stir the ice a few times before pouring drinks.

Frosting glasses. For a longer-lasting frost, dip the glasses into water and, while still dripping, place them in your refrigerator's freezer section (set at its coldest point) for two or three hours.

Sugar-frosting glasses. Glasses for appropriate cocktails, coolers, and liqueurs can be made more fascinating to the eyes and lips by frosting their rims with sugar. To administer this fancy finishing touch, make sure, first of all, that you use superfine sugar—not the regular granulated or confectioners'. Moisten the rim of each glass, inside and out, to a depth of about a quarter inch before dipping into sugar. There are four easy rites: (1) Anoint the rim with a small wedge of lemon or orange, invert the glass to shake off extra juice, then dip into sugar; (2) rub rim with lemon or orange peel, using the outside of the rind, then dip into sugar; (3) dip rim into grenadine, Falernum, or any other syrup—or any desired liqueur—then into sugar; (4) moisten rim with coffee liqueur, then dip into a mixture of 3 teaspoons superfine sugar mixed well with 1 teaspoon powdered instant coffee.

The contents of all sugar-frosted glasses, needless to add, should be sipped without benefit of a straw. For party purposes, a large number of glasses may be sugar-frosted and stored in the refrigerator or freezer until drinktime.

THE MECHANICS OF MIXING AND POURING

Filling the shaker. Ice should always go into the shaker first, alcohol last. By giving ice first place, all the ingredients that follow will be cooled on their way down. Furthermore, once you acquire the habit of adding the liquor last, it's unlikely that you'll inadvertently double the spirits or, worse yet, forget them altogether, both possible errors for hosts taking jolts along with their guests. The order of ingredients between ice and alcohol follows no dogmatic ritual; whether sugar should precede the lemon juice or vice versa isn't important as far as the final drink is concerned. One useful control for drinking hosts is to put the correct number of glasses for the needed drinks in front of the shaker before adding *anything*—a clear reminder of how many dashes of bitters, how many spoons of this or jiggers of that are necessary. Finally, never fill a shaker to the brim; allow enough room for all ingredients to be tossed back and forth, to set up the clear, pleasant rattle of ice.

Measuring. Guests at a pour-it-yourself bar should feel free to pour as many fingers as they please, but if the host himself is preparing any kind of mixed drinks, he should trust the jigger rather than his eye, just as the best professional barmen always do. In simple drinks such as Scotch and soda, as well as in more complicated tipple, too much liquor can be unpleasant and, in a way, as inhospitable as too little.

Stirring. To keep their icy clarity, cocktails such as martinis, manhattans, rob roys, and gimlets should always be stirred, not shaken (though it's no major disaster if you unwittingly shake rather than stir a martini: it will turn cloudy, but only for a few minutes). For proper dilution, stir every batch of cocktails at least twenty times. When carbonated water is added to tall drinks, stir as briefly as possible; most of the liquor rises to the top automatically, and excessive stirring only dissipates the sparkle in the water.

Shaking. Shake the shaker, not yourself. Don't just rock it—hold it well out in front of you and move it diagonally from lower left to upper right, or in any other convenient motion, with a pistonlike rhythm. In time the cold, icy feel of the cocktail shaker will tell you that the drinks have a creamy head and are ready for pouring. Shake one round of drinks at a time and rinse the shaker thoroughly after each use.

Pouring. When drinks have been shaken, pour them at once; don't let the cocktail shaker become a watery grave. If extra liquid is left in the shaker, strain it off at once; the so-called dividends left standing in ice will be weak replicas of the original drinks. Never pour drinks higher than a quarter inch from the rim of the glass. In the case of wine, a large glass should never be more than one-third to one-half full to permit swirling of the wine and liberation of its aromas. In large brandy snifters, a 1½-ounce drink is the maximum. When garnishes such as orange slices and pineapple sticks are being used, allow sufficient room to add them without causing the drink to overflow. When pouring more than one mixed drink, line up the glasses rim to rim, fill them half-full, then pour again to the same height in each glass.

FRUIT JUICES AND PEELS

Always try to use fresh fruit when you're making drinks. Lemons, limes, and oranges should be tamed on the cutting board before they're cut for squeezing. With the palm of your hand, lean on the fruit and roll it back and forth a few times, thus softening its flesh so that the juice will flow freely after it's cut. Peels should be cut just before serving to preserve the volatile oils. Use a twist cutter or a very sharp paring knife to shave off only the colored surface of the peel, in 1-by-½-inch sections.

SIMPLE SYRUP

In drinks calling for sugar, some barmen prefer sugar syrup to loose sugar, since it makes drinks velvety smooth and is often easier to use, since it blends without prolonged shaking or stirring. To make it, bring 1 cup of water to a boil and stir in 1 cup of sugar; simmer for 1½ minutes. By that time the mixture will have been reduced to approximately 1 cup, making it possible to substitute equal amounts of syrup for sugar in any bar recipe where it may be preferred.

Bar Measurements

Bottle sizes of all spirits and wines sold in the U.S., once indicated in ounces, are now shown in liter measurements. The system was mandated by the U.S. government in 1980 in order to stop the liquid shell game in which consumers were frequent, easy victims. A bottle of wine that looked like a fifth (one-fifth of a gallon, or 25.6 ounces) would often turn out to be 24 or 23 ounces when examined at home. Sizes of imported liqueurs ranged all over the place, tripping up the host who tried to estimate how many drinks a specific bottle would yield for party entertainment. The move to metrics applies to all spirits and wines except wines bottled abroad before January 1, 1979.

Undoubtedly, the traditional 1½-ounce bar jigger will continue to be the standard unit for mixing or measuring individual drinks. Other units of liquid measurements, such as dash, teaspoon, etc., are described below. They should help you take a recipe for a single drink and magnify it at will or reduce a giant-sized punch bowl to the desired amount of wassail.

Dash. For all drink recipes in this book, a dash means ⅛ teaspoon; two dashes will thus fill a ¼-teaspoon measure. Theoretically, a dash is the amount of liquid that squirts out of a bottle equipped with a dash stopper. Stoppers, however, vary in size, and to different liquor dispensers a dash means anything from three drops up. But dashes have potent flavor or they wouldn't be dashes; so it's important to be as accurate as possible.

Teaspoon. ⅓ tablespoon, or ⅙ ounce. Use a standard measuring teaspoon for the exact amount. The long-handled bar spoon, designed for mixing, will usually hold more and is useful for those who like a generous amount of sugar in mixed drinks, especially those made with lemon or lime juice.

Tablespoon. 3 teaspoons, or ½ ounce.

Pony. 1 ounce, or the small end of a double-ended measuring jigger. Also the usual capacity of the liqueur glass or the pousse-café glass.

Jigger. 1½ ounces. Also called a bar measuring glass, it's the standard measure for mixing individual drinks, though generous hosts use a 2-ounce jigger. Although jiggers are supposed to provide exact measurements, they're sometimes grossly inaccurate; so it's a good idea, if possible, to check any new jigger you buy with a lab measuring glass.

Wineglass. Used as a measuring term, it means 4 ounces, which is the old-fashioned wineglass filled to the brim. Though today wine is generally served in a much larger glass—one-third full to permit the wine to be swirled for releasing its bouquet—*wineglass* as a 4-ounce measure still appears in some drink recipes and in food recipes.

Hosts attempting to get the hang of the metric system should start with an old point of reference, namely the U.S. quart, or 32 ounces. It will be replaced by the liter, which is slightly larger—33.8 ounces. The liter is subdivided into milliliters; there are 1000 in a liter, and they're shown in Tables 1 and 2 as *ml*. Here, then, on the following page, are the new bottle sizes and their closest corresponding old sizes.

Needless to say, such colorful old containers as the demijohn—a narrow-necked bottle of either glass or stoneware containing from one to ten gallons—are out. Ditto for the tappit hen (about ⅗), the jeroboam (about ⅘), and the rehoboam (about 1⅕ gallons). Travelers to Europe may occasionally notice massive bottles of wine seldom shipped to the United States. These range from the Methuselah (1⅗ gallons) to the Nebuchadnezzar (about four

THE HOST AND HIS BAR 41

gallons). Bottles of these huge dimensions are hard to fabricate in uniformly exact capacities. The U.S. government is proposing to allow some bottles of these lusty sizes to be used, provided they are in exact liter sizes, such as four liters, five liters, etc.

For the quantities of liquor, mixers, etc., to buy for party purposes, see the drink calculators (Tables 3, 4, and 5) on pages 44–45.

Table 1

Spirits (Six Sizes)

Old Size Names	Old Size Fluid Ozs.	New Metric Size Fluid Ozs.	New Metric Size
Miniature	1.6	1.7	50 ml.
½ Pint	8.	6.8	200 ml.
Pint	16.	16.9	500 ml.
Fifth	25.6	25.4	750 ml.
Quart	32.	33.8	1 liter
½ Gallon	64.	59.2	1.75 liters

Table 2

Wines (Seven Sizes)

Old Size Names	Old Size Fluid Ozs.	New Metric Size Fluid Ozs.	New Metric Size
Miniature	2, 3, or 4	3.4	100 ml.
⅖ Pint	6.4	6.3	187 ml.
⅘ Pint	12.8	12.7	375 ml.
Fifth	25.6	25.4	750 ml.
Quart	32.	33.8	1 liter
⅖ Gallon	51.2	50.7	1.5 liters
⅘ Gallon	102.4	101.4	3 liters

Party Drinking

DRINK CALCULATOR

As a rule, the drinking curve rises headlong on holidays and weekends and descends at other times. Also, as men get older, their capacity for hoisting and draining the glass increases. Seniors drink more, and can hold more, than freshmen. The class of 1940 at its annual midwinter reunion polishes off considerably more than the class of 1970. The seventies raise more thunder about their drinking, but at the end of the evening, when the actual liquor tally is made, the older imbibers will be far ahead of the more youthful alumni. A party around a punch bowl will normally drink at least fifty percent more than a party where the host laboriously mixes drinks one by one to order. Furthermore, the place where one cracks his bottles often determines the amount of liquid cheer consumed. Liquor is downed at a dockside party in far greater volume than when dispensed from a boat's galley. Ale or beer drinkers cavorting at an outdoor lobster barbecue will kill kegs rather than the bottles of an indoor seafood party.

In estimating how much liquor to buy for any party where mixed drinks are served, you must start out with the specific recipes you have in mind. If, for instance, you plan to serve brandy sours, you must decide beforehand whether each drink will have a 1½-ounce or a 2-ounce

THE HOST AND HIS BAR 43

base. If you're serving tall coolers with rum and other spirits, you must go back to the base recipe, check each kind of spirit called for, and then expand it to any number up to infinity. Even when your goal isn't infinity, it's always best in your calculations to err on the side of too much. Certainly, if you're buying for your party the same spirits you'd normally stock in your liquor cabinet, additional bottles left over are good liquid assets. And in buying a half-dozen or dozen bottles at a time, you can usually tuck away a noticeable saving under the single-bottle price.

A useful guideline for parties, tested over and over, is simply this: Most of the crowd will consume two to three drinks at the usual cocktail hour at sundown, before a buffet, or before a sit-down dinner. After dinner, if you're serving highballs, you can again reasonably estimate two to three drinks per person, depending on how long guests remain after the dinner table has been cleared. At a knockdown, drag-out bachelor party, the two-to-three formula will expand to four-to-six. At a pretheater party, where everyone wants to keep an especially clear head, the formula may dip to one or two drinks per guest. The drink-calculation guide in Table 3 covers cocktails before dinner or postprandial highballs. If you're serving both, calculate both.

(Note: In the measurements below, the 25.4-ounce bottle is used instead of the old-fashioned "fifth," which was $2/10$ ounce more than the 25.4-ounce (750-milliliter) bottle. You will find that the word *fifth* is still used in this country when what is actually meant is the 25.4-ounce size. To be on the plus side, however, liters (33.8 ounces) may be purchased; generally there's a saving in the larger bottles. Finally, for further saving, one may buy the 1¾-liter size, often called the short half gallon. The disadvantage of this latter size is inconvenience in handling, especially if guests at parties are pouring their own drinks.)

Table 3
Cocktail and Highball Calculator

If you're the host for a party of	As a rule, they'll consume	If drinks are 1½ ozs., you'll need at least	If drinks are 2 ozs., you'll need at least
6	12–18 drinks	2 750 ml. (25.4 ozs.)	2 750 ml. (25.4 ozs.)
8	16–24 "	2 " "	2 " "
10	20–30 "	2 " "	3 " "
12	24–36 "	3 " "	3 " "
20	40–60 "	4 " "	5 " "
30	60–90 "	6 " "	8 " "

Table 4
Aperitif and Table-Wine Calculator

If you're serving predinner aperitif wines, not aperitif cocktails, or if you're serving sherry or port for a party of	Your guests will generally average	You should buy or have on hand ready for serving
6	6–12 drinks	2 750 ml. (25.4 ozs.)
8	8–16 "	2 " "
10	10–20 "	3 " "
12	12–24 "	3 " "
20	20–40 "	5 " "
30	30–60 "	8 " "

When serving a single red or white table wine throughout the meal and your party consists of	Your guests will generally average	You should buy or have on hand ready for serving
6	12–18 drinks	3 750 ml. (25.4 ozs.)
8	16–24 "	4 " "
10	20–30 "	5 " "
12	24–36 "	6 " "
20	40–60 "	10 " "
30	60–90 "	15 " "

Brandy and liqueurs are in a special category when served straight and not as an ingredient in dessert cocktails, liqueur frappés, etc. The usual serving in the small brandy glass as well as the larger brandy snifter is 1 ounce per person; the same goes for liqueurs served straight.

Table 5

Brandy and Liqueur Calculator

When pouring brandy or liqueurs as after-dinner drinks for a party of	As a rule they'll consume	You should buy or have on hand ready for serving
6	6–12 drinks	1 750 ml. (25.4 ozs.)
8	8–16 "	1 " "
10	10–20 "	1 " "
12	12–24 "	1 " "
20	20–40 "	2 " "
30	30–60 "	3 " "

In estimating carbonated waters such as club soda, tonic water, ginger ale, cola drinks, etc., a generous guideline is to allow a 28-ounce bottle for every two persons. Thus, a person consuming three gin and tonics would usually pour from 12 to 14 ounces for his three drinks. The smaller 10-ounce bottles of carbonated waters are easy when guests are pouring their own drinks at cocktail tables. Larger-size bottles are used when a bartender is doing the honors. If you're using your own soda water made with soda charges, keep plenty of charges in reserve. The usual charge makes one quart of soda.

At an all-beer party—a picnic, barbecue, or steak party —count on an average of three bottles of beer, ale, or stout per person.

WINES

Exploring Wines

As wine drinkers, Americans now judiciously sip more than two gallons of wine per person a year, as opposed to the one gallon they gulped a decade ago. At businessmen's luncheons, many of the doughtiest martini drinkers are now quaffing white wine instead. The seemingly endless assortment of imported and domestic wines now available in wineshops and on supermarket shelves in some states shows that wine is no longer the stiff symbol of the formal dinner table but something we're taking more and more with our daily bread. It will be some time before Americans reach the bibulous capacity of Frenchmen, who drink twenty-seven gallons a year, or Italians, who drink twenty-eight, but part of the great joy of wine drinking in this country is exploring the fragrances and flavors of wines from every important wine-growing country in the world, from vineyards before and behind the Iron Curtain, from the picturesque valley of the Rhine to the slopes of Mount Etna.

There are four main types of wine:

1. *Table wines.* They may be red, rosé, or white. They're called table wines because generally they're offered as part of the meal, poured at the dining table, although many dry white wines and fruity reds are now served at the cocktail hour. Most table wines are dry or semi-dry.

2. *Sparkling wines.* These are wines that undergo two fermentations, one when the grapes are first converted to alcohol and a second one in which the carbon dioxide is retained. The white-tie-and-tails class of these wines is French champagne, even though you may want to drink it wearing Levi's or ski pants before a roaring fire. The category includes sparkling wines from Italy, Germany, and the United States. Besides their obvious use at celebrations, they may be served at any event from wedding breakfasts to ship launchings, as well as with or before any meal.

3. *Dessert wines.* Sweet wines that may be served with or after the dessert or at other times of the day or night include many of the world's most eminent white wines, such as Sauternes from France with their marvelous balance of tartness and sugar, the German white wines made from late-picked grapes, and the American wines of this type. Also belonging to this class are the port wines and sweet sherries, which are not only dessert wines but belong to the class called fortified.

4. *Fortified wines.* A fortified wine is one to which brandy has been added, increasing the wine's alcohol content but, more importantly, stabilizing the wine so that the bottle may be opened and kept on the shelf without danger of imminent spoilage. There are two kinds of fortified wines: the ports and sherries previously mentioned, as well as Madeira, Marsala, etc.; and aromatized, or aperitif, wines. These include the vermouths, both dry and sweet, as well as such aperitifs as Dubonnet, Lillet, Cynar, etc. They are aromatized with a vast variety of spices, herbs, fruit peel, etc., to give them their characteristic, sometimes bitter, but always appetite-provoking features.

Wine Tasting

No phase of the wine experience is camouflaged with more mumbo jumbo than wine tasting. So thick is the mantle in which it's wrapped that the novice, canvassing the subject of wines, is made to feel that he or she must of necessity turn to the wine expert or panel of experts or wine judges at fairs and other places, the admonishing angels telling him or her what should or should not be liked.

If you are a beginner, the best way to learn to judge wine is to drink wine—not guzzle it in huge quantities but repeatedly taste the same type of wine, even in small amounts, day after day. In a reasonably short time, you'll find yourself noticing changes in wines the same way you'd spot changes in soups, sauces, or stews. Whether you're looking for an intense or light flavor, whether you're trying to associate the flavor of the raw grape with the finished wine, whether you're comparing American with European wines made from the same grape, the technique is a simple one. You do *not* have to go through the ritual slurping, sloshing, and spitting. That method should be reserved for the vineyards and the movies—it's ridiculous in your home. Wine makers don't do it in *their* homes.

First of all, you want a thin, clear, tulip-shaped glass with at least an eight-ounce capacity. Fill the glass one-third full; then, grasping it securely by the foot of the stem and using a white tablecloth as a background or holding the glass to the light, look at the wine's color and clarity, since both are clues to the soundness of a wine. A young red wine may range from a light to a deep-purplish red. If it's an old red wine, it may have a brownish tinge around the edge of the glass. If it's a rosé, it should look like a rosé, neither rusty nor a dark garnet. If it's a white wine, it may range from the lightest pale yellow, sometimes tinged with green, to deeper straw-colored yellow to deep gold. In both red and white wines, color is the guide to the wine's body (intensity of flavor). The lighter the color, the lighter the body; the deeper the color, the more heavy-bodied, or robust.

After assessing the clarity and color, set the glass on the table and, holding the bottom of the stem, revolve the glass carefully so that the wine swirls and laps against the side of the glass and releases its bouquet. Raise the glass and nose it, breathing deeply. In time you'll learn to recognize the smell that's technically called the aroma, the smell of the raw grape rather than the finished wine.

Next, sip the wine, taking a small amount, holding it briefly at the front of the mouth on the tongue, and then slowly swallowing it. Note the aftertaste—give it several moments to develop before you take more wine or food. The aftertaste, or finish, is considered by some winemen the most important of any of the taste sensations. In time, after drinking and tasting many wines, the aftertaste becomes the wine memory that you retain and recognize when you taste the same kind of wine again.

Serving Wine

When you pour wine at your own table, you don't assume the role of the restaurant sommelier, fluttering over the bottle, awaiting your guests' approval as though it were a life-or-death verdict. As a host, your first job is to make sure you've bought enough wine for two rounds, at least. If it's a hot day and guests haven't been drinking cocktails, it's possible for two people to finish a single bottle (three or four drinks apiece) of a chilled white wine, but this is the exception. Most likely before mealtime your guests will have had their cocktails, highballs, or aperitif wines; subsequent wine drinking at the dinner table will usually average out to two glasses per person, some taking more, some less.

So much for the basics. Now for the actual service.

1. If it's a white wine, champagne, or dessert wine, it should be chilled beforehand. Some fruity young red wines such as Beaujolais, zinfandel, or rosés are often preferred chilled, too. *How* chilly is a matter of personal choice. Here again, wine authorities can be counted on to confuse you. One will tell you to chill wine to a temperature between 31° and 41° F.; another says to serve it between 41° and 45° F.; and two California professors say, "Most dessert wines require a slight chilling to about 60° F." I, myself, don't recommend that you run around with a

thermometer to take its temperature. At a small party, you can chill wine in a champagne bucket; at very large parties, washtubs filled with ice are sometimes put on display. Fill the bucket or tubs with cracked ice and twirl the bottles occasionally. About a half hour's chilling is enough. If ice cubes rather than cracked ice are used, add water to the bucket or tub to hasten the chilling. Wine can also be chilled in the refrigerator for an hour or two (most are set between 35° and 40° F.) or in the freezer for about a half hour.

2. If white wine or any other wine is chilled in a bucket, wipe the entire bottle with a towel to prevent dripping at the table. If it's a red wine served at room temperature and is taken from the cellar with the dust of ages on it, wipe it well, too. Don't, however, wrap the bottle in a towel; guests are often as interested in the wine label as they are in the food that's being served. If you're serving a jug wine, pouring it from a carafe is easier and more attractive than attempting to handle the three-liter bottle at the table.

3. With a paring knife, cut off the foil capsule over the cork. Don't merely cut it level with the top of the bottle but at least an inch below, or remove it entirely. Sometimes it's grimy, and wine poured over it may pick up an off-flavor.

4. Wipe the top of the bottle with a clean towel. Moisten the towel if necessary to remove any grime.

5. For opening, use a corkscrew, which should always be longer than the cork. Insert the end of the corkscrew at the very center of the cork. Turn the corkscrew evenly; do not push it or attempt to force it in by leaning on it or you may force the cork into the bottle. If the cork seems to be slipping into the bottle, stop turning it or, again, the cork might be forced into the bottle. Withdraw the corkscrew as steadily as possible. Don't attempt to make it pop like a champagne bottle. If the cork seems to be breaking while you're withdrawing it, grasp its top with your fingers to keep it intact. If you are opening champagne, hold the cork covered with a towel in your right hand, and twist the bottle with your left hand.

6. Smell the cork. It should smell of wine. If it's a strong old wine, the cork will have a strong smell, which

is natural. (Don't confuse the wine smell with the smell of a rotten cork—a very rare occurrence. Such a cork has an out-and-out putrid smell that causes both the wine's odor and taste to be unmistakably bad, or "corky.") Wipe the rim of the bottle. Wipe the inside of the neck of the bottle if necessary.

7. If the cork breaks or falls into the bottle, or if there's an abundance of cork crumbs in the wine, the wine must be strained. Use a clean linen or silk cloth in a funnel, or use filter paper. Straining never helps the flavor of any wine, but in some cases it's unavoidable. If the neck of the bottle breaks (a very rare occurrence), the wine shouldn't be used.

8. Pour a little wine into your own glass for your own nosing and tasting. If there are a few cork crumbs, they will fall into your glass rather than your guests' glasses. If you'd like to have your wife, inamorata, or any guest to share in the tasting beforehand, do so. The preliminary glass for good humor as well as tasting is a good way of throwing off the yoke of convention, and guests are invariably flattered when you ask them to offer *their* judgment.

9. Pour the wine at each place at the table. (The old custom of formally filling the glasses of all the ladies before the men seems a bit quaint in the age of women's lib.) If you're serving wine at a buffet party, the glasses may be on the buffet table and should be filled just before the food is offered. Offer refills to guests, but don't ply them with wine, and don't insist that they kill the bottle just to avoid leftover wine.

10. The custom of keeping wine at the table in a wine basket with the bottle on its side has never caught on in this country. The original idea of the wine basket (a device for keeping the bottle at a forty-five-degree angle, and with a handle at the top for passing the wine) was to keep the sediment of the wine, if any, from flowing into the glasses. This proves an impractical idea because some sediment can still flow into the glass. The basket is useful—sediment or no sediment—for allowing guests to pass the wine around the table.

11. If you're serving sweet sherry or port with the coffee at the end of the dinner, you might bring the glasses

to the table with the coffee rather than clutter the table beforehand. It's an old custom among port lovers to pass the bottle from one guest to the next rather than have the host pour it at each place; the bottle is passed clockwise around the table in deference to an old superstition that the port would turn sour if passed otherwise.

Wine Dictionary

There are still Americans who buy names rather than wines, relying on the éclat of prestigious old labels, some dating from the last century. Smug high sniffers in American wineshops will pay any price for the status of certain wine names, particularly if they're French. No one can deny that France is the most celebrated wine country in the world and that the quantity of magnificent wines from its vineyards exceeds that of other wine countries. But there have been good, bad, and even bogus wines shipped to this country from France. And so a name should be taken for what it is: a means of identification and not necessarily a judgment of the contents of the bottle. The list below makes no attempt to include the ten thousand wines now available in American shops, but the most prominent names on labels, the ones that you're likely to hear about and that have become standards of reference, are included. Besides the names on bottle labels, there are wine terms that professional winemen use, heard in wineshops and at wine tastings; the meaning of these words and information concerning them are included.

Acidity. The pleasant bite and natural tartness of grapes and wines; not to be confused with sourness. Without acidity, wines would be insipid.

Aloxe-Corton. Township in the northern end of Côte

WINES 57

de Beaune in the Burgundy region of France; produces some of the best red and white wines of the region. The best bottlings eliminate the name Aloxe and are listed in hyphenated form as Corton-Charlemagne, a white wine, and Corton-Clos du Roi, a red wine.

Alsace. Province of France, near the German border, noted for its white wines. The wines resemble German wines in fruitiness and flavor and are made principally from the Riesling, Gewürztraminer, Sylvaner, and other grapes grown in Germany.

Amontillado. Type of Spanish sherry, neither as dry as fino or cocktail sherries nor as sweet as cream or dessert sherries.

Anjou. Area of France bordering on the Loire River; best known in the U.S. for its rosés and Muscadet.

Appelation contrôleé (A.C. for short). Official French term guaranteeing that a wine was made in a designated place from specific grapes or a combination of approved grapes and that production of the wine followed government regulations for growing grapes, vinification, etc. If there is a district, township, or vineyard listed, the A.C. assures its authenticity.

Aroma. Smell of the wine when young, revealing its grape but not necessarily duplicating the raw grape flavor. As wine ages, it develops a *bouquet* (see below).

Asti Spumante. Italy's noted sparkling white wine from the Piedmont area; somewhat more flowery in flavor and sweeter than very dry champagnes.

Astringency. The quality of a wine, produced by *tannin* (see below), particularly in red wines, that causes a feeling of puckerishness in the mouth.

Auslese (German). Wine made from a special selection of individual bunches of ripe grapes; some of them may have the *Botrytis* (see below) found in the great sauternes of France.

Baco Noir. French-American hybrid red wine grape cultivated in New York State; produces wines of well-developed flavor.

Balance. The qualities of a wine that result in a pleasant equilibrium, such as sweetness and tartness that complement each other. A wine may be tart or very sweet, but body, bouquet, smoothness, and all salient qualities are in such proportion that if one quality is tipped too much one way or the other, the wine will be out of balance.

Barbera. Grape used in both Italian and California red wines, noted for their *earthy* (see below), full flavor; sometimes slightly rough. Best Barberas, aged up to five years, develop into rounded, mellow wines.

Bardolino. Light, young Italian red wine produced in northern Italy.

Barolo. One of the greatest of the Italian red wines from Piedmont. Long-lived, its nuances of rich flavors place it in a class with the greatest of the world's red wines.

Barsac. Township in the Sauternes wine district of Bordeaux, France; noted for white wines somewhat less sweet and lighter than Sauternes.

Beaujolais. French red wine from southern Burgundy, renowned for lightness and fruitiness; extremely popular in both France and the U.S. May be served slightly chilled. In France some Beaujolais is consumed within days or weeks after bottling, called Beaujolais Nouveau. Some villages known for their fine Beaujolais are Brouilly, Fleurie, Morgon, and Moulin-à-Vent.

Beaulieu. Vineyard in California, established in 1900, one of the first to offer premium wines after Repeal in the thirties, with excellent reputation for Cabernet Sauvignon, particularly their Private Reserve label.

Beaune. City in the Burgundy region of France, center of its wine trade. The red and white wines produced west of the city are of excellent quality.

Beerenauslese (German). Term indicating wine made from individually picked, rather than bunches of, extremely ripe grapes, resulting in a rich, expensive white dessert wine.

Bernkastel. Small German town on the Moselle River. Its finest vineyard is Bernkasteler Doktor.

Blanc de blancs (French). Term meaning "white of whites"; applies to light, delicate white wines or champagne made from all white grapes rather than a mixture of white and dark grapes or all dark grapes. (Dark grapes yield white juice unless skins are retained during fermentation.)

Blanc fumé. White wine made from the Sauvignon Blanc grape. In France the wine labeled Pouilly-Fumé, made in the Loire Valley, is very dry and popular as a seafood accompaniment. California *blanc fumé* usually has less body than its French counterpart.

Body. Intensity rather than quality of flavor. Good body is the opposite of wateriness.

Bordeaux. City in southwestern France, adjoining the wine country that produces France's most prestigious wines, divided into five main districts: Médoc, Graves, Sauternes, Saint-Émilion, and Pomerol.

Bordeaux Supérieur. French wine bearing this label, indicating no château, is the common, mass-produced, blended wine of the Bordeaux area exported to the U.S. in large quantities. When the word *supérieur* is omitted, the wine has somewhat less alcoholic content.

Botrytis cinerea. Called "noble mold" by wine makers, *Botrytis* is a beneficent fungus that affects the skins of some late-harvested, very ripe grapes, resulting in a rare rich, sweet wine. In Germany it is known as *Edelfäule*, and in France as *pourriture noble*.

Bottle fermentation. Laborious, classical method of making sparkling wine in the bottle, known in France as the *méthode Champenoise*, in which sugar and yeast are added to still wine, inducing a second fermentation in the bottle. Stacked bottles in cellars must be turned by hand regularly over several years to bring the sediment to the neck of the bottle, from which it is eventually disgorged. Bottles are then given a *dosage*, or addition of syrup and spirits, and recorked. This method stands in contrast to the less expensive *bulk process* (see below).

Breed. A wine whose original type was one of great finesse and whose present quality reflects the source of which it is the progeny.

Brolio. One of Italy's finest Chiantis, named after a twelfth-century castle and its wine estate. The label does not show the symbolic black rooster of most Chiantis. Brolio Riserva is the best quality.

Brut. French term, also used in the U.S., indicating the driest of all champagnes, more dry than the grade labeled "extra dry."

Bulk process. Method of making sparkling wine in tanks where the wine is kept under pressure and later bottled under pressure. The method is faster and less expensive than making champagne in bottles, but the quality is inferior.

Burgundy. Famous wine-producing region of France. Its production is less than that of the Bordeaux area, but its wines are renowned. In the north of the area is the town of Chablis, with its dry, crisp white wines. Richest of the Burgundies are from the Côte d'Or, or "slope of gold," which is divided into the Côte de Nuits, with red Burgundies such as Chambertin, Romanée-Conti, and Richebourg; and the Côte de Beaune, with such fine reds as Corton, Pommard, etc., as well as magnificent whites such as Montrachet and Meursault. Farther south are Mâcon, with its dry white wines, and Beaujolais, known for its young, fruity reds. Wines from other areas of the world with the generic label "Burgundy" bear little resemblance to the genuine Burgundies.

Cabernet Sauvignon. Principal red grape used in making the greatest Bordeaux and California red wines. The best wines of this grape when young are often tart and tannic, but they age into wines with complex, mellow flavors.

California. Largest wine-growing area in the U.S. Wineries include huge operations such as E. & J. Gallo, Almadén, and Christian Brothers, which produce a large variety of products, including generic wines, premium table wines each made principally from a noted grape variety, dessert wines, fortified wines, sparkling wines, and brandy—an assortment one never finds in a single European winery. California is also the home of many so-called boutique wineries, which like their European counterparts, feature only a few premium wines. The best of California wines can now challenge the best in France. California wines with generic names such as Burgundy, Chablis, etc., are dependable in quality but not identical with the wines whose European names they bear.

Catawba. Light-red native American grape used in New York State and Ohio white and sparkling wines with a *foxy* flavor (see below).

Cave. French word for "cellar," or storage area.

Chablis. Town in the northern part of Burgundy, France, famed for crisp, dry white wines sometimes called "fish wines" because of their compatibility with seafood dishes.

Chambertin. Famed Burgundy vineyard that produces a red wine of immense prestige, which was a favorite of

Napoleon. The adjoining vineyard, Chambertin-Clos de Bèze, is considered equally great.

Chambolle-Musigny. Noted township in Burgundy, France, whose red wines are distinguished by their subtlety and delicacy of flavor.

Champagne. Sparkling white wine made in a delimited area of France, east of Paris. Most are blends of various years. A few bear vintage years. Although the word *champagne* appears on the labels of sparkling wines in other countries, the French product is matchless.

Character. The quality of a wine so definite and vivid as to be unmistakable. A wine such as rosé need not be great to have the pink color and fresh, fruity flavor that is rosé's character.

Château. French name for vineyard properties in the Bordeaux area. Some have castles or stately residences; others are simply plots of land among the 4000 wine-producing châteaux in Bordeaux. Among the most famous château names you may encounter are Ausone, Cheval-Blanc, Haut-Brion, Lafite-Rothschild, La Tour, Margaux, Mouton-Rothschild, Pétrus, and d'Yquem.

Châteauneuf-du-Pape. Red wine of the Rhône Valley in France, noted for its sturdy, full-bodied flavor; chosen by many Americans for its price advantage over the expensive Bordeaux wines.

Chelois. French-American hybrid grape that produces a medium-bodied red New York State wine.

Chenin Blanc. Great white wine grape of the Loire Valley in France, used in Vouvray; also cultivated in California. Most American Chenin Blanc wines, unlike their European counterparts, are slightly sweet.

Chewy. Term used to describe red wines of great body with mouth-filling flavor and a pronounced aftertaste.

Chianti. Word that to many Americans means the archetype of the best Italian red wines made in a delimited area of Tuscany. At one time most Chiantis were sent to the U.S. in raffia-covered bottles. Today the best Chiantis are in conventional bottles, labeled "Chianti Classico," and show a black cockerel on the label, symbol of the Chianti League, whose members are pledged to follow strict procedures for vineyard planting, harvesting, and vinification.

Claret. English term for Bordeaux red wines; used loosely for dry red wines of varying qualities from France, California, and elsewhere.

Clean. Leaving an uncluttered and distinct flavor in the mouth.

Clos (French). Vineyard or enclosure that may have stone walls.

Clos de Vougeot. Famed French vineyard of the Côte d'Or in Burgundy, owned by approximately a hundred individuals; produces red wines of varying quality, the best of which are noted for their dry, rich body and superb finish.

Coarse. Description of a rough, undeveloped flavor; sometimes a lot of flavor but with no finesse.

Complex. Having a number of perceivable flavors. Lemon juice added to a Coke drink makes it more complex in the taster's jargon. When young, fruity wines with the relatively simple flavor of grapes become older, their flavors —in the case of certain fine wines—acquire subtle overtones and are then said to be more complex.

Corky or **corked.** An almost rotten aroma given off by wine bottled with a defective cork; a rather rare defect, not to be confused with the normal smell of wine in a drawn cork.

Corton. Wine from the French village of *Aloxe-Corton* (see above).

Côte d'Or. French place name meaning, literally, "slope of gold"; a 36-mile-long area in Burgundy that includes two sections, Côte de Nuits and Côte de Beaune, home of the greatest Burgundies.

Côte Rôtie. Area of the Rhône Valley in France noted for red wines of deep color and rich body.

Cru (French). Term for "growth," using the word not in the sense of increased size but as the tract of vineyard land and the wines it produces. When a noted vineyard is officially classified as *cru classé*, it may be designated as first growth for the best class, second growth for the next best, etc.

Crust. Deposit left in a bottle of port wine after aging. The wine is usually decanted before serving to eliminate the deposit.

Cuvée (French). Term for vatful or tankful, referring to a specific batch of wine or specific blend, separating it from others of the same label.

Decant. To slowly pour wine (usually a very old red wine) from its original bottle into a carafe in order to eliminate the sediment in the bottle.

Deidesheimer. German white wine from the town of Deidesheim in *Rheinpfalz* (see below); usually from the Riesling grape, renowned for its rich body and bouquet.

Delaware. Eastern U.S. native pink grape, which makes a flowery, sweet, somewhat tart wine often used in New York State champagne making.

Demi-sec (French). Term meaning, literally, "half-dry," applying to champagne.

Depth. Flavor that is both rich and of good duration.

Diamond. Eastern U.S. white grape, also known as Moore's Diamond, used for spicy, tart white wine and champagne.

Dôle. Red, full-bodied Swiss wine from the Rhône Valley.

Dom Pérignon. Seventeenth-century French cellarmaster, legendary inventor of champagne.

Dosage. Mixture of syrup and spirits, added to champagne after the deposit from fermentation is removed from the bottles and before the final corking. The amount of sugar in the syrup determines whether the wine is dry or of varying degrees of sweetness.

Dry. Opposite of sweet. When the term *dry* is applied to champagne, however, it means the champagne is comparatively not as free of sugar as *brut* (see above).

Earthy. Flavor given to certain wines because of the soil in which the grapes are grown, reminiscent of freshly turned earth in a complimentary sense. If earthiness is exaggerated, the wine is coarse.

Echezeaux. Highly rated French red Burgundy wine from a number of different vineyards in the Côte de Nuits.

Edelfäule (German). Term for *Botrytis* (see above).

Emerald Riesling. White wine made from grapes that are a cross between the Riesling and Muscadelle grapes, which yield flavors that are fruity, slightly tart, and spicy. The best brands are noted for a good balance of acid and sugar.

Entre-Deux-Mers (French). Term meaning "between two seas"; actually an area between two rivers, the Dordogne and the Garonne, in Bordeaux, from which are shipped many pleasant dry white wines of fair quality and reasonable price.

Epernay. Town east of Paris in the Champagne area, known as a busy trade center for champagne.

Est! Est!! Est!!! Latin term meaning "It is"; the name of a slightly sweet white wine discovered in the twelfth century by a German bishop's valet who, traveling ahead of the bishop to check the wine and food, scribbled the word *Est!* on walls of taverns where the food and wine were good. He chalked the word three times for the wine he found in the town of Montefiascone, north of Rome.

Estate bottled. In areas where the word *château* is not used to describe a wine property, the term *estate bottled* sometimes appears on labels to indicate the wine was bottled on the same property where the grapes were grown—an assurance of authenticity.

Finesse. Just as a delicious consommé is consummate, or finished, with subtle—not overbearing—flavor accents, a wine with finesse has delicacy and distinction.

Finger Lakes. Region of western New York State that produces the most important wines of the eastern U.S.

Finish. Aftertaste, or lingering sensation in the mouth after a wine has been swallowed; one of the most important criteria in judging a wine's flavor.

Fino. Extremely dry, light, pale sherry, often served chilled as an aperitif wine.

Flabby. Descriptive term for wines so soft and weak in flavor as to almost completely lack character.

Flat. Term that applies both to sparkling wines that have lost their effervescence and to still wines with low acidity or dull flavor.

Flinty. Descriptive metaphor of a dry white wine with a crisp, almost hard flavor, such as French Chablis, recalling flint striking steel.

Flowery. Evocative of fragrant blossoms but not perfumy in the artificial sense. Flowery wines are easy and delicate on the nostrils.

Folle Blanche. White grape that produces a light, tart wine known best as one of the wines from which cognac is distilled. It is also grown in California and sometimes is used as a blending ingredient in *Chenin Blanc* (see above).

Fortified. Sweet dessert wines and aperitif wines to which brandy has been added are said to be fortified, although the term does not appear on the labels. The addition of brandy raises the alcoholic content of the wines from the legal limit of 14 percent for table wines to approximately 20 percent. Wines thus fortified may be opened and kept on the shelf without danger of spoilage.

Foxy. Term describing the flavor of wines from indigenous American grapes that Leif Ericson found in Vineland the Good. European wine drinkers dislike wines of this type, which taste so much like the original grapes. California wines from European root stocks do not have a foxy flavor. Foxy wines are beloved by millions of Americans, especially in the eastern U.S.

Frascati. Italian white wine, dry and of medium body, produced in a town southeast of Rome.

Freemark Abbey. Winery in Napa Valley, California, that produces premium Pinot Chardonnay and Cabernet Sauvignon wines.

Fresh. Young flavor of wines that are at their best within a year or two of their bottling, such as Beaujolais wines, rosés, and many whites.

Funchal. Town on the island of Madeira where Madeira wines are aged and from which they are shipped.

Gallo. The huge winery of E. & J. Gallo in California, once known mainly for popular jug wines; now also produces excellent varietal wines. Their Hearty Burgundy, a generic label, has been rated by some wine connoisseurs as one of the finest buys in red table wines.

Gamay. Red grape from which the famed French Beaujolais is made. Similar wines produced in California may have the names Gamay Beaujolais or Napa Gamay on their labels.

Geisenheim. Town in the Rheingau area of Germany noted for excellent Riesling wines.

Generic. When a wine label bears the specific place name of a wine from another country, purporting to be the class of wine represented by the place name, it is called generic. Thus, Rhine wine made in the U.S. is the generic name for wine of a similar type, made from similar grapes, in Germany. American wines labeled with the names of

French wines, such as Burgundy, Chablis, and Sauternes (or sauterne, as it is called in California), are not a duplicate of, and sometimes bear little resemblance to, the same wines from France. Generic names as used in the U.S. and other countries have no geographical significance, and wines bearing such names vary from mediocre to good and must be judged strictly on an individual basis.

Gewürztraminer. A white wine grape from the German word *Gewürz*, meaning "spice." Wine of this grape produced in the Alsace, Germany, and California has overtones called spicy that, however, do not convey the intensity of such spices as cloves, nutmeg, etc. The wine has a mildly pungent, easygoing floweriness of such individuality that a rank beginner would be unlikely to confuse it with any other wine.

Graves. Area of the Bordeaux district in France, an important part of which contains a gravelly soil, that produces red and white wines. In the U.S., the white Graves are generally more popular than the reds, although one of the reds, Château Haut-Brion, is rated as one of the world's finest.

Gray Riesling. In France this white wine grape, called *Chauché Gris*, is held in low esteem. In California its flavor is more satisfying and vivid. The wine of the same name is popular and is often compared to *Sylvaner* (see below).

Green. Term used to describe young wines rough in flavor and often with strong acidity.

Grenache. Red grape used for some dessert wines but best known for its distinctive rosé.

Grignolino. Red wine grape whose original home was Piedmont, Italy; is grown successfully in California for light, fruity wines and is used for blending with other red table wines.

Growth. English word for *cru* (see above).

Gumpoldskirchen. Noted wine-producing area of Austria, which produces fruity white wines similar to German Riesling, Gewürztraminer, etc.

Hallgarten. Wine town high in the hills of the Rheingau, Germany, noted for wines with sturdy body, fine balance, and clean aftertaste.

Hard. Stubborn flavor of tannin that time, in the case

of many fine wines, softens. If it fails to soften, hardness becomes harshness.

Haut Sauternes (French). Term meaning, literally, "high" Sauternes, or a white wine made from grapes grown on one of the more northerly vineyards, or higher vineyards, in the Sauternes area of France, theoretically more exposed to the sun and therefore sweeter than other Sauternes. The term is not a dependable guide to quality.

Hermitage. Wine from a town in the Rhône Valley in France that produces red and white wines. In the U.S., the reds, dark in color with fine, rich body, are more popular than the whites.

Hock. English term for German white wines, probably an abbreviation of Hockheimer, a white wine from the area near Wiesbaden.

Hungary. One of the most productive of the east European wine countries. Although little Hungarian table wine is sold in the U.S., their Tokay, a sweet, very rich white dessert wine, enjoys great prestige.

Inferno. Red wine from Lombardy, Italy, made from the Nebbiolo grape; of decidedly dark color; hard when young, but after three to four years in the bottle, it becomes a superb red wine that bears no resemblance to its name.

Inglenook. California winery at Rutherford, in Napa Valley; noted for popular red and white jug wines and very outstanding Cabernet Sauvignon wines.

Jerez. City in southern Spain, center of the sherry trade, around which are extensive vineyards that produce sherry.

Johannisberg. Famed German village and its castle, called Schloss Johannisberg, on the Rhine; source of some of the most eminent German Riesling wines. When "Johannisberg Riesling" appears on a California wine label, it simply means the wine was made from the white Riesling grape. Most non-German Rieslings are softer than, and lack the finesse and body of, the true Johannisberg Rieslings.

Kabinett. Term on German wine labels that indicates the driest class of wines.

Kornell, Hanns. Owner of California champagne cellars that bear the same name; produces champagne following the French method of *bottle fermentation* (see above). The Kornell label has long been one of the most prestigious for champagne made in this country.

Krug, Charles. Winery in the Napa Valley, California, that offers a very large selection of premium varietal wines under the Charles Krug label, as well as less expensive wines identified as C.K.

Lacrima Christi. Soft Italian red and white table wines whose name means "tears of Christ"; originally grown near Mount Vesuvius, now also produced in other parts of Italy.

Lambrusco. Italian slightly sparkling, slightly sweet red wine, popular in Italy as an accompaniment to fatty foods; in tremendous favor with young U.S. wine drinkers.

Liebfraumilch. Blended German semi-dry white wine from many different vineyards; very popular in the U.S. The quality of various labels and the consistency of quality vary with the shipper.

Livermore. California valley southeast of San Francisco, with warm climate; produces noted white wines from Sauvignon Blanc and Semillon grapes.

Long. Characteristic of a wine that leaves a pronounced, pleasant aftertaste.

Mâcon. Southern Burgundy town and surrounding area, best known in the States for a dry white wine made from Pinot Chardonnay grapes and sold at comparatively reasonable prices. The label may indicate just Mâcon or both Pinot Chardonnay and Mâcon. Famed for *Pouilly-Fuissé* (see below).

Madeira. Fortified wine from an island in the Atlantic belonging to Portugal. Resembling sherry in flavor, it ranges from Sercial, the lightest and driest, to Malmsey, the darkest and sweetest.

Maderized, or **maderisé** (French). Term for white or rosé wine unintentionally turned brown because of oxidation and, therefore, on its way to complete spoilage.

Malaga. Spanish seaport and province known for its sweet, fortified wine, which resembles sherry; also a California grape used for dessert wines.

Manzanilla. Extremely dry wine of the sherry type, produced near Jerez, Spain.

Marsala. Sicilian dessert wine fortified with brandy;

comes in both sweet and dry types, the latter less sweet but a far cry from bone-dry table wines.

Martini, Louis M. One of California's most respected wine makers, whose winery is in Napa Valley. "Special Selections" on his labels indicates outstanding wines. "Mountain" designation on his labels means wines grown in elevated vineyards.

Masson, Paul. Large California winery noted for its wide selection of moderately priced varietal wines as well as some proprietary blends, such as Rubion, Baroque, etc.

May wine. German white wine flavored with the herb woodruff, often served with a floating strawberry.

Médoc. Important wine district of Bordeaux, France; produces some of the greatest French red wines.

Mellow. Characteristic of a wine that is soft and full-flavored; may be used to describe either dry or sweet wine.

Mendocino. California county north of Sonoma, known originally for production of jug wines from Zinfandel and other red grapes; now a source of noted varietal wines, home of several outstanding small wineries as well as Cresta Blanca, producing a large variety of table wines.

Merlot. Red wine grape grown both in France and in California, used mostly for blending with Cabernet Sauvignon to add roundness and softness; used almost entirely in the great Bordeaux wine from Pomerol, Château Pétrus.

Meursault. Burgundy village renowned for white wine with a rich, spirited flavor and fine aftertaste.

Mirassou. California winery started in 1854, noted in recent years for plantings in both Santa Clara and Monterey counties; its wide selection of varietal wines is known for rich bouquets and vigorous flavors.

Mis en bouteilles au château (French). Term of the Bordeaux area of France, printed on a wine label to indicate the wine was bottled on vineyard property where the grapes were grown; in other areas this is often indicated as "Estate bottled."

Mondavi, Robert. Well-known owner of a California winery, once associated with Charles Krug winery; produces very distinguished varietal wines, including Cabernet Sauvignon and Fumé Blanc, among others.

Montrachet. Most prestigious of all French white Burgundies; distinguished labels are Le Montrachet, Chevalier-Montrachet, and Bâtard-Montrachet.

Moselblümchen (German). Word meaning, literally, "little flower of the Moselle." White wine from the Moselle River area in Germany. Like Liebfraumilch of the Rhine, it may be blended from different grapes or diverse vineyards.

Moselle. German river that meets the Rhine at Coblenz. On its banks are grown Riesling grapes, from which some of Germany's best white wines, known for their special delicacy, are produced. These wines are always sold in tall green bottles. (Rhine wines are in brown bottles.)

Mousseux (French). Term for sparkling wines that are not made in the French Champagne area, such as Bourgogne Mousseux, or sparkling Burgundy.

Muscadet. Crisp, dry white wine from the Loire Valley in France, sometimes slightly bubbly; favored as an accompaniment to seafood.

Muscat. Sweet grapes, either black or white, used for dessert wines; not to be confused with Muscatel wine of the winos, made from the Muscat of Alexandria.

Must. Juice drawn from the grapes in the initial step of wine making.

Musty. Unpleasant flavor of wine reminiscent of old or moldy wood in casks.

Nahe. Valley of the Nahe River, in Germany, a tributary of the Rhine; the home of less expensive German wines made from Riesling and Sylvaner grapes.

Napa Gamay. The red wine grape used in France for Beaujolais, called simply Gamay, is known in California as Napa Gamay and is the component of many red wines that are at their best when young.

Napa Valley. California's most prestigious wine-growing region, north of San Francisco.

Nebbiolo. Italian grape, also grown in California, used for some of Italy's most noted and big-flavored red wines made in the Piedmont area.

Nerveux (French). Term meaning, literally, "nervous." When applied to wine, it means vigorous and well balanced.

New York State. Next to California, the largest wine-growing area in the U.S., most of it concentrated in the Finger Lakes section, where native American grapes (*Vitis labrusca,* below) thrive.

Niagara. Native New York State white grape used for a

semi-dry white wine and as a table grape; also a region alongside the Niagara River where native and hybrid grapes are grown for wine.

Nierstein. German town of the Rhinehessen region, noted for estate-bottled wines of great delicacy.

Nose. Sensory effect of a wine on the nose; therefore, its bouquet. Also a verb meaning to judge a wine with the olefactory sense.

Nuits-Saint-Georges. Village in the Côte-de-Nuits, which along with *Pommard* (see below) produces two of the wines from Burgundy, France, most familiar to U.S. wine shoppers. The best of the Nuits-Saint-Georges wines are known for their big flavor and rich bouquet.

Nutty. Term often used to describe medium-dry sherries of full flavor reminiscent of walnuts.

Oloroso. Full-bodied, deeply fragrant sherry usually blended into sweet cream sherry.

Oppenheim. Town of the Rhinehessen in Germany that produces white wines with soft but good body, made from Sylvaner or Riesling grapes.

Originalabfüllung (German). Term on German wine labels indicating the wine was bottled on the estate where the grapes were grown.

Orvieto. Italian white wine from Umbria, in both dry and semi-dry types.

Pauillac. Township of the Haut-Médoc area in Bordeaux, home of red wines from some of the highest-ranking châteaux in France.

Pays (French). Term meaning "country," applied to locally produced wine sold in or near the vineyards; sometimes unknown outside of the immediate countryside, sometimes bearing no label, the wine is called *vin de pays*.

Pétillant (French). Term that describes wine with a very slight sparkle. Examples are some Swiss wines and Portuguese crackling rosé.

Petite-Sirah. Grape that produces deeply colored, robust red wines; widely cultivated in California.

Piesport. Small village along the Moselle River in Germany, known for delicate, mellow wines of great distinction.

Pinot Blanc. White grape used in France, Italy, and California largely for blending.

Pinot Chardonnay. White grape, sometimes called simply Chardonnay, from which are made the great French white Burgundies as well as noted California white wines. Shy-bearing vines yield a comparatively small harvest, and the wines are therefore expensive. The wines range in color from light yellow to light or medium gold; flavors are usually rich, with pronounced body and aroma.

Pinot Noir. Dark grapes used for eminent French red Burgundies, for much French champagne, and for California red wines.

Piquant. The quality of a wine with lively but pleasant acidity and vivid flavor.

Pomerol. Township of Bordeaux, France, famed for red wines of rich flavor and velvety smoothness; home of the illustrious Château Pétrus.

Pommard. Township in the Côte de Beaune, source of one of the most popular French red Burgundies imported in the U.S. Unless the label shows a vineyard designation, the wine may be Pommard blended with wine from other sources.

Port. Fortified dessert wine from Portugal, quite sweet and both richer and more subtle than American wines sold as port. The youngest is ruby port, with a fresh, fruity flavor; older ports are called tawny, with a brownish tinge to the color, as well as greater age and flavor. Almost all ports are blends. Vintage port, or port of a distinguished year, is rather rare in U.S. wineshops. White port, with a comparatively small sugar content and a young, fruity flavor, is popular in some European countries as an aperitif wine.

Pouilly-Fuissé. Very dry French white Burgundy with a vivacious, fruity flavor; made from Pinot Chardonnay grapes.

Pouilly-Fumé. French white wine of the Loire Valley, usually less dry than Pouilly-Fuissé, but with full, extremely pleasant flavor; made from Sauvignon Blanc grapes.

Powerful. Term applied to wines with extraordinary, mouth-filling flavor and bold bouquet.

Qualitätswein (German). Term on German wine labels indicating wine from one of eleven specified regions, made from approved grapes. The wine must pass a chemical analysis and tasting panel before the term may be used on the label; it must carry an official approval number, or A.P., on the label. In this category of wines, sugar may be added before fermentation to increase the alcoholic content.

Qualitätswein mit Prädikat (German). *Qualitätswein* (see above) with special attributes. No added sugar is permitted for fermentation. Within this superior class are the following grades, all described in this section: Kabinett, Spätlese, Auslese, Beerenauslese, and Trockenbeerenauslese.

Retsina. Greek table wine to which resin has been added, resulting in a flavor reminiscent of turpentine; thought to have been originally used as a preservative, now popular among natives, who accept its strong flavor.

Rheingau. Most famous wine-growing region of Germany, on the right bank of the Rhine River, extending west from Wiesbaden. Its rich white wines of big flavor are produced mainly from the Riesling grape.

Rheinhessen. Second to the Rheingau in prestige, the Rheinhessen region is south of the Rheingau and on the west bank of the Rhine River. Sylvaner is the principal grape.

Rheinpfalz (also known as **Pfalz** and **Palatinate**). Large wine-growing region in Germany, south of Rheinhessen, extending to the Alsace in France. Most of its wines, with a few outstanding exceptions, such as those from the town of Deidesheim, do not enjoy the international prestige of German wines from Rheingau and Rheinhessen.

Rhine wine. Term that originally applied only to German white wine made from grapes grown on the slopes of the Rhine River; now widely used in other parts of the world where Riesling and Sylvaner grapes are grown. All Rhine wine from Germany is sold in tallish brown bottles.

Rhône. River that flows from the Swiss Alps through southeastern France; home of two red wines popular in the U.S.: Hermitage and Châteauneuf-du-Pape.

Riesling. Famed white wine grape of Germany, sometimes identified as White Riesling. In other countries it is sometimes called Johannisberg Riesling (see *Johannisberg*, above). Not to be confused with *Emerald* or *Gray Riesling* grapes (see both, above), which produce wines of much different flavor. The true Riesling is known for its rich, vivid flavor.

Rioja. Red wine from a district in northern Spain. Rioja is slow to mature but develops a sturdy, big flavor. In some instances, the best riojas rival the better red wines of Bordeaux, France.

Romanée-Conti. One of the most illustrious and most expensive of the top red Burgundies in France, from a vineyard in the Côte d'Or that produces about 500 cases of wine a year.

Rosé. A type of light, young, fruity wine with a pink color from red grapes the skins of which are allowed to remain only briefly with the juice.

Rough. Wine term that, unlike *earthy*, is never used in a complimentary sense; describes a wine that may lack maturity, be unpleasantly puckerish, or leave a coarse aftertaste.

Rounded. Like the term *balance*, rounded describes a wine whose qualities complement each other. The wine may not be illustrious, but no one quality can be faulted, and the aftertaste is completely satisfying.

Sack. Old English word for sherry.

Saint-Emilion. French township in the Bordeaux area, noted for eminent châteaux that produce red wines with a big, beautifully rounded flavor.

Saint-Estèphe. French township in the Haut-Médoc district of Bordeaux that produces red wines with robust flavor, requiring ample time to mature.

St. Jean, Chateau. Small California winery noted for rich Rieslings made from late-picked grapes.

Saint-Julien. Township in the Haut-Médoc district of Bordeaux, France, known for elegant red château wines as well as more moderately priced wines labeled simply "St.-Julien."

Saumur. Wine area bordering the Loire River in France; produces pleasantly light red, white, rosé, and sparkling wines.

Sauternes. French wine district in Bordeaux famed for sweet, rounded white wines, including the great Château d'Yquem. Note that the French word is spelled ending in *s*; in California, where weak imitations of the French prototype are produced, the word is spelled *sauterne*.

Sauvignon Blanc. White grape used for California varietal wines, sometimes appearing on labels as just Sauvignon; used in France for making Graves and as a partner with Sémillon grapes in making Sauternes.

Schloss (German). Term meaning "castle." Like the French word *château*, *schloss* refers to a vineyard and its buildings, which may or may not include a castle.

Sec (French). Term for "dry," characterizing beverages that lack sweetness. The term is wildly inconsistent when applied to champagne, since a French *sec* champagne is quite sweet.

Sekt (German). Sparkling wine.

Sémillon. White grape used in combination with Sauvignon Blanc for producing French Sauternes. In California it's employed for a medium-bodied white wine in both sweet and dry versions.

Seyval. White American hybrid grape that yields a fruity, dry wine; grown in the eastern U.S., it sometimes appears on labels as Seyval-Blanc.

Sherry. Spain's great wines from the district in southern Spain whose principal city is Jerez. All are fortified with brandy. Flavors run the spectrum from the palest of finos, usually served as an appetizer wine, to medium-dry amontillados, all the way to deep, sweet olorosos or cream sherries. Sherries are developed, aged, and blended in the solera system, a method of wine making in which younger wines are gradually moved in limited quantities at a time into casks containing older wines. The younger wines take on the rich flavor, deep color, and full-bodied maturity of the senior sherries sooner than if they had remained alone in their original casks.

Short. Term describing wine that leaves a brief flavor or very limited flavor in the mouth.

Simi. California winery with an excellent reputation for its rosé made from Cabernet Sauvignon grapes, zinfandel, and Chardonnay wines.

Soave. Italian dry white wine known for its suave feel in the mouth; produced in an area near Verona.

Soft. Term to describe a pleasing wine whose qualities are harmonious but never insipid; sometimes used to describe wines with a low alcoholic content.

Solera. See *Sherry*, above.

Sommelier (French). Term for wine waiter who often wears customary chain and cellar keys. An outstanding sommelier knows wines in general and, more specifically, the quality of all wines in his cellar.

Sonoma. Historic wine town and county north of San Francisco, California; home of many small, old-fashioned wineries as well as noted modern vineyards.

Spätlese (German). Term meaning late grape harvest or wines made from grapes of such a harvest, ripened to pronounced sweetness.

Spicy. Although conventional spices or herbs are not included in wine making (except in the case of *May wine*, above), the term refers to wines of the Alsatian or German types, particularly Gewürztraminer, whose provocative and pleasant flavor is reminiscent of spices.

Spritzer (German). Cold mixed drink of white wine, usually Rhine wine, and sparkling water.

Spritzig (German). Term for wine with a small natural sparkle, usually not visible, but noticeable in the mouth.

Stag's Leap. Small California winery in Napa Valley noted for its magnificently full, rich Cabernet Sauvignon wines.

Sterling. California winery at the north end of the Napa Valley, distinguished for its Cabernet Sauvignon and two white wines, Sauvignon Blanc and Pinot Chardonnay.

Sulfury. Wine in which sulfur dioxide, widely used to prevent oxidation, flavor deterioration, and spoilage, may have been used excessively, leaving a pungent, unpleasant flavor.

Sylvaner. Abundant white grape of the Alsace and Germany, sometimes called Franken Riesling; wine noted for its soft, fruity flavor. In California, Sylvaner wine is sometimes labeled "Riesling" or used in blending with the true White Riesling, although its flavor is less complex and less assertive than the Riesling.

Tannin. Substance in wine that makes it astringent or puckerish in the mouth. Tannin is important in red wines needing long age, during which it acts as an antioxidant and, as the wine matures, generally diminishes in strength and becomes acceptable as a flavor component.

Tart. Sharp to the taste. As in many fresh fruits, a

measure of tartness in wine, when not excessive, adds to the wine's taste appeal and balance.

Tavel. District in the Rhône Valley, France, that produces outstanding rosé wine.

Taylor Wine Company. Biggest winery in New York State; includes the Pleasant Valley Wine Company, makers of the well-known Great Western champagne. Taylor New York State wines are made from native as well as hybrid grapes. Taylor's western arm, the Taylor California Cellars, are producers of well-known generic wines such as Chablis and Burgundy.

Tokay. Hungarian sweet, rich white dessert wine, in rare supply and quite expensive. The Hungarian label reads, "Tokaji Aszú."

Traminer. Name of a grape variety of which the *Gewürztraminer* (see above) is the best quality.

Trockenbeerenauslese (German). Term for a white wine made from dried berries of very select, late-harvested grapes. Wine of this name is made from grapes affected with *Botrytis* (see above), deliberately left on the vine until they are almost raisins, with a maximum of sweetness and greatly reduced moisture content, resulting in a fabulously rich flavor.

Valpolicella. Light- to medium-bodied fruity red wine from the Veneto province of Italy.

Valtellina. Hearty, full-bodied Italian red wine from Lombardy.

Varietal wine. Wine labeled by the principal grape used in its making. The name of the vineyard may or may not be stated.

Verdicchio. Italian white wine from east-central Italy, medium-bodied, sometimes with a pungent aftertaste; may be in an amphora-type bottle.

Vigorous. Term to describe wines of pronounced, assertive flavor; applied to both young, strong wines and older ones.

Vin ordinaire (French). Term for common table wine. It may be local or shipped from another area and is unidentified by label, may vary in quality from poor to good, and is often sold in restaurants by the carafe or glass.

Vintage. Specific year's grape harvest. Where vintages vary considerably in quality from one year to the next, as they do in Europe, vintage years on a bottle are important. California vintage differences from one year to the next are less drastic but still noticeable and important. A great majority of the wines in shops are blends of different years. In certain areas, fine wines may be produced in a poor year and poor wines in a fine year.

Vitis labrusca. Species of grapes growing on the North American continent before any white men landed; produces wines with *foxy* (see above) flavor, reminiscent of bottled grape juice or grape jam. Still heavily cultivated and used in making many eastern U.S. wines.

Vitis vinifera. Species of grapes that were originally cultivated in Europe and were transplanted to California, producing wines that not only resemble European wines but in a few outstanding cases equal or surpass them.

Volnay. Notable, delicate, soft red Burgundy wine from Côte de Beaune in France.

Vouvray. Fruity, dry white wine of the Loire Valley in France, popular in the U.S. Some Vouvray is also made into a sparkling wine.

Woody. The literal flavor of wood in wines held too long in the cask or in casks whose wood conveyed an unacceptable flavor.

Zeltingen. Town on the Moselle River in Germany, source of delicate white wines with good body, made from Riesling grapes.

Zinfandel. Red wine grape of European origin that flourishes in California but is not now cultivated in Europe. Flavor overtones of the wine are frequently described as berrylike. It may be a young, fruity wine or an older one with the capacity for aging into a rich, complex wine.

COCKTAILS

The most overwhelmingly popular of all potables, the open sesame to brunch parties, lunch parties, dinner parties, midnight supper parties, and the next morning's revival parties, the cocktail is undoubtedly America's most noted contribution to the world of bibulous pleasure. The stories concerning the origin of the word *cocktail* are nearly as many and varied as the mixtures themselves. Among them, the following legends have enjoyed long vintage life:

The word came from the French word *coquetel*, once used to describe a mixed drink in the Bordeaux region.

Southern army officers were once served a luscious mixed drink by a lovely southern belle. Her name? Octelle, suh!

A distinguished American general was invited to the court of a Mexican monarch whose daughter appeared with a drink in the royal cup of gold encrusted with rubies. When the obvious question of who would drink first racked all the king's men, the daughter solved the problem very intelligently by drinking the libation herself. The stunning princess's name was, of course, Coctel.

Western horse traders whose nags weren't worth the price of their pelts, on sale day, fed their horses liquor whose effects made them cock their tails and come to life with incredible spirit.

Morning tipplers in New Amsterdam, visiting inns for a pick-me-up, would invariably run into Dutch barmaids who (you guessed it) used the tails of roosters for sweeping away last night's litter.

A young Irish lass (this one by James Fenimore Cooper) not only managed to procure and roast chickens from Tory farmers for her Revolutionary guests, but decorated their drinks with feathers from the cocks' tails.

Whether or not these stories are any truer than Bunyan's blue ox, it's clear that the cocktail goes deep into America's drinking heritage. And even today, Americans remain the foremost masters and idolaters of the cocktail.

Cocktails range from appetite-awakening bone-dry martinis to velvety dessert cocktails that correctly climax a rich feast. Men taking the lead at their own cocktail parties should weigh the counsel in the section on "Barmanship." In time, as your cocktail repertoire expands, the ups and downs of the cocktail shaker will become second nature. But even the most polished perfectionists at their bars follow certain well-tested guidelines for cocktails, hence the following review of the more important considerations in drink making:

1. Inferior liquors aren't masked in cocktails. A fine gin will seem even finer in a martini. The same goes for whiskeys, rums, vodkas, and vermouths.

2. Don't imitate free-pouring bartenders in public bars. Use standard measures, whether they be teaspoons, jiggers, ounces, cups, or quarts. When you multiply quantities for party drinking, be mathematically accurate.

3. Ice must be hard, cold, and clean—not weeping. Fresh ice at 0° F. or below will produce a much brisker drink than lazy ice turning to water.

4. Though cocktails must be icy cold (proper dilution is part of the art), they shouldn't be watery. Anyone can begin shaking cocktails. An artist knows when to stop. Normally 2 to 2½ ounces poured into a cocktail shaker will grow to approximately 4 ounces after proper shaking. Use a 4½-ounce glass or 6-ounce glass for larger cocktails.

5. Use the proper glass for each cocktail, and be sure that it's sparkling clean and prechilled. The glass should

first chill the hand and then the lips; the icy cocktail itself will take care of the rest.

6. You should, of course, use fresh ingredients in your cocktails, especially when it comes to fruit juices.

7. Cocktails with fruit juices, eggs, syrups, etc., are normally shaken; those containing only liquor and vermouth are stirred (although one of the most eminent martini men of modern times, Somerset Maugham, insisted that his martinis be *shaken*). The stirred cocktail is clear; the shaken cloudy.

8. Make your own personal recipe changes only with the greatest care, remembering that some cocktails are dominated by a single straight, powerful flavor—the martini by gin, for instance, or the negroni by Campari—while others are a medley of flavors: liquors, fortified wines, juices, bitters, fruits, etc. A fine cocktail of the latter type is always in delicate balance; even its aftertaste leaves a pleasant sense of the tart and the sweet, the strong and the weak. Sometimes adding or subtracting an eighth of a teaspoon will make a noticeable difference. Be creative if you will, but create slowly and deftly. A new drink is always an evolution.

The cocktails that follow are designed for a 4½-ounce cocktail glass, except in those cases where an old-fashioned or other glass is used. The parsimonious 3-ounce cocktail glasses are now skeletons in most liquor closets; not only does the larger cocktail provide more sumptuous bliss for guests, but it's a boon to the host since it means fewer refills and the coveted chance to sit down, drink, and enjoy the revels.

After-Dinner Cocktails

On a dinner or late-supper menu, the after-dinner cocktail can take the place of the dessert or supplement it. As a libation, it's frankly sweet and toothsome. It goes perfectly with a platter of cheese and crackers, a fresh fruit bowl, or both. It graciously replaces the ubiquitous pie and the gooey ice cream. For the harried host who has neither the time to make nor the energy to shop for a fresh dessert, it's a deliverance. Freshly concocted, any of the following are an imaginative way to conclude a brunch, lunch, or dinner.

AFTER-DINNER CHARADE

1 oz. Sciarada
½ oz. peppermint schnapps
½ oz. heavy cream

Shake extremely well with ice. Strain into prechilled cocktail glass.

AMARETTO CREAM

1 oz. amaretto
1 oz. Muscari
½ oz. heavy cream

Shake well with ice. Strain into cocktail glass or over rocks.

BANSHEE

1 oz. banana liqueur
½ oz. white crème de cacao
1 inch ripe banana, sliced
½ oz. cream or milk
½ cup crushed ice

Put all ingredients into blender. Blend 10 seconds. Pour into deep-saucer champagne glass.

BERRIES AND CREAM

1 oz. blackberry-flavored brandy
1 oz. strawberry liqueur
1 oz. nondairy creamer
½ oz. lime juice

Shake well with ice. Strain into prechilled cocktail glass or serve over rocks. Fresh heavy sweet cream may be used, but it tends to curdle when mixed with the lime juice.

BLUE ANGEL

½ oz. blue curaçao
½ oz. parfait amour
½ oz. brandy
½ oz. lemon juice
½ oz. heavy cream

Shake well with ice. Strain into prechilled cocktail glass. Cool and incredibly smooth.

BOURBON CREAM

1 oz. bourbon
½ oz. Wild Turkey liqueur
1 oz. heavy sweet cream

Shake well with ice. Strain into prechilled cocktail glass.

BRAVE BULL

1 oz. Kahlúa
1 oz. tequila
1 piece lemon peel

Pour Kahlúa and tequila over rocks in an old-fashioned glass. Stir well. Add ice if necessary to fill glass. Twist lemon peel over drink and drop into glass.

CADIZ

¾ oz. amontillado sherry
¾ oz. blackberry liqueur
½ oz. Triple Sec
½ oz. heavy cream

Shake well with ice. Strain over rocks in prechilled old-fashioned glass.

CALM VOYAGE

½ oz. Galliano or Roiano
½ oz. passion-fruit syrup
2 teaspoons lemon juice
½ oz. light rum
½ egg white
⅓ cup crushed ice

Put all ingredients into blender. Blend at low speed 10–15 seconds. Pour into prechilled deep-saucer champagne glass. Mendelssohn is good accompaniment on this trip.

CARAMEL COW

2 ozs. (¼ measuring cup) vanilla ice cream
1 oz. Caramella
½ oz. crème de cacao
1½ ozs. milk

Pour all ingredients into blender. Blend at high speed 10 seconds. Pour over rocks in 8-oz. old-fashioned glass. Stir well.

CARA SPOSA

1 oz. coffee liqueur
1 oz. curaçao
½ oz. heavy cream
⅓ cup crushed ice

Put all ingredients into blender. Blend at low speed 10–15 seconds. Pour into prechilled deep-saucer champagne glass. Although any kind of coffee liqueur may be used in this drink, the espresso-coffee liqueur is especially pleasant.

CHERRY RUM

1¼ ozs. light rum
¾ oz. cherry liqueur
½ oz. heavy cream
⅓ cup crushed ice

Put all ingredients into blender. Blend at low speed 10–15 seconds. Pour into prechilled deep-saucer champagne glass.

CHIQUITA PUNCH

1½ ozs. banana liqueur
1½ ozs. orange juice
1½ ozs. cream
¾ oz. grenadine
¾ cup crushed ice

Put all ingredients into blender. Blend at high speed 10 seconds. Pour into prechilled old-fashioned glass.

CHOCOLATE BLACK RUSSIAN

2 ozs. (¼ measuring cup) chocolate ice cream
1 oz. Kahlúa
½ oz. vodka
1½ ozs. milk

Pour all ingredients into blender. Blend at high speed 10 seconds. Pour over rocks in 8-oz. glass. Stir well.

CHOCOLATE ECLAIR

2 ozs. (¼ measuring cup) chocolate ice cream
1 oz. Choclair
½ oz. light rum
1½ ozs. milk
1 tablespoon sweet chocolate shavings

Pour chocolate ice cream, Choclair, light rum, and milk into blender. Blend at high speed 10 seconds. Pour over rocks in 8-oz. glass. Stir well. Sprinkle chocolate shavings on top.

CHOCOLATE MINT

2 ozs. (¼ measuring cup) chocolate ice cream
1 oz. peppermint schnapps
½ oz. vodka
1½ ozs. milk

Pour all ingredients into blender. Blend at high speed 10 seconds. Pour over rocks in 8-oz. glass. Stir well.

CHOCOLATE RUM

1 oz. light rum
½ oz. white crème de cacao
½ oz. white crème de menthe
½ oz. heavy cream
1 teaspoon 151-proof rum

Shake light rum, crème de cacao, crème de menthe, and cream well with ice. Strain into prechilled cocktail glass. Float 151-proof rum on top.

CHOCOLATIER

2 ozs. (¼ measuring cup) chocolate ice cream
1 oz. dark Jamaica rum
½ oz. crème de cacao
1½ ozs. milk
1 tablespoon sweet chocolate shavings

Pour chocolate ice cream, rum, crème de cacao, and milk into blender. Blend at high speed 10 seconds. Pour over rocks in 8-oz. glass. Stir well. Sprinkle chocolate shavings on top.

COCO AMOR

1 oz. CocoRibe
½ oz. amaretto
½ oz. lemon juice

Shake extremely well with ice. Strain into prechilled cocktail glass with sugar-frosted rim.

COCO BANANA

1 oz. CocoRibe
½ oz. banana liqueur
½ oz. heavy cream

Shake extremely well with ice. Strain into prechilled cocktail glass.

COCONUT MINT

1 oz. CocoRibe
½ oz. peppermint schnapps
½ oz. heavy cream
1 tablespoon chocolate shavings

Shake CocoRibe, peppermint schnapps, and cream extremely well with ice. Strain into prechilled cocktail glass. Float chocolate shavings on drink.

COFFEE CREAM

1 oz. coffee liqueur
1 oz. California brandy
1 oz. heavy cream

Shake well with ice. Strain into large cocktail glass or over rocks.

COFFEE GRASSHOPPER

¾ oz. coffee liqueur
¾ oz. white crème de menthe
¾ oz. cream

Shake well with ice. Strain into prechilled cocktail glass.

COFFEE ROIANO

1½ ozs. Roiano
½ oz. coffee liqueur
½ oz. heavy cream
⅓ cup crushed ice

Put all ingredients into blender. Blend at low speed 10–15 seconds. Pour into prechilled deep-saucer champagne glass. May be served not only at the end of a meal but at any time of the day.

CREAMY CHARADE

1 oz. Sciarada
½ oz. vodka
½ slightly beaten egg white
½ oz. lemon juice
½ oz. heavy sweet cream

Shake all ingredients extremely well with ice. Strain into prechilled large cocktail glass.

DULCET

1 oz. vodka
½ oz. curaçao
½ oz. anisette
½ oz. apricot liqueur
1 teaspoon lemon juice
½ brandied apricot

Shake vodka, curaçao, anisette, apricot liqueur, and lemon juice well with ice. Strain over cracked ice or rocks in prechilled old-fashioned glass. Add brandied apricot.

FROZEN BANANA MINT

1 oz. banana liqueur
1 oz. peppermint schnapps
⅓ cup sliced ripe banana
¾ cup crushed ice
2 large mint leaves

Pour banana liqueur, peppermint schnapps, sliced banana, and crushed ice into blender. Blend at high speed 10 seconds. Pour into 8-oz. glass. Float mint leaves on drink.

FROZEN BLACK CURRANT

1 oz. crème de cassis
1 oz. pineapple juice
½ oz. brandy
⅓ cup crushed ice
1 slice orange

Put crème de cassis, pineapple juice, brandy, and crushed ice into blender. Blend at low speed 10–15 seconds. Pour into prechilled deep-saucer champagne glass. Add orange slice.

FROZEN COCO BANANA

2 ozs. CocoRibe
1/3 cup sliced ripe banana
1/2 cup crushed ice
1/2 oz. lemon juice

Whirl all ingredients in blender at high speed 10 seconds. Pour into deep-saucer champagne glass.

GAELIC GLEE

1 1/2 ozs. Irish cream liqueur
1/2 oz. coffee liqueur
1/2 oz. light rum
Freshly grated nutmeg

Shake Irish cream liqueur, coffee liqueur, and rum extremely well with ice. Strain into prechilled cocktail glass. Sprinkle with nutmeg.

GINGERMAN

2 ozs. (1/4 measuring cup) chocolate ice cream
1 oz. ginger-flavored brandy
1/2 oz. light rum
1 1/2 ozs. milk

Pour all ingredients into blender. Blend at high speed 10 seconds. Pour over rocks in 8-oz. glass. Stir well.

GOLD CADILLAC

3/4 oz. crème de cacao
3/4 oz. Galliano
3/4 oz. heavy cream
1/3 cup crushed ice

Put all ingredients into blender. Blend at low speed 10–15 seconds. Pour into prechilled deep-saucer champagne glass. For another version, omit crushed ice, shake well with ice, and strain into prechilled cocktail glass.

GOLDEN FROG

½ oz. Strega
½ oz. Galliano
½ oz. vodka
½ oz. lemon juice
¾ cup crushed ice

Put all ingredients into blender. Blend at high speed 10 seconds. Pour into prechilled old-fashioned glass.

GRASSHOPPER

¾ oz. white crème de cacao
¾ oz. green crème de menthe
¾ oz. heavy cream

Shake well with ice. Strain into prechilled cocktail glass.

GRASS SKIRT

1 oz. CocoRibe
½ oz. light rum
1 oz. pineapple juice
½ oz. lime juice

Shake well with ice. Strain into prechilled large cocktail glass with sugar-frosted rim.

IL MAGNIFICO

¾ oz. Tuaca liqueur
¾ oz. curaçao
¾ oz. heavy cream
⅓ cup crushed ice

Put all ingredients into blender. Blend at low speed 10–15 seconds. Pour into prechilled deep-saucer champagne glass. May be served before, with, or after the espresso.

IRISH ALEXANDER ON THE ROCKS

¾ oz. blended Irish whiskey
¾ oz. Irish coffee liqueur
¾ oz. heavy cream

Shake all ingredients well with ice. Pour into prechilled old-fashioned glass. Add ice cubes to fill glass to rim. Stir.

KALANI WAI

1 oz. Midori
1 oz. green crème de menthe
1 oz. heavy cream

Shake well with ice. Strain into large cocktail glass or over rocks.

LADY IN GREEN

1 oz. pistachio liqueur
1 oz. green crème de menthe
½ oz. heavy cream

Shake well with ice. Strain over rocks in 8-oz. glass. Stir.

MAUI

1 oz. Midori
1 oz. Cointreau or Triple Sec
½ oz. lemon juice

Shake well with ice. Strain into large cocktail glass or over rocks.

MOCHA MINT

¾ oz. coffee liqueur
¾ oz. white crème de menthe
¾ oz. crème de cacao

Shake well with ice. Strain into prechilled sugar-and-coffee-frosted cocktail glass.

NUMERO UNO

1 oz. amaretto
1 oz. tequila
1 oz. heavy cream
Ground cinnamon

Shake amaretto, tequila, and cream well with ice. Strain into large cocktail glass. Sprinkle with cinnamon.

ORACABESSA

1 oz. banana liqueur
½ oz. lemon juice
½ oz. 151-proof rum
1 slice banana
1 slice lemon

Dip banana slice into lemon juice or orange juice to prevent discoloration. Shake banana liqueur, lemon juice, and rum well with ice. Strain over rocks in old-fashioned glass. Add banana and lemon slices.

ORANGE COMFORT

½ oz. Southern Comfort
½ oz. anisette
¾ oz. orange juice
½ oz. lemon juice
1 slice cocktail orange in syrup

Shake Southern Comfort, anisette, orange juice, and lemon juice well with ice. Strain into prechilled cocktail glass. Garnish with cocktail-orange slice.

ORANGE FLOWER

1 oz. curaçao
½ oz. cherry liqueur
½ oz. orange juice
1 teaspoon lemon juice
1 dash orange-flower water
⅓ cup crushed ice

Put all ingredients into blender. Blend at low speed 10–15 seconds. Pour into prechilled deep-saucer champagne glass. Exhilarating finale for a roast-goose dinner.

PARSON WEEMS

2 ozs. (¼ measuring cup) chocolate ice cream
½ oz. cherry-flavored brandy
½ oz. maraschino liqueur
½ oz. California brandy
1½ ozs. milk

Pour all ingredients into blender. Blend at high speed 10 seconds. Pour over rocks in 8-oz. glass. Stir well.

PAYOFF

2 ozs. (¼ measuring cup) vanilla ice cream
¾ oz. amaretto
¾ oz. California brandy
1½ ozs. milk
1 tablespoon toasted slivered almonds

Pour vanilla ice cream, amaretto, California brandy, and milk into blender. Blend at high speed 10 seconds. Pour over rocks in 8-oz. glass. Stir well. Sprinkle almonds on top.

PINK ALMOND

½ oz. crème de noyaux
½ oz. orgeat or orzata
1 oz. blended U.S. whiskey
½ oz. kirschwasser
½ oz. lemon juice
1 slice lemon

Shake crème de noyaux, orgeat, whiskey, kirschwasser, and lemon juice well with ice. Strain over rocks in prechilled old-fashioned glass. Add lemon slice.

PINK CARNATION

2 ozs. (¼ measuring cup) vanilla ice cream
½ oz. cranberry liqueur
½ oz. cherry-flavored brandy
½ oz. California brandy
1½ ozs. milk

Pour all ingredients into blender. Blend at high speed 10 seconds. Pour over rocks in 8-oz. glass. Stir well.

PINK COCONUT

1½ ozs. CocoRibe
½ oz. nondairy creamer
½ oz. lime juice
1 teaspoon grenadine

Shake all ingredients extremely well with ice. Strain into prechilled cocktail glass.

PINK RIBBON

1 oz. strawberry liqueur
½ oz. Triple Sec
½ oz. California brandy
½ oz. lemon juice

Shake all ingredients well with ice. Strain into sugar-frosted cocktail glass.

PINK SQUIRREL

1 oz. crème de noyaux
1 oz. white crème de cacao
¾ oz. heavy cream

Shake all ingredients well with ice. Strain into prechilled sugar-frosted cocktail glass. Pinker and smoother than a pink lady.

PISTACHIO CREAM

2 ozs. (¼ measuring cup) vanilla ice cream
1 oz. pistachio liqueur
½ oz. California brandy
1½ ozs. milk

Pour all ingredients into blender. Blend at high speed 10 seconds. Pour over rocks in 8-oz. glass. Stir well.

RUSSIAN CARAMEL

1 oz. Caramella
1 oz. vodka
1 oz. heavy cream
Freshly grated nutmeg

Shake Caramella, vodka, and cream well with ice. Strain into large cocktail glass. Sprinkle nutmeg on drink.

RUSSIAN COFFEE

¾ oz. coffee liqueur
¾ oz. vodka
¾ oz. heavy cream
⅓ cup crushed ice

Put all ingredients into blender. Blend at low speed 10–15 seconds. Pour into prechilled deep-saucer champagne glass.

SHERRIED COFFEE

1¼ ozs. oloroso sherry
1¼ ozs. coffee liqueur
2 teaspoons heavy cream

Shake sherry and coffee liqueur well with ice. Strain over rocks in prechilled old-fashioned glass. Float cream on top.

SNIFTER

¾ oz. Galliano
¾ oz. California brandy
1 teaspoon white crème de menthe
⅓ cup finely crushed ice

Pour liquors into prechilled brandy snifter. Add crushed ice. Stir. May be served with or without straw.

SOFT LANDING

1 oz. anisette
½ oz. Cointreau
¼ teaspoon vanilla extract
2 ozs. heavy sweet cream

Shake all ingredients well with ice. Strain over ice in prechilled old-fashioned glass.

SOUTHERN PEACH

1 oz. Southern Comfort
1 oz. peach liqueur
½ oz. heavy cream
1 slice fresh or brandied peach

Shake Southern Comfort, peach liqueur, and cream well with ice. Strain over rocks or coarsely cracked ice in prechilled old-fashioned glass. Add peach slice. It's peaches and cream brought up to date.

STRAWBERRY KISS

1 oz. strawberry liqueur
½ oz. kirschwasser
½ oz. light rum
½ oz. orange juice
1 teaspoon lemon juice
1 large strawberry

Shake strawberry liqueur, kirschwasser, rum, orange juice, and lemon juice well with ice. Strain into prechilled sugar-frosted cocktail glass. Add strawberry.

SWEET OFFERING

1 oz. Caramella
½ oz. crème de cacao
½ oz. light rum
½ oz. lime juice

Shake all ingredients well with ice. Strain into large cocktail glass.

SWEET TALK

1 oz. blackberry-flavored brandy
½ oz. California brandy
½ oz. heavy cream

Shake all ingredients very well with ice. Strain into cocktail glass.

SWEET WILLIAM

¾ oz. pear brandy
¾ oz. apricot liqueur
¾ oz. heavy cream
Ground cinnamon

Shake pear brandy, apricot liqueur, and cream very well with ice. Strain into prechilled cocktail glass. Sprinkle with cinnamon.

ULTRA SUEDE

½ oz. Irish cream liqueur
½ oz. white crème de cacao
½ oz. banana liqueur
½ oz. lime juice
Shaved sweet chocolate

Shake Irish cream liqueur, crème de cacao, banana liqueur, and lime juice well with ice. Strain into prechilled cocktail glass. Sprinkle with chocolate. (To shave chocolate, rub a bar of sweet chocolate over the coarse holes of a metal grater.)

YELLOW FINGERS

1 oz. gin
1 oz. blackberry brandy
½ oz. banana liqueur
½ oz. heavy cream

Shake all ingredients well with ice. Strain into prechilled saucer champagne glass.

FRAPPES

Frappés are even more pleasing than ice cream and cake as a finale for a feast. Cool, clean, and rich, they're a mixture of liqueurs poured over finely crushed ice. You can serve them freshly made, but we prefer to swizzle them up beforehand and store them in the freezer until the drinking lamp is lit. When you take them out, you'll find that an ice cap has formed on top of each drink. But the cap will loosen after a minute or two, and the drink can be sipped from the rim with or without a short straw.

ALL-WHITE FRAPPE

½ oz. anisette
¼ oz. white crème de menthe
½ oz. white crème de cacao
1 teaspoon lemon juice

Stir without ice. Pour over crushed ice in deep-saucer champagne glass.

BANANA RUM FRAPPE

½ oz. banana liqueur
½ oz. light rum
½ oz. orange juice

Stir without ice. Pour over crushed ice in deep-saucer champagne glass. Cool postscript for an Oriental dinner.

BRANDY APRICOT FRAPPE

¾ oz. California brandy
½ oz. apricot-flavored brandy
¼ oz. crème de noyaux

Stir without ice. Pour over crushed ice in deep-saucer champagne glass.

CHARTREUSE COGNAC FRAPPE

¾ oz. yellow Chartreuse
¾ oz. cognac

Stir without ice. Pour over crushed ice in deep-saucer champagne glass.

CHERRY GINGER FRAPPE

1 oz. cherry liqueur
¼ oz. kirschwasser
¼ oz. ginger-flavored brandy
1 brandied cherry
1 piece preserved ginger in syrup

Stir cherry liqueur, kirschwasser, and ginger-flavored brandy without ice. Pour over crushed ice in deep-saucer champagne glass. Pierce brandied cherry and preserved ginger with cocktail spear and place over rim of glass.

CHOCOLATE ORANGE FRAPPE

¾ oz. white crème de cacao
¾ oz. orange juice
1 teaspoon Galliano or Roiano

Stir without ice. Pour over crushed ice in deep-saucer champagne glass.

COFFEE GRAND MARNIER

½ oz. coffee liqueur
½ oz. Grand Marnier
½ oz. orange juice
1 slice orange

Stir coffee liqueur, Grand Marnier, and orange juice without ice. Pour over crushed ice in deep-saucer champagne glass. Add orange slice.

COGNAC MENTHE FRAPPE

1 oz. green crème de menthe
½ oz. cognac
2 large mint leaves

Stir crème de menthe and cognac without ice. Pour over crushed ice in deep-saucer champagne glass. Tear each mint leaf partially and place on drink.

CRANBERRY FRAPPE

½ oz. cranberry liqueur
½ oz. cherry-flavored brandy
½ oz. orange juice

Stir without ice. Pour over crushed ice in deep-saucer champagne glass.

DUTCH PEAR FRAPPE

1¼ ozs. pear brandy
¾ oz. Vandermint liqueur
½ oz. heavy cream
½ cup finely crushed ice
Sweetened whipped cream

Pour pear brandy, Vandermint, heavy cream, and ice into blender. Blend at low speed 20 seconds. Pour into prechilled old-fashioned glass. Add ice cubes if necessary to fill glass to rim. Top with dollop of whipped cream. Make this drink just before serving.

GRAND MARNIER QUETSCH

1 oz. Grand Marnier
¼ oz. quetsch
¼ oz. orange juice
1 slice lemon

Stir Grand Marnier, quetsch, and orange juice without ice. Pour over crushed ice in deep-saucer champagne glass. Add lemon slice. Mirabelle or slivovitz may be used in place of quetsch, since all are plum brandies.

KUMMEL BLACKBERRY FRAPPE

¾ oz. kümmel
¾ oz. blackberry liqueur or blackberry-flavored brandy
1 teaspoon lemon juice

Stir without ice. Pour over crushed ice in deep-saucer champagne glass.

MIXED MOCHA FRAPPE

¾ oz. coffee liqueur
¼ oz. white crème de menthe
¼ oz. crème de cacao
¼ oz. Triple Sec

Sugar-frost rim of deep-saucer champagne glass. Fill with crushed ice. Stir liqueurs without ice and pour over ice in glass.

PERNOD CURAÇAO FRAPPE

¾ oz. Pernod
¾ oz. curaçao
1 teaspoon lemon juice
2 teaspoons orange juice
1 thin slice orange

Stir Pernod, curaçao, lemon juice, and orange juice without ice. Pour over crushed ice in deep-saucer champagne glass. Add orange slice.

SAMBUCA COFFEE FRAPPE

1 oz. sambuca
½ oz. coffee liqueur
Roasted coffee beans

Stir the sambuca and coffee liqueur without ice. Pour over crushed ice in deep-saucer champagne glass. Place the glass on a saucer along with about a half-dozen coffee beans to munch while sipping. It's an Italian custom; the more distinguished the guest, the more coffee beans placed alongside his sambuca.

SHERRIED CORDIAL MEDOC FRAPPE

1 oz. Cordial Médoc
½ oz. amontillado sherry

Stir without ice. Pour over crushed ice in deep-saucer champagne glass.

SLOE LIME FRAPPE

1 oz. sloe gin
½ oz. light rum
1 slice lime

Stir sloe gin and light rum without ice. Pour over crushed ice in deep-saucer champagne glass. Add lime slice. Sip without straw.

SOUTHERN COMFORT STRAWBERRY FRAPPE

¾ oz. Southern Comfort
¾ oz. strawberry liqueur
Orange peel
1 slice lemon

Stir Southern Comfort and strawberry liqueur without ice. Pour over crushed ice in deep-saucer champagne glass. Twist orange peel above drink and drop into glass Add lemon slice. Sip on a summer evening under the stars.

POUSSE-CAFE

This showy little drink is one of the oldest bits of nonsense known to bartenders—and, needless to say, the number of drinkers who never stop loving nonsense is greater than ever. If not a cocktail by definition, it is for after-dinner imbibing, and thus we include it here.

The pousse-café is a series of liqueurs poured into a small, straight-sided pousse-café glass so that each forms a layer. Since the liqueurs are of different weights or densities, the heaviest stays on the bottom, the next heaviest directly above it, and so on. The main problem that bedevils the pousse-café specialist is that the densities of liqueurs of the same flavor often vary from one brand to the next. One man's menthe may not rise above another man's parfait amour. Since the density of a liqueur is not indicated on the bottle's label, a certain amount of trial and error may be necessary in building a pousse-café. As a general guide, remember that frequently the higher a liqueur's alcohol content, the lower its density. This doesn't apply in all cases, but it's something of a help. The so-called *demi-sec* liqueurs are lighter than the sweet crèmes, and U.S. fruit-flavored brandies are lighter than liqueurs. If you're in doubt about a recipe, make an experimental pousse-café before the guests arrive, and when you find a formula that works, stick to it as long as you're using the same brands of liqueurs.

To keep the ingredients from mingling, pour them slowly over the back of a teaspoon, with the tip of the spoon held against the inside of the glass. Pour slowly and steadily, keeping your eye on the liquid as it flows. If you follow this procedure carefully, the layers should stay separate; you may find, in fact, that a liqueur poured in the wrong order will seep down or rise up to its proper level and stay there intact. For a party, you can make a large number of pousse-cafés beforehand, and if you place them carefully in the refrigerator, each small rainbow will remain undisturbed until you need it.

A pousse-café may be of three, four, or five layers. Each layer needn't be equal, but each should be of a distinctly different color when held at eye level. Nonalcoholic liquids such as syrups and cream may be poured along with the liqueurs or other spirits. Here are twelve pousse-café combinations, with the heaviest liquid listed first and the lighter ones in ascending order. To both create and divert conversation, make an assortment with several combinations on the same tray.

1. White crème de cacao, cherry liqueur, kümmel, and a dab of whipped cream.
2. Green crème de menthe, Galliano, blackberry liqueur, and kirschwasser.
3. Banana liqueur, Peter Heering or Cherry Karise, and cognac.
4. Peach liqueur, kirsch liqueur (not kirschwasser), and Pernod.
5. Orzata or orgeat, crème de noyaux, curaçao, and sweet cream mixed with enough crème de noyaux to make cream pink.
6. Passion-fruit syrup, green crème de menthe, strawberry liqueur, and ouzo.
7. Grenadine, brown crème de cacao, Drambuie, and sweet cream flavored with crème de menthe.
8. Crème de noyaux, anisette, Tuaca, and a dab of whipped cream.
9. Grenadine, brown crème de cacao, Triple Sec, and Sciarada.
10. Brown crème de cacao, maraschino liqueur, Rosémint, yellow Chartreuse, and cognac.
11. Parfait amour, cherry liqueur, anisette, and sweet cream flavored with a small amount of parfait amour.
12. Strawberry liqueur, cream, Cointreau, and Sciarada.

Aperitifs

AMERICANO

1¼ ozs. Campari
1¼ ozs. sweet vermouth
Lemon peel
Club soda (optional)

Stir Campari and sweet vermouth well with ice. Strain into prechilled cocktail glass. Twist lemon peel above drink and drop into glass. If you prefer, a Delmonico or old-fashioned glass may be used instead—with a rock or two and a splash of soda.

APPLE BYRRH

1 oz. calvados
½ oz. Byrrh
½ oz. dry vermouth
½ teaspoon lemon juice
Lemon peel

Shake calvados, Byrrh, vermouth, and lemon juice well with ice. Strain into prechilled cocktail glass. Twist lemon peel above drink and drop into glass. Then pass the Gruyère-and-anchovy canapés.

BASTARDO

1 oz. dry vermouth
1 oz. sweet vermouth
½ oz. California brandy
2 dashes Angostura bitters
Iced club soda
1 slice lemon

Pour dry vermouth, sweet vermouth, brandy, and bitters over rocks in old-fashioned glass. Stir well. Add splash of soda. Add lemon slice.

BITTERSWEET

1¼ ozs. sweet vermouth
1¼ ozs. dry vermouth
2 dashes Angostura bitters
1 dash orange bitters
Orange peel

Stir both kinds of vermouth and both kinds of bitters well with ice. Strain into prechilled cocktail glass. Twist orange peel above drink and drop into glass. Salted shelled pistachios go well with this taste teaser.

BUTTERFLY

¾ oz. dry vermouth
¾ oz. sweet vermouth
½ oz. red Dubonnet
½ oz. orange juice

Shake everything well with ice. Strain over rocks into prechilled old-fashioned glass. This combination of orange juice and three fortified wines is extremely light.

BYRRH BRANDY

¾ oz. Byrrh
¾ oz. cognac
¾ oz. dry vermouth

Combine and stir well with ice. Strain into prechilled cocktail glass.

BYRRH CASSIS

1½ ozs. Byrrh
¼ oz. crème de cassis
½ oz. lemon juice
1 slice lemon
Iced club soda (optional)

Shake Byrrh, crème de cassis, and lemon juice well with ice. Strain over rocks in prechilled old-fashioned glass. Add lemon slice—and a splash of soda if desired.

BYRRH COCKTAIL

1¼ ozs. Byrrh
1¼ ozs. gin
Lemon peel

Stir Byrrh and gin well with ice. Strain into prechilled cocktail glass or over rocks in prechilled old-fashioned glass. Twist lemon peel above drink and drop into glass.

CALIFORNIAN

1½ ozs. sweet vermouth
1 oz. blended U.S. whiskey
2 ozs. orange juice
1 teaspoon orgeat

Combine and shake well with ice. Strain over large ice cube in prechilled old-fashioned glass. Be sure the orange juice is freshly squeezed from ripe California navels or Valencias in midseason.

CANADIAN AND CAMPARI

1 oz. Canadian whisky
½ oz. Campari
1 oz. dry vermouth
Lemon peel

Stir whisky, Campari, and vermouth well with ice. Strain into prechilled cocktail glass. Twist lemon peel above drink and drop into glass. A perfect drink to sip while anticipating the antipasto.

CARDINAL I

¾ oz. gin
¾ oz. Campari
¾ oz. dry vermouth
Lemon peel

Stir gin, Campari, and vermouth well with ice. Strain into prechilled cocktail glass. Twist lemon peel above drink and drop into glass. (If you're wondering where and what Cardinal II is, you'll find it among the rum cocktails.)

COMBO

2½ ozs. dry vermouth
½ teaspoon curaçao
¼ teaspoon Angostura bitters
½ teaspoon sugar
1 teaspoon cognac

Shake everything well with ice. Strain over rocks in prechilled old-fashioned glass. An elusive, but not illusive, glow is created by this combination of aperitif flavors.

CYNAR SOUR

1 oz. Cynar
1 oz. California brandy
2 ozs. orange juice
1 oz. lemon juice
½ slice orange

Shake Cynar, California brandy, orange juice, and lemon juice well with ice. Strain into old-fashioned glass. Garnish with orange slice.

DIABOLO

1½ ozs. imported dry white port
1 oz. dry vermouth
¼ teaspoon lemon juice
Lemon peel

Shake port, vermouth, and lemon juice well with ice. Strain into prechilled cocktail glass. Twist lemon peel above drink and drop into glass.

DUBONNET COCKTAIL

1¼ ozs. red Dubonnet
1¼ ozs. gin
Lemon peel

Stir Dubonnet and gin well with ice. Strain into prechilled cocktail glass. Twist lemon peel above drink and drop into glass.

FINO

1¼ ozs. fino sherry
1½ ozs. sweet vermouth
1 slice lemon

Stir sherry and vermouth well with ice. Strain over rocks in prechilled old-fashioned glass. Garnish with lemon slice.

FLORIDIAN

1½ ozs. dry vermouth
½ oz. Forbidden Fruit
1 teaspoon Falernum
2 ozs. grapefruit juice
2 dashes orange bitters
1 slice lime

Shake vermouth, Forbidden Fruit, Falernum, grapefruit juice, and bitters well with ice. Strain over large ice cube in prechilled old-fashioned glass. Garnish with lime slice.

GIN AND CAMPARI

1¼ ozs. gin
1¼ ozs. Campari
Orange peel

Stir gin and Campari well with ice. Strain over rocks in prechilled old-fashioned glass. Twist orange peel above drink and drop into glass. Savor it in sips.

LILLET COCKTAIL

1½ ozs. Lillet
1 oz. gin
Lemon peel

Stir Lillet and gin well with ice. Strain into prechilled cocktail glass. Twist lemon peel above drink and drop into glass.

LILLET NOYAUX

1½ ozs. Lillet
1 oz. gin
¼ teaspoon crème de noyaux
Orange peel

Stir Lillet, gin, and crème de noyaux well with ice. Strain into prechilled cocktail glass. Twist orange peel above drink and drop into glass. The scintillating flavor of Lillet is even more pleasant when this drink is poured on the rocks.

MANHATTAN MILANO

1 oz. kirschwasser
2 ozs. sweet vermouth
1 brandied cherry

Pour kirschwasser and vermouth into mixing glass with ice. Stir very well. Strain into prechilled large cocktail glass. Add cherry. Use regular maraschino cherry if brandied cherries are unavailable.

MON DIEU

1 oz. blond Dubonnet
1 oz. red Dubonnet
1 oz. California brandy
1½-inch piece California orange peel, freshly cut

Pour both kinds of Dubonnet and brandy over ice in old-fashioned glass. Stir very well. Light a match. With other hand, bend orange peel sharply and hold flame to it to make a twinkling flare. Drop peel into glass.

NEGRONI

¾ oz. Campari　　　　　　　¾ oz. sweet vermouth
¾ oz. gin

Stir well with ice. Strain into prechilled cocktail glass. Similar to the Cardinal I except that the vermouth is sweet instead of dry. May be served on the rocks with a twist of lemon or splash of soda or both.

PICON ON THE ROCKS

1½ ozs. Amer Picon　　　　　Club soda
½ oz. lemon juice　　　　　　1 slice lemon

Pour Amer Picon and lemon juice over rocks in prechilled old-fashioned glass. Add a splash of soda. Stir. Garnish with lemon slice.

PICON PUNCH

1½ ozs. Amer Picon　　　　　1 tablespoon cognac
¼ teaspoon grenadine　　　　Lemon peel
Iced club soda

Pour Amer Picon, grenadine, and a splash of soda over rocks in a prechilled old-fashioned glass. Stir. Float cognac on top of drink. Twist lemon peel above drink and drop into glass. Although Amer Picon is a sweet liqueur, Frenchmen for over a century have sipped it avidly before mealtime. There's just enough bitterness to balance the sweet.

PLUM APERITIF

1½ ozs. dry vermouth　　　　¼ oz. prunelle
½ oz. cognac　　　　　　　　1 slice lemon

Stir vermouth, cognac, and prunelle well with ice. Strain over rocks in prechilled old-fashioned glass. Add lemon slice. A small jar of fresh beluga caviar will make the *mise en scène* perfect.

PUNT E MES NEGRONI

¾ oz. Punt e Mes
¾ oz. gin
¾ oz. sweet vermouth

Stir well with ice. Strain into prechilled cocktail glass. May be served on the rocks with a twist of lemon or splash of soda or both. Punt e Mes is one of those Italian aperitifs that cause you first to shudder, then instantly to ask for more.

RUM APERITIF

1 oz. dry vermouth
1 oz. light rum
1 teaspoon dark Jamaica rum
1 teaspoon raspberry syrup
½ oz. lemon juice
Lemon peel

Shake vermouth, both kinds of rum, raspberry syrup, and lemon juice well with ice. Strain into prechilled cocktail glass. Twist lemon peel above drink and drop into glass. This aperitif could just as well be included among the rum cocktails. The effect in either case is the same: a ravenous appetite.

SANCTUARY

1 oz. red Dubonnet
½ oz. Amer Picon
½ oz. Cointreau
½ oz. lemon juice
1 slice lemon

Shake Dubonnet, Amer Picon, Cointreau, and lemon juice well with ice. Strain over rocks in prechilled old-fashioned glass. Add lemon slice. Pass hot hors d'oeuvres.

SILVER KIRSCH

1½ ozs. Positano
1 oz. kirschwasser
½ oz. lemon juice
½ egg white
1 teaspoon sugar
⅓ cup crushed ice

Mix all ingredients in blender for 10 seconds at high speed. Pour into prechilled old-fashioned glass.

SLOE VERMOUTH

1 oz. sloe gin (creamy cap) *½ oz. lemon juice*
1 oz. dry vermouth

Shake well with ice. Strain into prechilled cocktail glass. A soft *divertissement* on a lazy afternoon.

SOFT ROCK

1 oz. California brandy *1 slice cocktail orange in*
2 ozs. Lillet *syrup*
3 ozs. orange juice

Shake brandy, Lillet, and orange juice well with ice. Strain over ice in old-fashioned glass. Add orange slice.

SOUTHWEST ONE

¾ oz. vodka *¾ oz. Campari*
¾ oz. orange juice

Shake well with ice. Strain into prechilled glass. Named after the London district in which the popular drink originated.

TRIO

¾ oz. dry vermouth *¾ oz. gin*
¾ oz. sweet vermouth

Stir well with ice. Strain into prechilled cocktail glass. A drink for rebels from the dry-martini crowd.

VERMOUTH CASSIS

2¼ ozs. dry vermouth
½ oz. crème de cassis
Iced club soda

Pour vermouth and crème de cassis over one or two rocks in a prechilled old-fashioned glass, a large wineglass, or an 8-oz. highball glass. Stir. Add soda, which Frenchmen use to stretch the drink into a long aperitif. Americans seem to prefer the drink less diluted. A *vin blanc* cassis is the same drink with dry white wine used instead of vermouth. A slice of lemon may be used as a garnish if desired.

VERMOUTH MARASCHINO

2 ozs. dry vermouth
½ oz. maraschino liqueur
½ oz. lemon juice
2 dashes orange bitters
1 maraschino cherry

Shake vermouth, maraschino liqueur, lemon juice, and bitters well with ice. Strain over large ice cube in prechilled old-fashioned glass. Garnish with cherry.

VERMOUTH SCIARADA

2½ ozs. chilled dry vermouth
½ oz. Sciarada
1 slice lemon

Pour vermouth and Sciarada over rocks in 8-oz. tall or squat glass. Stir well. Add lemon slice. May also be served in large stemmed wineglass.

VERMOUTH TRIPLE SEC

1 oz. dry vermouth
½ oz. Triple Sec
1 oz. gin
2 dashes orange bitters
Lemon peel

Shake vermouth, Triple Sec, gin, and bitters well with ice. Strain into prechilled cocktail glass. Twist lemon peel above drink and drop into glass.

ZAZA

2 ozs. red Dubonnet
1 oz. gin
1 slice orange

Stir Dubonnet and gin well with ice. Strain over rocks in prechilled old-fashioned glass. Place the orange slice on the rocks. Your nose should catch the aroma of the orange before your lips meet the drink. While there are many versions of this Dubonnet cocktail, these are the proportions we like best.

Apple-Brandy Cocktails

APPLE AND GINGER

1½ ozs. applejack
¾ oz. ginger-flavored
  brandy
½ oz. lemon juice
½ teaspoon sugar

Shake well with ice. Strain into prechilled cocktail glass. A cool alfresco drink.

APPLE BLOSSOM

1½ ozs. applejack
1 oz. apple juice
½ oz. lemon juice
1 teaspoon maple syrup
⅓ cup crushed ice
1 slice lemon

Put applejack, apple juice, lemon juice, maple syrup, and crushed ice into blender. Blend at low speed 10–15 seconds. Pour into prechilled deep-saucer champagne glass. Add lemon slice.

APPLECAR

¾ oz. applejack
¾ oz. Cointreau or curaçao
¾ oz. lemon juice

Shake well with ice. Strain into prechilled cocktail glass. The appleman's sidecar.

APPLE DUBONNET

1 oz. calvados
1 oz. red Dubonnet
1 slice lemon

Stir calvados and Dubonnet well with ice. Strain over rocks in prechilled old-fashioned glass. Add lemon slice.

APPLE GRAND MARNIER

1 oz. calvados
½ oz. Grand Marnier
½ oz. cognac
Lemon peel
Orange peel

Stir calvados, Grand Marnier, and cognac well with ice. Strain over rocks in prechilled old-fashioned glass. Twist lemon peel and orange peel above drink and drop into glass.

APPLEHAWK

1¼ ozs. applejack
1¼ ozs. unsweetened grapefruit juice
½ teaspoon sugar

Shake well with ice. Strain into prechilled cocktail glass.

APPLEJACK MANHATTAN

1¾ ozs. applejack
¾ oz. sweet vermouth
1 dash orange bitters
1 maraschino cherry

Stir applejack, vermouth, and bitters well with ice. Strain into prechilled cocktail glass. Add cherry.

APPLEJACK RABBIT

1½ ozs. applejack
½ oz. lemon juice
½ oz. orange juice
1 teaspoon maple syrup

Shake well with ice. Strain into prechilled sugar-frosted cocktail glass. Salted nuts or toasted coconut chips are good companions.

APPLEJACK SOUR

2 ozs. applejack
½ oz. lemon juice
1 teaspoon sugar
½ slice lemon

Shake applejack, lemon juice, and sugar well with ice. Strain into prechilled whiskey-sour glass. Add lemon slice.

APPLE LILLET

1 oz. calvados
1 oz. Lillet
1 slice orange

Stir calvados and Lillet well with ice. Strain over rocks in prechilled old-fashioned glass. Add orange slice. A perfect drink to kill time while waiting for the hot onion soup.

APPLE SUISSESSE

Grenadine
Superfine sugar
2 ozs. applejack
½ slightly beaten egg white
½ oz. heavy sweet cream
½ cup crushed ice

Dip rim of old-fashioned glass in grenadine, then in superfine sugar to make frosted rim. Place in freezer to chill. Pour applejack, 1 teaspoon sugar, egg white, cream, and crushed ice into blender. Blend at high speed 10 seconds. Pour into prechilled glass.

BITTER APPLE

2 ozs. applejack
2 dashes Angostura bitters
Iced club soda
Lemon peel

Pour applejack and bitters into prechilled old-fashioned glass. Add ice slices or cubes to fill glass. Add a splash of soda. Stir well. Twist lemon peel over drink and drop into glass. Aromatic, potent, and dry.

BLENHEIM

1 oz. applejack
½ oz. apricot-flavored brandy
¾ oz. lemon juice
1 teaspoon grenadine
1 dash orange bitters

Shake well with ice. Strain into prechilled sugar-frosted cocktail glass.

FROZEN APPLE

1½ ozs. applejack
½ oz. lime juice
½ egg white
1 teaspoon sugar
⅓ cup crushed ice

Put all ingredients into blender. Blend at low speed 10–15 seconds. Pour into prechilled deep-saucer champagne glass. A cocktail to pave the way for a roast suckling pig.

FROZEN APPLE AND BANANA

1½ ozs. applejack
½ oz. banana liqueur
½ oz. lime juice
⅓ cup crushed ice
1 slice banana

Put applejack, banana liqueur, lime juice, and ice into blender. Blend at low speed 10–15 seconds. Pour into prechilled deep-saucer champagne glass. Add banana slice.

FROZEN APPLECART

1½ ozs. applejack
¼ cup diced Delicious apple, peeled
⅓ cup crushed ice
½ oz. lemon juice
1 teaspoon sugar

Put all ingredients into blender. Blend at high speed 10 seconds. Pour into deep-saucer champagne glass or outsize cocktail glass.

JACK ROSE

2 ozs. applejack
½ oz. lime juice or lemon juice
1 teaspoon grenadine

Shake well with ice. Strain into prechilled cocktail glass. The classic applejack drink.

POLYNESIAN APPLE

1¼ ozs. applejack
¾ oz. pineapple juice
½ oz. California brandy
1 pineapple stick

Shake applejack, pineapple juice, and brandy well with ice. Strain over rocks in prechilled old-fashioned glass. Add pineapple stick. A standby cocktail when spareribs are slowly turning on the spit over charcoal.

PUERTO APPLE

1¼ ozs. applejack
¾ oz. light rum
½ oz. lime juice
1½ teaspoons orgeat or orzata
1 slice lime

Shake applejack, rum, lime juice, and orgeat well with ice. Strain over rocks in prechilled old-fashioned glass. Add lime slice.

RABBIT'S FOOT

¾ oz. applejack
¾ oz. light rum
½ oz. orange juice
½ oz. lemon juice
¼ oz. grenadine
1 slice orange

Shake applejack, rum, orange juice, lemon juice, and grenaline well with ice. Strain into prechilled old-fashioned glass. Add ice to fill glass. Garnish with orange slice.

Brandy Cocktails

ALABAMA

1 ¾ ozs. brandy
½ oz. lemon juice
1 teaspoon curaçao
½ teaspoon sugar
Orange peel

Shake brandy, lemon juice, curaçao, and sugar well with ice. Strain into prechilled sugar-frosted cocktail glass. Twist orange peel above drink and drop into glass.

APRICOT AND RASPBERRY SOUR

1 oz. apricot-flavored brandy or apricot liqueur
½ oz. framboise (white raspberry brandy)
½ oz. lemon juice
1 oz. orange juice
Iced club soda
½ slice orange
1 fresh raspberry or maraschino stem cherry

Shake apricot-flavored brandy, framboise, lemon juice, and orange juice well with ice. Strain into whiskey-sour glass. Add splash of soda. Stir. Garnish with orange slice and raspberry.

APRICOT SOUR

1½ ozs. apricot-flavored
   brandy
½ oz. lemon juice
1 oz. orange juice

Iced club soda
½ slice orange
1 maraschino stem cherry

Shake apricot-flavored brandy, lemon juice, and orange juice well with ice. Strain into whiskey-sour glass. Add splash of soda. Stir. Garnish with orange slice and cherry.

BAYOU

1¾ ozs. brandy
¼ oz. peach liqueur
½ oz. mango nectar

2 teaspoons lime juice
1 slice fresh or brandied
   peach

Shake brandy, peach liqueur, mango nectar, and lime juice well with ice. Strain over rocks in prechilled old-fashioned glass. Garnish with peach slice.

BOMBAY

1 oz. brandy
½ oz. dry vermouth
½ oz. sweet vermouth
½ teaspoon curaçao

¼ teaspoon Pernod
1 slice fresh or canned
   mango

Shake brandy, both kinds of vermouth, curaçao, and Pernod well with ice. Strain over rocks in prechilled old-fashioned glass. Add mango slice. Serve before a curry dinner.

BRANDIED APRICOT

1½ ozs. brandy
½ oz. apricot-flavored
   brandy

½ oz. lemon juice
Orange peel

Shake brandy, apricot-flavored brandy, and lemon juice well with ice. Strain into prechilled sugar-frosted cocktail glass. Twist orange peel above drink and drop into glass.

BRANDIED CORDIAL MEDOC

1½ ozs. brandy
½ oz. Cordial Médoc
½ oz. lemon juice
Orange peel

Shake brandy, Cordial Médoc, and lemon juice well with ice. Strain into prechilled cocktail glass. Twist orange peel above drink and drop into glass. Either California brandy or cognac may be used with good results.

BRANDIED GINGER

1½ ozs. brandy
½ oz. ginger-flavored brandy
1 teaspoon lime juice
1 teaspoon orange juice
1 piece preserved ginger in syrup

Shake brandy, ginger-flavored brandy, lime juice, and orange juice well with ice. Strain over rocks in prechilled old-fashioned glass. Garnish with preserved ginger.

BRANDTINI

1½ ozs. brandy
1 oz. gin
1 teaspoon dry vermouth
Lemon peel or cocktail olive

Stir brandy, gin, and vermouth well with ice. Strain into prechilled cocktail glass. Twist lemon peel above drink and drop into glass, or serve with cocktail olive.

BRANDY ALEXANDER

¾ oz. brandy
¾ oz. crème de cacao
¾ oz. heavy cream

Shake well with ice. Strain into prechilled cocktail glass.

BRANDY AND AMER PICON

2 ozs. cognac
½ oz. Amer Picon
Lemon peel
Orange peel

Stir cognac and Amer Picon well with ice. Strain over rocks in prechilled old-fashioned glass. Twist lemon peel and orange peel above drink and drop into glass.

BRANDY CASSIS

1¾ ozs. brandy
½ oz. lemon juice
2 teaspoons crème de cassis
Lemon peel

Shake brandy, lemon juice, and crème de cassis well with ice. Strain into prechilled cocktail glass. Twist lemon peel above drink and drop into glass.

BRANDY CRUSTA

Peel of ½ lemon, in one spiral
2 ozs. brandy
½ oz. curaçao
2 teaspoons lemon juice
1 dash bitters
1 teaspoon maraschino liqueur

Place lemon peel and cracked ice or rocks in prechilled sugar-frosted old-fashioned glass. Shake brandy, curaçao, lemon juice, bitters, and maraschino liqueur well with ice. Strain into glass.

BRANDY FINO

1½ ozs. brandy
½ oz. very dry sherry
½ oz. Drambuie
½ slice orange
Lemon peel

Shake brandy, sherry, and Drambuie well with ice. Strain over rocks in prechilled old-fashioned glass. Add orange slice. Twist lemon peel above drink and drop into glass.

BRANDY GUMP

2 ozs. brandy
½ oz. lemon juice
½ teaspoon grenadine

Shake well with ice. Strain into prechilled cocktail glass. A good one to relax with after an all-day sail.

BRANDY MANHATTAN

2 ozs. brandy
½ oz. sweet vermouth
1 dash bitters (optional)
1 maraschino cherry

Stir brandy, vermouth, and bitters well with ice. Strain into prechilled cocktail glass. Add cherry. For a dry brandy manhattan, use dry instead of sweet vermouth.

BRANDY MELBA

1½ ozs. brandy
¼ oz. peach liqueur
¼ oz. raspberry liqueur
½ oz. lemon juice
2 dashes orange bitters
1 slice fresh or brandied peach

Shake brandy, peach liqueur, raspberry liqueur, lemon juice, and bitters well with ice. Strain into prechilled cocktail glass. Add peach slice. If raspberry liqueur isn't available, raspberry syrup may be substituted.

BRANDY SOUR

2 ozs. brandy
½ oz. lemon juice
¼ oz. orange juice
½ to 1 teaspoon sugar
½ slice lemon

Shake brandy, lemon juice, orange juice, and sugar well with ice. Strain into prechilled whiskey-sour glass. Add lemon slice. Softer than a whiskey sour.

CHAMPS-ELYSEES

1½ ozs. cognac
½ oz. yellow Chartreuse
½ oz. lemon juice

1 dash Angostura bitters
(optional)

Shake well with ice. Strain over rocks in prechilled old-fashioned glass. Bitters may be omitted for a more pronounced Chartreuse flavor.

CHERRY BLOSSOM

1¼ ozs. brandy
¾ oz. wild-cherry liqueur
2 teaspoons lemon juice

¼ teaspoon curaçao
¼ teaspoon grenadine

Shake well with ice. Strain into prechilled sugar-frosted cocktail glass. Dip rim of glass in wild-cherry liqueur before dipping in sugar.

CLASSIC

1½ ozs. brandy
½ oz. lemon juice

¼ oz. maraschino liqueur
¼ oz. curaçao

Shake well with ice. Strain into prechilled cocktail glass. More tart than earlier versions of the brandy classic.

DAME MELBA

¾ oz. peach-flavored
   brandy
¾ oz. framboise
   (unsweetened raspberry
   brandy)

½ oz. lemon juice

Shake very well with ice. Strain into sugar-frosted cocktail glass.

DEAUVILLE

1 oz. brandy
½ oz. lemon juice
½ oz. apple brandy
½ oz. Triple Sec

Shake well with ice. Strain into prechilled cocktail glass.

DRY COLD DECK

1¾ ozs. brandy
½ oz. dry vermouth
¼ oz. white crème de menthe

Shake well with ice. Strain into prechilled cocktail glass. A sophisticated stinger.

FEMINA

1½ ozs. brandy
½ oz. Benedictine
½ oz. orange juice
1 slice cocktail orange in syrup

Shake brandy, Benedictine, and orange juice well with ice. Strain over rocks in prechilled old-fashioned glass. Add orange slice. Not biting in the "sour" tradition, but cool and comforting.

FOXHOUND

1½ ozs. brandy
½ oz. cranberry juice
1 teaspoon kümmel
1 teaspoon lemon juice
½ slice lemon

Shake brandy, cranberry juice, kümmel, and lemon juice well with ice. Strain over rocks in prechilled old-fashioned glass. Add lemon slice. Serve before a dinner of pheasant or partridge.

FRAMBOISE SOUR

1 oz. framboise
¾ oz. lime juice
2 level teaspoons sugar
1 wedge prepared cocktail orange in syrup
1 fresh raspberry, if available

Pour framboise, lime juice, and sugar into cocktail shaker with ice. Shake about double the usual time for proper dilution. Pour into prechilled whiskey-sour glass. Garnish with cocktail orange and raspberry.

FROUPE

1¼ ozs. brandy
1¼ ozs. sweet vermouth
1 teaspoon Benedictine

Stir well with ice. Strain into prechilled cocktail glass. Like a sunset's afterglow.

FROZEN BRANDY AND PORT

1½ ozs. brandy
1 oz. port
1 small egg
1 teaspoon powdered sugar
⅓ cup crushed ice
Grated nutmeg

Put brandy, port, egg, sugar, and ice into blender. Blend 20 seconds at low speed. Pour into prechilled saucer champagne glass. Sprinkle with nutmeg. Also known as a coffee flip when crushed ice is omitted and drink is shaken with ice in regular cocktail shaker.

FROZEN BRANDY AND RUM

1½ ozs. brandy
1 oz. golden rum
½ oz. lemon juice
1 egg yolk
1½ teaspoons sugar
⅓ cup crushed ice

Put all ingredients into blender. Blend 15–20 seconds at low speed. Pour into prechilled saucer champagne glass. Soothing.

HARVARD

1½ ozs. brandy
½ oz. dry vermouth
1 teaspoon grenadine
2 teaspoons lemon juice

Shake well with ice. Strain into prechilled cocktail glass. Drier than earlier versions, but still crimson.

HILLSBOROUGH

1 oz. California brandy
1 oz. Muscari
½ oz. lemon juice
Lemon peel

Shake brandy, Muscari, and lemon juice well with ice. Strain into cocktail glass. Twist lemon peel above drink and drop into glass.

JAPANESE

2 ozs. brandy
¼ oz. orgeat or orzata
¼ oz. lime juice
1 dash Angostura bitters
Lime peel

Shake brandy, orgeat, lime juice, and bitters well with ice. Strain into prechilled cocktail glass. Twist lime peel above drink and drop into glass.

LA JOLLA

1½ ozs. brandy
½ oz. banana liqueur
2 teaspoons lemon juice
1 teaspoon orange juice

Shake well with ice. Strain into prechilled sugar-frosted cocktail glass.

McBRANDY

1½ ozs. brandy
1 oz. apple juice
1 teaspoon lemon juice
1 slice lemon

Shake brandy, apple juice, and lemon juice well with ice. Strain into prechilled cocktail glass. Add lemon slice. Serve before a dinner of roast ham or duck.

PHOEBE SNOW

1¼ ozs. brandy
1¼ ozs. red Dubonnet
¼ teaspoon Pernod

Shake well with ice. Strain into prechilled cocktail glass.

PICASSO

1½ ozs. cognac
½ oz. red Dubonnet
½ oz. lime juice
1 teaspoon sugar
Orange peel

Shake cognac, Dubonnet, lime juice, and sugar well with ice. Strain into prechilled cocktail glass. Twist orange peel above drink and drop into glass.

POLONAISE

1½ ozs. brandy
½ oz. blackberry liqueur or blackberry-flavored brandy
½ oz. very dry sherry
1 teaspoon lemon juice
2 dashes orange bitters

Shake well with ice. Strain over rocks in prechilled old-fashioned glass.

QUAKER

1½ ozs. brandy
½ oz. rum
½ oz. lemon juice
1 teaspoon raspberry syrup
or grenadine
Lemon peel

Shake brandy, rum, lemon juice, and raspberry syrup well with ice. Strain into prechilled cocktail glass. Twist lemon peel above drink and drop into glass. Two rounds of these and all will be Friends.

SANTA FE

1½ ozs. brandy
½ oz. grapefruit juice
½ oz. dry vermouth
1 teaspoon lemon juice

Shake all ingredients well with ice. Strain into prechilled sugar-rimmed cocktail glass.

SARATOGA

2 ozs. brandy
½ oz. pineapple juice
1 teaspoon lemon juice
½ teaspoon maraschino
   liqueur
1 dash Angostura bitters

Shake well with ice. Strain into prechilled cocktail glass.

SIDECAR

¾ oz. brandy
¾ oz. Cointreau, curaçao,
   or Triple Sec
¾ oz. lemon juice

Shake well with ice. Strain into prechilled cocktail glass. All three ingredients may be varied to suit one's taste. For a strong brandy accent, use 1½ ozs. brandy, ½ oz. Cointreau, and ½ oz. lemon juice. One of the most venerable of traditional cocktails.

SLOE BRANDY

2 ozs. brandy
½ oz. sloe gin (creamy cap)
1 teaspoon lemon juice
Lemon peel

Shake brandy, sloe gin, and lemon juice well with ice. Strain into prechilled cocktail glass. Twist lemon peel above drink and drop into glass.

SOUTH PACIFIC

1½ ozs. brandy
½ oz. lemon juice
¼ oz. crème d'ananas
¼ oz. white crème de menthe
1 pineapple stick

Shake brandy, lemon juice, crème d'ananas (pineapple liqueur), and crème de menthe well with ice. Strain over rocks in prechilled old-fashioned glass. Garnish with pineapple stick.

SPLASHDOWN

1½ ozs. California brandy
½ oz. Galliano
½ oz. lime juice
1 oz. orange juice
1 teaspoon orgeat or orzata
1 slice lime

Shake brandy, Galliano, lime juice, orange juice, and orgeat well with ice. Strain over ice in prechilled old-fashioned glass. Add lime slice.

STINGER

1¼ ozs. brandy
1¼ ozs. white crème de menthe

Shake well with ice. Strain into prechilled cocktail glass. For a dry stinger, increase brandy to 2 ozs. and reduce crème de menthe to ½ oz. May be offered before or after dinner. Frequently served with a glass of ice water on the side.

THUMPER

1¾ ozs. brandy
¾ oz. Tuaca liqueur
Lemon peel

Stir brandy and Tuaca well with ice. Strain into prechilled old-fashioned glass. Add ice cubes or ice slices to fill glass. Stir well. Twist lemon peel above drink and drop into glass. One of Italy's oldest liqueurs shines in this drink.

VIA VENETO

1¾ ozs. brandy
½ oz. sambuca
½ egg white

2 teaspoons lemon juice
1 teaspoon sugar

Shake well with ice. Strain over rocks in prechilled old-fashioned glass. An engaging patio drink that's a little on the sweet side.

WATERBURY

1½ ozs. brandy
½ oz. lime juice
½ egg white

½ teaspoon grenadine
½ teaspoon powdered sugar

Shake well with ice. Strain into prechilled sugar-frosted cocktail glass.

Champagne Cocktails

AMERICANA

*1 teaspoon 100-proof
  bourbon*
½ teaspoon sugar
1 dash bitters

4 ozs. iced brut champagne
*1 slice fresh or brandied
  peach*

Stir bourbon, sugar, and bitters in prechilled champagne glass. Add champagne and peach slice. Stir very gently.

CARIBBEAN CHAMPAGNE

½ teaspoon light rum
½ teaspoon banana liqueur
1 dash orange bitters

4 ozs. iced brut champagne
1 slice banana

Pour rum, banana liqueur, and bitters into prechilled champagne glass. Add champagne. Stir very gently. Add banana slice.

CHAMPAGNE FRAISE

½ teaspoon strawberry liqueur
½ teaspoon kirschwasser
4 ozs. iced brut *champagne*
1 large fresh strawberry

Pour strawberry liqueur and kirsch into prechilled champagne glass. Tilt glass so that liqueurs coat bottom and sides of glass. Add champagne. Float strawberry on drink. (Measure ½ teaspoons precisely—don't overpour.)

CHAMPAGNE MANHATTAN

1 oz. Canadian whisky
¼ oz. sweet vermouth
1 dash bitters
3 ozs. iced brut *champagne*
1 brandied cherry

Stir whisky, vermouth, and bitters well with ice. Strain into prechilled champagne glass. Add champagne and brandied cherry. Stir very gently.

CHAMPAGNE NORMANDE

1 teaspoon calvados
½ teaspoon sugar
1 dash Angostura bitters
4 ozs. iced brut *champagne*

Stir calvados, sugar, and bitters in prechilled champagne glass. Add champagne. Stir very gently.

CHAMPAGNE NOYAUX

½ oz. crème de noyaux
1 teaspoon lime juice
1 large toasted almond
4 ozs. iced brut *champagne*
1 slice lime

Stir crème de noyaux and lime juice in prechilled champagne glass. Add almond. Pour champagne into glass. Stir slightly. Float lime slice on top.

CHAMPAGNE OLD-FASHIONED

½ oz. Grand Marnier
½ oz. Forbidden Fruit
1 dash orange bitters

4 ozs. iced brut *champagne*
1 slice lemon

Into prechilled old-fashioned glass, pour liqueurs and bitters. Add champagne. Stir very gently. Launch with lemon slice.

CHAMPAGNE POLONAISE

1 teaspoon blackberry liqueur

½ teaspoon cognac
4 ozs. iced brut *champagne*

Pour blackberry liqueur and cognac into prechilled sugar-frosted champagne glass. Add champagne. Stir very gently.

CHARTREUSE CHAMPAGNE

½ teaspoon green Chartreuse
½ teaspoon cognac

4 ozs. iced brut *champagne*
Lemon peel

Pour Chartreuse, cognac, and champagne into prechilled champagne glass. Stir very gently. Twist lemon peel above drink and drop into glass. Toast the Carthusian order.

CHERRY CHAMPAGNE

½ oz. iced Peter Heering
4 ozs. iced brut *champagne*

½ pitted fresh cherry

Pour Peter Heering into stem of prechilled hollow-stemmed champagne glass. Add champagne. Float cherry on drink.

CLASSIC CHAMPAGNE COCKTAIL

½ teaspoon sugar
1 dash Angostura bitters
4 ozs. iced brut *champagne*
Lemon peel

Stir sugar and bitters in prechilled champagne glass. Add champagne. Usually, the sparkle of the champagne will blend the ingredients, and little if any stirring is necessary. Twist lemon peel above drink and drop into glass.

MELBA CHAMPAGNE

½ oz. Himbeergeist (raspberry brandy, not liqueur)
4 ozs. iced brut *champagne*
1 fresh or thawed frozen raspberry
Raspberry sherbet, hard-frozen

Pour Himbeergeist into prechilled champagne glass. Add champagne and the raspberry. With a fruit-baller, scoop out a single small ball of sherbet. Float on champagne. Stir very gently.

ORANGE CHAMPAGNE

Peel of ½ orange, in one spiral
2 teaspoons curaçao
4 ozs. iced brut *champagne*

Place orange peel in prechilled champagne glass. Add curaçao and champagne. Stir very gently.

SPARKLING GALLIANO

½ oz. Galliano
½ teaspoon lemon juice
4 ozs. iced brut *champagne*
Cucumber peel, 1½ inches long, ½ inch wide

Pour Galliano and lemon juice into prechilled champagne glass. Stir very gently. Add champagne and cucumber peel. Drink to the stars.

Gin Cocktails

ALEXANDER'S SISTER

¾ oz. gin
¾ oz. white or green crème de menthe
¾ oz. heavy cream

Shake well with ice. Strain into prechilled cocktail glass.

ALEXANDER WITH COFFEE

¾ oz. gin
¾ oz. coffee liqueur
¾ oz. heavy cream

Shake well with ice. Strain into prechilled sugar-frosted cocktail glass. (Moisten rim of glass with coffee liqueur before dipping in sugar.) Especially good with espresso-coffee liqueur. Like all alexanders, which are really sweet cocktails, this one is both a pre- and postprandial drink.

ALEXANDER WITH GIN

¾ oz. gin
¾ oz. crème de cacao
¾ oz. heavy cream

Shake well with ice. Strain into prechilled cocktail glass. (An alexander made with a brandy base instead of gin will be found among the brandy cocktails.)

ALEXANDER WITH PRUNELLE

¾ oz. gin
¾ oz. prunelle

¾ oz. cream
Ground cinnamon

Shake gin, prunelle, and cream well with ice. Strain into prechilled cocktail glass. Sprinkle lightly with cinnamon.

BENNETT

1½ ozs. gin
½ oz. lime juice
1 teaspoon sugar

2 dashes Angostura bitters
Lime peel

Shake gin, lime juice, sugar, and bitters well with ice. Strain into prechilled cocktail glass. Twist lime peel above drink and drop into glass.

BERLINER

1½ ozs. gin
¼ oz. dry kümmel

½ oz. dry vermouth
¼ oz. lemon juice

Shake well with ice. Strain into prechilled cocktail glass. Best appreciated with freshly made, well-buttered smoked-salmon canapés.

BISCAYNE

1 oz. gin
½ oz. light rum
½ oz. Forbidden Fruit

½ oz. lime juice
1 slice lime

Shake gin, rum, Forbidden Fruit, and lime juice well with ice. Strain over rocks in prechilled old-fashioned glass. Add lime slice.

BISHOP'S COCKTAIL

1 oz. gin *1 slice lemon*
1 oz. Stone's ginger wine

Stir gin and ginger wine well with ice. Strain over rocks in old-fashioned glass. Add lemon slice.

BLUE DEVIL

1½ ozs. gin *½ oz. lemon juice*
½ oz. blue curaçao *1 slice lemon*

Shake gin, curaçao, and lemon juice well with ice. Strain into prechilled cocktail glass garnished with lemon slice. A gentle blues chaser.

BONNIE PRINCE

1¼ ozs. gin *¼ oz. Drambuie*
½ oz. Lillet

Shake well with ice. Strain into prechilled cocktail glass. Inspired by gin drinkers with both French and Scottish blood in their veins.

BRITTANY

1½ ozs. gin *¼ oz. lemon juice*
½ oz. Amer Picon *Orange peel*
¼ oz. orange juice

Shake gin, Amer Picon, orange juice, and lemon juice well with ice. Strain into prechilled cocktail glass. Twist orange peel above drink and drop into glass.

BRONX

1½ ozs. gin
½ oz. orange juice
¼ oz. dry vermouth
¼ oz. sweet vermouth

Shake well with ice. Strain into prechilled cocktail glass. For a drier bronx, omit sweet vermouth and increase gin to 1¾ ozs. One of the few inventions of the Prohibition era really worth retaining when made with fine gin rather than the notorious bathtub variety.

CHATHAM

1¼ ozs. gin
½ oz. ginger-flavored brandy
¼ oz. lemon juice
1 small piece preserved ginger in syrup

Shake gin, ginger-flavored brandy, and lemon juice well with ice. Strain into prechilled cocktail glass. Garnish with preserved ginger.

CHERRY SLING

1½ ozs. gin
½ oz. cherry liqueur
½ oz. lime juice

Shake well with ice. Strain into prechilled cocktail glass. Use a tart cherry liqueur such as Peter Heering or Cherry Karise for best results.

CLOISTER

1½ ozs. gin
½ oz. grapefruit juice
¼ oz. lemon juice
¼ oz. yellow Chartreuse

Shake well with ice. Strain into prechilled cocktail glass. A contemplative kind of drink, perfect for an autumn sundown.

CLOVER CLUB

1½ ozs. gin
¾ oz. lemon juice

1 teaspoon grenadine or
raspberry syrup
½ egg white

Shake well with ice. Strain into prechilled cocktail glass.

CLOVER CLUB ROYAL

1½ ozs. gin
¾ oz. lemon juice

1 teaspoon grenadine or
raspberry syrup
½ egg yolk

Shake well with ice. Strain into prechilled cocktail glass. A trifle richer than the clover club, above, this velvety cocktail is even smoother when made with ⅓ cup crushed ice in a blender and poured over the rocks in an old-fashioned glass.

COCONUT GIN

1½ ozs. gin
½ oz. lemon juice

¼ oz. maraschino liqueur
¼ oz. cream of coconut

Cream of coconut, from the can, should be well mixed before using. Shake all ingredients well with ice. Strain into prechilled sugar-frosted cocktail glass. Sets up a beautiful indoor tropical breeze.

COLD GIN TODDY

2 ozs. gin
½ teaspoon sugar

Lemon peel

Shake gin and sugar well with plenty of ice and strain into old-fashioned glass filled with large cubes or slices of ice. Twist lemon peel above drink and drop into glass.

COPENHAGEN

1 oz. gin
1 oz. aquavit
¼ oz. dry vermouth
1 large stuffed olive

Stir gin, aquavit, and vermouth well with ice. Strain into prechilled cocktail glass. Add olive.

CORDIAL MEDOC

1 oz. gin
½ oz. Cordial Médoc
½ oz. dry vermouth
¼ oz. lemon juice

Shake well with ice. Strain into prechilled cocktail glass. For a bon-voyage cocktail party before flying to Paris.

CORDIAL MEDOC SOUR

1½ ozs. gin
½ oz. Cordial Médoc
½ oz. lemon juice
½ slice orange

Shake gin, Cordial Médoc, and lemon juice well with ice. Strain into prechilled whiskey-sour glass. Garnish with orange slice.

DUNDEE

1 oz. gin
½ oz. Scotch
½ oz. Drambuie
¼ oz. lemon juice
Lemon peel

Shake gin, Scotch, Drambuie, and lemon juice well with ice. Pour over rocks in prechilled old-fashioned glass. Twist lemon peel above drink and drop into glass.

FOGGY DAY

1½ ozs. gin
¼ oz. Pernod
1 slice lemon
Lemon peel

Shake gin and Pernod well with ice. Strain over rocks in prechilled old-fashioned glass. Rub outside of lemon peel around rim of glass and drop peel into glass. Add lemon slice.

GENOA

¾ oz. gin
¾ oz. grappa
½ oz. sambuca
½ oz. dry vermouth
1 cocktail olive

Stir gin, grappa, sambuca, and vermouth well with ice. Strain into prechilled cocktail glass. Add olive.

GIMLET

2 ozs. gin ½ oz. Rose's lime juice

Stir extremely well with ice. Strain into prechilled cocktail glass. Long stirring is absolutely essential to present this English classic in its best light. The above formula, 4-to-1, may be made 5-to-1, if desired, by adding ½ oz. gin. Glass may be sugar-frosted by moistening rim with Rose's lime juice before dipping in sugar.

GIN AND LIME

1½ ozs. gin
½ oz. fresh lime juice
½ oz. orange juice
1 teaspoon Rose's lime juice
Lime peel

Shake gin, fresh lime juice, orange juice, and Rose's lime juice well with ice. Strain into prechilled cocktail glass. Twist lime peel above drink and drop into glass. A superb cocktail to sip with English potted shrimp or anchovy-paste canapés.

GIN AQUAVIT

1½ ozs. gin
½ oz. aquavit
½ oz. lemon juice
1 teaspoon sugar
½ egg white
1 teaspoon heavy cream

Shake well with ice. Strain into prechilled old-fashioned glass containing two or three ice cubes. A light, foamy drink to serve before passing a platter of Danish open sandwiches.

GIN CASSIS

1½ ozs. gin
½ oz. lemon juice
½ oz. crème de cassis

Shake well with ice. Strain into prechilled cocktail glass, or into prechilled old-fashioned glass with one or two rocks.

GIN DAIQUIRI

1½ ozs. gin
½ oz. light rum
½ oz. lime juice
1 teaspoon sugar

Shake well with ice. Strain into prechilled sugar-frosted cocktail glass.

GIN OLD-FASHIONED

¼ teaspoon sugar
1 or 2 dashes Angostura bitters
1¾ ozs. gin
Lemon peel

Put sugar and bitters into prechilled old-fashioned glass. Stir until sugar dissolves, adding a teaspoon of water if necessary to complete the process. Add gin and two or three ice cubes or large pieces of coarsely cracked ice. Stir well. Twist lemon peel above drink and drop into glass. Old-fashioneds are frequently garnished with orange slice, lemon slice, pineapple, cherry, etc., but knowledgeable old-fashioned men shun the fruit salad.

GIN SIDECAR

¾ oz. high-proof English gin
¾ oz. Triple Sec
¾ oz. lemon juice

Shake well with ice. Strain into prechilled cocktail glass. The gin substitutes for brandy in this version of the sidecar.

GIN SOUR

1½ ozs. gin
½ oz. lemon juice
¼ oz. orange juice
1 teaspoon sugar
½ slice orange
1 maraschino cherry

Shake gin, lemon juice, orange juice, and sugar well with ice. Strain into prechilled whiskey-sour glass. Garnish with orange slice and cherry.

GIN SOUTHERN

1½ ozs. gin
½ oz. Southern Comfort
¼ oz. grapefruit juice
¼ oz. lemon juice

Shake well with ice. Strain into prechilled cocktail glass. For drinking men who appreciate verandas and magnolia blossoms.

GOLDEN HORNET

1½ ozs. gin
½ oz. amontillado sherry
½ oz. Scotch
Lemon peel

Stir gin and sherry well with ice. Strain over two rocks in prechilled old-fashioned glass. Float Scotch on top. Twist lemon peel over drink and drop into glass.

GRANVILLE

1½ ozs. gin
¼ oz. Grand Marnier
¼ oz. calvados
¼ oz. lemon juice

Shake well with ice. Strain into prechilled cocktail glass.

GREEN DEVIL

1½ ozs. gin
½ oz. lime juice
¼ oz. green crème de menthe
2 sprigs mint

Shake gin, lime juice, and crème de menthe well with ice. Strain over two or three rocks in prechilled old-fashioned glass. Tear several mint leaves to release aroma before adding to drink as garnish.

HUDSON BAY

1 oz. gin
½ oz. cherry liqueur
½ oz. orange juice
¼ oz. lime juice
¼ oz. 151-proof rum
1 slice lime

Shake gin, cherry liqueur, orange juice, lime juice, and rum well with ice. Strain into prechilled cocktail glass. Add lime slice. A winter or summer cocktail with prodigious thawing powers.

JAMAICA GLOW

1½ ozs. gin
½ oz. dry red wine
½ oz. orange juice
1 teaspoon dark Jamaica rum
1 slice lime

Shake gin, wine, orange juice, and rum well with ice. Strain into prechilled sugar-frosted cocktail glass. Add lime slice. This relic of plantation days is still a magnificent reviver for surf riders and scuba divers.

JOULOUVILLE

1 oz. gin
½ oz. apple brandy
½ oz. lemon juice
¼ oz. sweet vermouth
¼ teaspoon grenadine

Shake well with ice. Strain into prechilled cocktail glass.

KEY COCKTAIL

1½ ozs. gin
½ oz. lime juice
¼ oz. dark Jamaica rum
¼ oz. Falernum
1 pineapple stick

Shake gin, lime juice, rum, and Falernum well with ice. Strain into prechilled cocktail glass. Garnish with pineapple stick.

MARTINI

(See page 157 for a separate discussion of this immensely popular cocktail and its many variations.)

MATINEE

1 oz. gin
½ oz. sambuca
½ egg white
1 teaspoon heavy cream
½ oz. lime juice

Shake all ingredients well with ice. Strain into prechilled cocktail glass. A comfortable midafternoon cocktail. May also be served as a pick-me-up the morning after with a spray of freshly ground nutmeg.

MINTED GIN

1½ ozs. gin
½ oz. lemon juice
1 teaspoon sugar
2 sprigs fresh mint
1 slice lemon
½ slice orange

Shake gin, lemon juice, and sugar well with ice. Strain into prechilled old-fashioned glass with rocks. Garnish drink with lemon and orange slices. Tear mint leaves before placing on rocks. A perfect drink for unwinding after eighteen holes on the fairway.

MOLDAU

1½ ozs. gin
½ oz. plum brandy
¼ oz. orange juice
¼ oz. lemon juice
1 brandied cherry

Shake gin, plum brandy, orange juice, and lemon juice well with ice. Strain into prechilled old-fashioned glass with two or three ice cubes. Garnish with brandied cherry.

MORRO

1 oz. gin
½ oz. golden rum
½ oz. lime juice
½ oz. pineapple juice
1 teaspoon sugar

Shake well with ice. Strain into prechilled sugar-frosted glass. Moisten rim of glass with Falernum before dipping in sugar. Once tasted, the marriage of gin and rum is one of those unions that no man in his right drinking sense would dream of putting asunder. Fruit juices in this drink help fortify the nuptials.

ORANGE BLOSSOM

1½ ozs. gin
1 oz. orange juice
½ slice orange

Shake gin and orange juice well with ice. Strain into prechilled sugar-frosted cocktail glass. Glass may be sugar-frosted by moistening rim with orange peel before dipping in sugar. Add orange slice.

ORANGE BLOSSOM, FROZEN

1½ ozs. gin
2 ozs. orange juice
½ oz. curaçao
½ oz. lemon juice
2 drops orange-flower water
¼ cup cracked ice
½ slice orange

Put gin, orange juice, curaçao, lemon juice, orange-flower water, and ice into blender. Spin 5–8 seconds. Pour into deep-saucer champagne or old-fashioned glass. Place orange slice on top.

PINK GIN

2 ozs. gin   2 dashes Angostura bitters

In Britain, the custom is simply to stir these ingredients at room temperature in a small cocktail glass. For American tastes, it's more pleasant if the gin and bitters are well stirred with ice and then poured into a prechilled glass. This is one of the drinks that sustained Sir Francis Chichester so beautifully on his long, lonely trip round the world.

PINK LADY

1½ ozs. gin
¼ oz. lime juice
1 teaspoon heavy cream
1 teaspoon grenadine
½ egg white

Shake well with ice. Strain into prechilled cocktail glass. Glass may be sugar-frosted by moistening rim with grenadine before dipping in sugar.

PIROUETTER

1 oz. gin
½ oz. Grand Marnier
1 oz. orange juice
1 teaspoon lemon juice
Orange peel

Shake gin, Grand Marnier, orange juice, and lemon juice well with ice. Strain into prechilled cocktail glass. Twist orange peel above drink and drop into glass.

POLISH SIDECAR

¾ oz. gin
¾ oz. Polish or Polish-style blackberry liqueur
¾ oz. lemon juice

Shake well with ice. Strain into prechilled cocktail glass. A large fresh blackberry, if available, is a pleasant garnish for this drink.

POMPANO

1 oz. gin
½ oz. dry vermouth
1 oz. grapefruit juice
4 dashes orange bitters
1 slice orange

Shake gin, vermouth, grapefruit juice, and bitters well with ice. Strain over rocks in prechilled old-fashioned glass. Garnish with orange slice. A perfect cocktail for Florida- or Caribbean-bound vacationers.

PRINCETON

1¼ ozs. gin
¾ oz. dry vermouth
½ oz. lime juice

Shake well with ice. Strain into prechilled cocktail glass. Like the bronx, this is one of very few drinks born in Prohibition days really worth retaining. Named for the great seat of learning, which, during the Noble Experiment, distinguished itself even more for its prowess in soaking up bathtub gin.

RED CLOUD

1½ ozs. gin
½ oz. apricot liqueur
½ oz. lemon juice
1 teaspoon grenadine
1 dash bitters

Shake well with ice. Strain into prechilled cocktail glass.

RED LIGHT

1 oz. gin
½ oz. sloe gin
½ oz. Italian vermouth
½ oz. lemon juice

Shake all ingredients well with ice. Strain over ice in prechilled old-fashioned glass.

RENAISSANCE

1½ ozs. gin
½ oz. dry sherry
½ oz. heavy cream
Freshly grated nutmeg

Shake gin, sherry, and cream well with ice. Strain into prechilled cocktail glass. Spray with nutmeg. A drink to savor after a lengthy tour of art galleries.

RENDEZVOUS

1½ ozs. gin
½ oz. kirschwasser
¼ oz. Campari
Lemon peel

Shake gin, kirschwasser, and Campari well with ice. Strain into prechilled cocktail glass. Twist lemon peel above drink and drop into glass. An appetite arouser best sipped while a double-thick filet is browning over the charcoals.

RIGHT ON

1 oz. gin
½ oz. apricot-flavored brandy
½ oz. Cointreau
½ oz. lemon juice
Lemon peel

Shake gin, apricot-flavored brandy, Cointreau, and lemon juice well with ice. Strain into prechilled cocktail glass. Twist lemon peel above drink and drop into glass.

ROCKY DANE

1 oz. gin
½ oz. dry vermouth
½ oz. Peter Heering
¼ oz. kirsch
Lemon peel

Shake gin, vermouth, Peter Heering, and kirsch well with ice. Strain over rocks in prechilled old-fashioned glass. Twist lemon peel above drink and drop into glass.

ROSE

1 oz. gin
½ oz. apricot-flavored brandy
½ oz. dry vermouth
½ oz. lemon juice
1 teaspoon grenadine
Lemon peel

Shake gin, apricot-flavored brandy, vermouth, lemon juice, and grenadine well with ice. Strain into prechilled cocktail glass. Twist lemon peel above drink and drop into glass.

ST.-LO

1½ ozs. gin
½ oz. calvados
½ oz. lemon juice
1 teaspoon sugar

Shake well with ice. Strain into prechilled cocktail glass.

SAN SEBASTIAN

1 oz. gin
¼ oz. rum
½ oz. grapefruit juice
¼ oz. curaçao
½ oz. lemon juice

Shake well with ice. Strain into prechilled cocktail glass. Recommended for galley bartenders after a lazy Sunday-afternoon sail.

SEVILLE

1 oz. gin
½ oz. fino sherry
½ oz. orange juice
½ oz. lemon juice
½ teaspoon sugar

Shake well with ice. Strain into prechilled sugar-rimmed glass.

SOUTH SIDE

2 ozs. gin
½ oz. lemon juice
1 teaspoon sugar
2 sprigs fresh mint

Shake gin, lemon juice, and sugar well with ice. Strain into prechilled cocktail glass. Tear several leaves of each mint sprig before adding to drink. Although not as well known as the mint julep, the south side is a delightful summery cocktail with a delicate mint accent.

STRAWBERRY SWIG

1½ ozs. gin
½ oz. strawberry liqueur
¼ oz. lime juice
1 dash orange bitters
1 slice lime

Shake gin, strawberry liqueur, lime juice, and bitters well with ice. Strain into prechilled old-fashioned glass with several rocks. Garnish with lime slice.

STREGA SOUR

1½ ozs. gin
½ oz. lemon juice
½ oz. Strega
1 slice lemon

Shake gin, lemon juice, and Strega well with ice. Strain into prechilled sugar-frosted cocktail glass. Moisten rim of glass with Strega before dipping in sugar. Garnish with lemon slice.

TURF

1 oz. gin
1 oz. dry vermouth
¼ oz. Pernod
¼ oz. lemon juice
1 slice lemon

Shake gin, vermouth, Pernod, and lemon juice well with ice. Strain over rocks in prechilled old-fashioned glass. Add lemon slice.

VERBOTEN

1 oz. gin
½ oz. Forbidden Fruit
½ oz. lemon juice
½ oz. orange juice
1 brandied cherry

Shake gin, Forbidden Fruit, lemon juice, and orange juice well with ice. Strain into prechilled cocktail glass. Garnish with brandied cherry.

WHITE ROSE

1¼ ozs. gin
½ oz. orange juice
½ oz. lime juice
1 teaspoon sugar
½ egg white

Shake well with ice. Strain into prechilled cocktail glass. There are dozens of different recipes bearing the name white rose. This balmy concoction is designed for sipping in the vicinity of a glowing fireplace.

WOODSTOCK

1½ ozs. gin
1 oz. lemon juice
¼ oz. maple syrup
1 dash orange bitters

Shake well with ice. Strain into frosty cocktail glass. A drink from the ski country.

THE MARTINI

Over the years, the martini, most famous of all cocktail-hour thoroughbreds, has evolved into a drink that is practically all gin with only the faintest hint of vermouth. This preference for drier and drier martinis (while *dry* usually means less sweet, in reference to martinis it means less vermouth) has spawned some strange equipment and a countless number of jokes. Some barmen ritualize the exacting vermouth formula with a long ℞ dropper; some spray their vermouth from atomizers. The fanatical, reaching the *reductio ad absurdum,* claim they waft the vermouth bottle-top over the gin or mutter the word *vermouth* under their breath while stirring their raw concoction in the mixing glass. It would be unfortunate if the use of vermouth in the martini became extinct, for its bite, however faint, is trenchant. It turns cold gin into a civilized cocktail.

Most topflight barmen make their martinis with about ten or twelve parts gin to one part dry vermouth. The drink may be served "up," meaning in a regular stemmed cocktail glass, or on the rocks in an old-fashioned glass. You can drop a twist of lemon peel into the glass or rub the rim with the peel before adding it to the drink. The martini's most common garnish is an olive, pitted or stuffed. With a cocktail-onion garnish, it turns into a gibson.

A martini must be piercingly cold; at its best, both gin and vermouth are prechilled in the refrigerator, well stirred with ice, and poured into a prechilled glass. Energetic stirring with the ice is all-important; the dilution makes the drink both smooth and palatable. Those who merely combine gin and vermouth beforehand and then refrigerate without stirring wind up serving raw slugs to guests who are quickly cargoed and who completely miss the pleasure of a well-made martini.

Although vermouth is the spirited minor ingredient, a bottle opened for pouring and left standing in the liquor cabinet for weeks will lose its bell-ringing zest. To retain as much as possible of the flavor of the aromatic herbs used in making vermouth, store the opened bottle in the refrigerator. It's a good idea for the martini man to buy his vermouth in pint bottles and make frequent replacements.

Here are several variations on the familiar martini theme:

12-to-1 MARTINI

2 ozs. gin   1 teaspoon dry vermouth

8-to-1 MARTINI

2 ozs. gin   ¼ oz. dry vermouth

4-to-1 MARTINI

2 ozs. gin   ½ oz. dry vermouth

GIBSON

As noted, any of the above martini mixtures garnished with a cocktail onion.

BLENTON

1½ ozs. gin   1 dash Angostura bitters
¾ oz. dry vermouth

Stir well with ice. Strain into prechilled cocktail glass. A martini variation so old that it's new. Total effect on the palate: warming and elevating.

BLOODHOUND

1 oz. gin   ½ oz. strawberry liqueur
½ oz. dry vermouth   1 large strawberry
½ oz. sweet vermouth

Shake gin, both kinds of vermouth, and strawberry liqueur well with ice. Strain into prechilled cocktail glass. Drop strawberry into glass. The best dry vermouth for this one is Chambery Fraise.

CORDIAL MARTINI

1¼ ozs. gin
¼ oz. dry vermouth
¼ oz. Cordial Médoc
Lemon peel

Stir gin, vermouth, and Cordial Médoc well with ice. Strain into prechilled cocktail glass or over rocks. Twist lemon peel over drink and drop into glass.

FINO MARTINI

2 ozs. gin
½ oz. fino sherry

Stir well with ice. Strain into prechilled cocktail glass. Add olive or lemon twist. Serve with a side dish of freshly toasted, salted almonds.

FLYING DUTCHMAN

2 ozs. gin
¼ oz. dry vermouth
Curaçao

Into a prechilled cocktail glass, pour enough curaçao so that when the glass is slowly twirled, it will coat the sides. Stir gin and vermouth well with ice. Strain into glass.

GIN AND IT

2 ozs. gin
Italian sweet vermouth

Stir gin well with ice. Into a prechilled cocktail glass, pour enough vermouth so that when the glass is slowly twirled, it will coat the sides. Add the gin. The English drink is often served at room temperature. The "It" stands for the Italian vermouth. A gin and French is the same drink with French dry vermouth instead.

KNICKERBOCKER

2 ozs. gin
½ oz. dry vermouth
¼ oz. sweet vermouth

Stir well with ice. Strain into prechilled cocktail glass. Serve without benefit of cherry, olive, or lemon twist. This version of the martini appeals to those who like vermouth in both sweet and dry forms.

MARSALA MARTINI

¾ oz. gin
¾ oz. dry vermouth
¾ oz. dry Marsala
Lemon peel

Stir gin, vermouth, and Marsala well with ice. Strain into prechilled cocktail glass. Twist lemon peel above drink and drop into glass.

MARTINEZ

2 ozs. gin
½ oz. dry vermouth
½ teaspoon maraschino liqueur
2 dashes orange bitters

Stir well with ice. Strain into prechilled cocktail glass. Martini men with a strain of Spanish in their veins go for this one. Alleged to have been the original martini.

MARTINI, HOLLAND STYLE

2 ozs. Dutch genever gin
½ oz. dry vermouth
Lemon peel

Stir gin and vermouth well with ice. Strain into prechilled cocktail glass. Twist lemon peel above drink and drop into glass.

PAISLEY MARTINI

2¼ ozs. gin
¼ oz. dry vermouth

1 teaspoon Scotch

Stir well with ice. Strain into prechilled cocktail glass. The flavor of the Scotch in this 9-to-1 martini is just subtle enough to let the drinker know that something delightfully offbeat is in his glass.

PERFECT

1½ ozs. gin
½ oz. dry vermouth

½ oz. sweet vermouth

Stir well with ice. Strain into prechilled cocktail glass. Add olive or twist of lemon peel if desired. Modern martini men would call this an "imperfect" martini, but *perfect* is its traditional name.

PERNOD MARTINI

2 ozs. gin
½ oz. dry vermouth

⅛ teaspoon Pernod

Stir well with ice. Strain into prechilled cocktail glass. Very pleasant with an onion-stuffed olive. Some bartenders pour a soupçon of Pernod into the glass, swirl it around, and then add the martini.

RACQUET CLUB

2 ozs. gin
½ oz. dry vermouth

2 dashes orange bitters

Shake, don't stir, with ice in silver cocktail shaker until shaker is completely frosted. Strain into cocktail glass so cold it's somewhat uncomfortable to hold.

SAKETINI

2 ozs. gin   ½ oz. sake

Stir well with ice. Strain into prechilled cocktail glass. If desired, an olive or twist of lemon peel may be added. The saketini is a reminder that dry vermouth and rice wine bear an uncanny resemblance to each other.

SWEET MARTINI

2 ozs. gin   Orange peel
½ oz. sweet vermouth

Stir gin and vermouth well with ice. Strain into prechilled cocktail glass. Twist orange peel above drink and drop into glass. While *sweet martini* sounds like a contradiction in terms, the drink is not only tolerable but titillating.

Rum Cocktails

ACAPULCO

1½ ozs. light rum
½ oz. lime juice
¼ oz. Triple Sec
½ egg white
½ teaspoon sugar
2 fresh mint leaves

Shake rum, lime juice, Triple Sec, egg white, and sugar well with ice. Strain into prechilled cocktail glass. Tear each mint leaf partially and drop into glass.

APRICOT LADY

1½ ozs. light rum
1 oz. apricot-flavored brandy
½ oz. lime juice
½ teaspoon curaçao
½ egg white
¼ cup crushed ice
½ slice orange

Put rum, apricot-flavored brandy, lime juice, curaçao, egg white, and ice into blender. Blend 15 seconds at low speed. Pour into prechilled old-fashioned glass. Add ice cubes or ice slices to fill glass to rim. Place orange slice on top.

APRICOT PIE

1 oz. light rum
1 oz. sweet vermouth
½ teaspoon apricot-flavored brandy
½ teaspoon lemon juice
¼ teaspoon grenadine
Orange peel

Shake rum, vermouth, apricot-flavored brandy, lemon juice, and grenadine well with ice. Strain into prechilled cocktail glass. Twist orange peel above drink and drop into glass.

BACARDI

1½ ozs. light or golden Bacardi rum
½ oz. lime juice
1 teaspoon grenadine

Shake well with ice. Strain into prechilled cocktail glass or over rocks in a prechilled old-fashioned glass. The proprietary name Bacardi, a rum originally distilled in Cuba but now made in Puerto Rico and other Spanish-speaking lands, has long been the title of this classic rum cocktail.

BANANA DAIQUIRI

1½ ozs. light rum
½ oz. lime juice
1 oz. orange juice
1 oz. banana liqueur
⅓ cup finely crushed ice

Mix all ingredients in blender at high speed 10 seconds. Pour into 6-oz. saucer champagne glass or outsize cocktail glass.

BANANA MANGO

1½ ozs. light rum
¼ oz. banana liqueur
½ oz. mango nectar
½ oz. lime juice
1 slice fresh mango

Shake rum, banana liqueur, mango nectar, and lime juice well with ice. Strain over rocks in prechilled old-fashioned glass. Add mango slice.

BEACHCOMBER

1½ ozs. light rum
½ oz. lime juice
½ oz. Triple Sec
¼ teaspoon maraschino liqueur

Shake well with ice. Strain into prechilled sugar-rimmed cocktail glass.

BEACHCOMBER'S GOLD

1½ ozs. light rum
½ oz. dry vermouth
½ oz. sweet vermouth

Stir well with ice. Strain into prechilled deep-saucer champagne glass. Add cracked ice or ice slices to fill glass. The same mixture of rum and both kinds of vermouth is also known as the rum perfect, usually served in a regular cocktail glass without added ice. Either way, it's delightful.

BEE'S KNEES

1½ ozs. light rum
¾ oz. orange juice
½ oz. lime juice
1 teaspoon sugar
2 dashes orange bitters
Orange peel

Shake rum, orange juice, lime juice, sugar, and bitters well with ice. Strain into prechilled cocktail glass. Twist orange peel above drink and drop into glass. A speakeasy heirloom whose orange accent is most mellow.

BETWEEN THE SHEETS

¾ oz. light rum
¾ oz. California brandy
¾ oz. Cointreau
½ oz. lemon juice

Shake well with ice. Strain into prechilled cocktail glass. An exhilarating variation on the rum sidecar.

BLACK DEVIL

2 ozs. light rum
½ oz. dry vermouth
1 black olive

Stir rum and vermouth well with ice. Strain into prechilled cocktail glass. Add black olive.

BOLERO

1½ ozs. light rum
¾ oz. apple brandy
¼ teaspoon sweet vermouth
Lemon peel

Stir rum, apple brandy, and vermouth well with ice. Strain into prechilled sugar-frosted cocktail glass. Twist lemon peel above drink and drop into glass.

BOLO

1½ ozs. light rum
½ oz. lemon juice
½ oz. orange juice
½ teaspoon sugar
½ slice lemon

Shake rum, lemon juice, orange juice, and sugar well with ice. Strain into prechilled cocktail glass or prechilled whiskey-sour glass. Garnish with lemon slice.

BORINQUEN

1½ ozs. light rum
½ oz. passion-fruit syrup
¾ oz. lime juice
½ oz. orange juice
1 teaspoon 151-proof rum
½ cup crushed ice

Put all ingredients into blender. Blend at low speed 10 seconds. Pour into prechilled double old-fashioned glass. Add ice cubes or cracked ice to fill glass. Garnish with gardenia, if available.

BRASS HAT

1 oz. light rum
½ oz. Galliano
½ oz. apricot liqueur
½ oz. lime juice
1 slice lime

Shake light rum, Galliano, apricot liqueur, and lime juice well with ice. Strain into prechilled cocktail glass. Add lime slice.

BUSHRANGER

1 oz. light rum
1 oz. red Dubonnet
2 dashes Angostura bitters
Lemon peel

Shake rum, Dubonnet, and bitters well with ice. Strain into prechilled cocktail glass. Twist lemon peel above drink and drop into glass.

CARDINAL COCKTAIL II

2 ozs. light rum
¼ oz. orzata
1 teaspoon grenadine
¼ oz. Triple Sec
1 oz. lime juice
1 slice lime

Shake rum, orzata, grenadine, Triple Sec, and lime juice well with ice. Strain into prechilled old-fashioned glass. Add ice cubes to bring liquid to rim. Garnish with lime slice.

CARIB

1 oz. light rum
1 oz. gin
½ oz. lime juice
1 teaspoon sugar
1 slice orange

Shake rum, gin, lime juice, and sugar well with ice. Strain over rocks in prechilled old-fashioned glass. Garnish with orange slice.

CASABLANCA

2 ozs. golden rum
1 dash Angostura bitters
1 teaspoon lime juice
¼ teaspoon curaçao
¼ teaspoon maraschino liqueur

Shake well with ice. Strain into prechilled cocktail glass.

CHERRY DAIQUIRI

1½ ozs. light rum
½ oz. lime juice
½ oz. tart cherry liqueur
¼ teaspoon kirschwasser
Lime peel

Shake rum, lime juice, cherry liqueur, and kirschwasser well with ice. Strain into prechilled cocktail glass. Twist lime peel above drink and drop into glass.

CHINA

2 ozs. golden rum
¼ teaspoon grenadine
¼ teaspoon passion-fruit syrup
1 teaspoon curaçao
1 dash Angostura bitters

Shake well with ice. Pour into prechilled cocktail glass. A slightly sweet drink, but not a dessert cocktail; one to set the mood for a roast-duck dinner.

COLUMBIA

1½ ozs. light rum
½ oz. strawberry syrup
½ oz. lemon juice
1 teaspoon kirschwasser

Shake well with ice. Strain into prechilled sugar-frosted cocktail glass. The kirschwasser, though small in proportion, comes through vividly.

CONCH SHELL

4 ozs. light rum   ½ oz. lime juice

Shake well with ice. Strain over rocks in prechilled double old-fashioned glass. Allow at least an hour for polishing this one off.

CONTINENTAL

1¾ ozs. light rum
½ oz. lime juice
½ teaspoon sugar
½ teaspoon green crème de menthe

Shake well with ice. Strain into prechilled cocktail glass. A light bracer before a seafood dinner.

CORKSCREW

1½ ozs. light rum
½ oz. dry vermouth
½ oz. peach liqueur
1 slice lime

Shake rum, vermouth, and peach liqueur well with ice. Strain into prechilled cocktail glass. Add lime slice.

CREOLE

1½ ozs. light rum
1 dash Tabasco sauce
1 teaspoon lemon juice
Iced beef bouillon or consommé (undiluted)
Salt and pepper

Put two large ice cubes into prechilled old-fashioned glass. Add rum, Tabasco, and lemon juice. Stir well. Fill glass with beef bouillon. Sprinkle with salt and pepper. Stir again. A pleasant pick-me-up or prebrunch cocktail.

CUBA LIBRE COCKTAIL

1 oz. light rum
½ oz. 151-proof rum
½ oz. cola drink
½ oz. lime juice
½ teaspoon sugar
Lime peel

Shake both kinds of rum, cola drink, lime juice, and sugar well with ice. Strain into prechilled cocktail glass. Twist lime peel above drink and drop into glass. Not to be confused with cuba libre, a tall rum-cola drink that's somewhat slower in its liberating effects.

CULROSS

1½ ozs. golden rum
½ oz. Lillet
1 teaspoon apricot-flavored brandy
1 teaspoon lime juice

Shake well with ice. Strain into prechilled cocktail glass as a straight-up drink or over the rocks in a prechilled old-fashioned glass. Equally good either way.

DAIQUIRI

2 ozs. light rum
½ oz. lime juice
½ teaspoon sugar

Shake well with ice. Pour into prechilled sugar-frosted cocktail glass or over the rocks in an old-fashioned glass. Sugar may be increased if a sweeter daiquiri is desired.

DERBY DAIQUIRI

1½ ozs. light rum
½ oz. lime juice
1 oz. orange juice
½ oz. simple syrup
⅓ cup crushed ice

Put all ingredients into blender. Blend 10–15 seconds at low speed. Pour into prechilled oversize cocktail glass or deep-saucer champagne glass.

DEVIL'S TAIL

1½ ozs. golden rum
1 oz. vodka
½ oz. lime juice
¼ oz. grenadine
¼ oz. apricot liqueur
⅓ cup crushed ice
Lime peel

Put rum, vodka, lime juice, grenadine, apricot liqueur, and ice into blender. Blend at low speed 10–15 seconds. Pour into prechilled deep-saucer champagne glass. Twist lime peel above drink and drop into glass. Powerful, but pleasant rather than pugnacious.

EL PRESIDENTE

1½ ozs. golden rum
½ oz. dry vermouth
1 teaspoon dark Jamaica rum
1 teaspoon curaçao
2 teaspoons lime juice
¼ teaspoon grenadine

Shake well with ice. Strain into prechilled cocktail glass. Hail to the chief.

FERN GULLY

1 oz. dark Jamaica rum
1 oz. light rum
½ oz. cream of coconut
½ oz. lime juice
2 teaspoons orange juice
1 teaspoon orzata
⅓ cup crushed ice

Put all ingredients into blender. Blend 10–15 seconds at low speed. Pour into prechilled deep-saucer champagne glass. More rummy than the usual frozen daiquiri, but delicious.

FORT LAUDERDALE

1½ ozs. golden rum
½ oz. sweet vermouth
¼ oz. orange juice
¼ oz. lime juice
1 slice cocktail orange in syrup

Shake rum, vermouth, orange juice, and lime juice well with ice. Strain over rocks in prechilled old-fashioned glass. Add orange slice.

FROSTY DAWN COCKTAIL

1½ ozs. light rum
1 oz. orange juice
½ oz. Falernum
¼ oz. maraschino liqueur

Shake well with ice. Strain over rocks in prechilled old-fashioned glass.

FROZEN APPLE DAIQUIRI

1½ ozs. light rum
½ oz. apple juice
½ oz. lemon juice
⅓ cup crushed ice
1 teaspoon sugar
1 wedge apple, with skin

Put rum, apple juice, lemon juice, crushed ice, and sugar into blender. Blend 10–15 seconds at low speed. Pour into prechilled deep-saucer champagne glass. Add apple wedge.

FROZEN BANANA DAIQUIRI

1½ ozs. light rum
½ oz. lime juice
½ medium-size very ripe banana, sliced
½ cup finely crushed ice
1 to 2 teaspoons sugar, to taste

Mix all ingredients in blender at low speed 10–15 seconds. Pour into 6-oz. saucer champagne glass or outsize cocktail glass.

FROZEN BERKELEY

1½ ozs. light rum
½ oz. California brandy
½ oz. passion-fruit syrup
½ oz. lemon juice
⅓ cup crushed ice

Put all ingredients into blender. Blend 10–15 seconds at low speed. Pour into prechilled deep-saucer champagne glass.

FROZEN DAIQUIRI

1½ to 2 ozs. light rum
½ oz. lime juice
½ to 1 teaspoon sugar
½ cup crushed ice

Put all ingredients into blender. Blend at low speed 10–15 seconds. Pour into prechilled deep-saucer champagne glass. May be served with a small straw. The drink may be made rummier by floating a teaspoon of 151-proof rum on top of the daiquiri in the glass, or the drink may be made with golden rum or any of the heavier-bodied rums, such as Jamaica, Barbados, or Martinique.

FROZEN GUAVA DAIQUIRI

1½ ozs. light rum
1 oz. guava nectar (not syrup)
½ oz. lime juice
1 teaspoon banana liqueur
⅓ cup crushed ice

Put all ingredients into blender. Blend 10–15 seconds at low speed. Pour into prechilled deep-saucer champagne glass.

FROZEN GUAVA-ORANGE DAIQUIRI

1½ ozs. light rum
¾ oz. guava syrup
½ oz. lime juice
½ oz. orange juice
⅓ cup crushed ice

Put all ingredients into blender. Blend 10–15 seconds at low speed. Pour into prechilled deep-saucer champagne glass.

FROZEN MINT DAIQUIRI

2 ozs. light rum
½ oz. lime juice
6 large mint leaves
1 teaspoon sugar
½ cup crushed ice

Put all ingredients into blender. Blend 20 seconds at low speed. Pour into prechilled deep-saucer champagne glass. Perfect prelude to a lamb-chop dinner.

FROZEN PASSION-FRUIT DAIQUIRI

1½ ozs. light rum
½ oz. passion-fruit syrup
½ oz. lime juice
½ oz. orange juice
¼ oz. lemon juice
⅓ cup crushed ice

Put all ingredients into blender. Blend at low speed 10–15 seconds. Pour into prechilled deep-saucer champagne glass.

FROZEN PEACH DAIQUIRI

1½ ozs. light rum
½ oz. lime juice
¼ cup frozen sliced peaches, thawed
½ oz. syrup from frozen peaches
⅓ cup crushed ice

Put all ingredients into blender. Blend at low speed 10–15 seconds. Pour into prechilled deep-saucer champagne glass. You'll find the rich flavor of the frozen peaches and their syrup peachier than the fresh fruit for this drink.

FROZEN PINEAPPLE DAIQUIRI

1½ ozs. light rum
½ oz. lime juice
½ teaspoon sugar
4 canned pineapple chunks, drained
⅓ cup crushed ice

Put all ingredients into blender. Blend 10–15 seconds at low speed. Pour into prechilled deep-saucer champagne glass. The canned pineapple is actually better than the fresh for this fruity cocktail.

FROZEN SESAME DAIQUIRI

1½ ozs. rum
½ oz. sesame-seed syrup (ajonjoli)
½ oz. lime juice
½ oz. dry vermouth
½ oz. orange juice
⅓ cup crushed ice

Put all ingredients into blender. Blend at low speed 10–15 seconds. Pour into prechilled deep-saucer champagne glass.

FROZEN SOURSOP DAIQUIRI

1½ ozs. light rum
¼ oz. dark Jamaica rum
1 oz. guanabana (soursop) nectar
¼ oz. lime juice
¼ cup sliced banana
⅓ cup crushed ice

Put all ingredients into blender. Blend 10–15 seconds at low speed. Pour into prechilled deep-saucer champagne glass. The delicious soursop is now shipped to the States as a canned nectar.

GAUGUIN

2 ozs. light rum
½ oz. passion-fruit syrup
½ oz. lemon juice
¼ oz. lime juice
⅓ cup crushed ice
1 maraschino cherry

Put rum, passion-fruit syrup, lemon juice, lime juice, and ice into blender. Blend at low speed 10–15 seconds. Pour into prechilled deep-saucer champagne glass. Add cherry.

GOLDEN GATE

¾ oz. light rum
¾ oz. gin
1 teaspoon 151-proof rum
½ oz. lemon juice
½ oz. crème de cacao
½ teaspoon Falernum
1 slice orange

Shake light rum, gin, 151-proof rum, lemon juice, crème de cacao, and Falernum well with ice. Strain over rocks in a prechilled old-fashioned glass. Add orange slice. Leaves a rich afterglow.

GUANABANA

1½ ozs. light rum
1 oz. guanabana (soursop) nectar
1 teaspoon lime juice

Shake well with ice. Strain into prechilled cocktail glass. Drink must be icy cold.

HURRICANE

1 oz. light rum
1 oz. golden rum
½ oz. passion-fruit syrup
2 teaspoons lime juice

Shake well with ice. Strain into prechilled cocktail glass. Quantities may be doubled and drink poured over rocks in a coconut shell or double old-fashioned glass.

ISLE OF THE BLESSED COCONUT

1½ ozs. light rum
½ oz. cream of coconut
½ oz. lime juice
¼ oz. lemon juice
¼ oz. orange juice
½ teaspoon sugar
⅓ cup crushed ice

Put all ingredients into blender. Blend at low speed 10–15 seconds. Pour into prechilled deep-saucer champagne glass. Serve with a bowl of toasted coconut slices.

JADE

1¾ ozs. golden rum
½ teaspoon green crème de menthe
½ teaspoon curaçao
1½ teaspoons lime juice
1 teaspoon sugar
1 slice lime

Shake rum, crème de menthe, curaçao, lime juice, and sugar well with ice. Strain into prechilled cocktail glass. Add lime slice. Minty, but not overpowering.

LEEWARD

1½ ozs. light rum
½ oz. calvados
½ oz. sweet vermouth
Lemon peel

Shake rum, calvados, and vermouth well with ice. Strain over rocks in prechilled old-fashioned glass. Twist lemon peel above drink and drop into glass. Pass anchovy canapés sprinkled with chopped hard-boiled egg.

MAI TAI

3 ozs. light rum
½ oz. lime juice
¼ teaspoon Triple Sec
¼ teaspoon orzata
½ teaspoon sugar
1 slice lime
1 sprig mint
1 pineapple stick

Shake rum, lime juice, Triple Sec, orzata, and sugar well with ice. Strain into prechilled double old-fashioned glass. Add enough cracked ice or ice cubes to fill glass. Tear one or two mint leaves partially to release flavor. Garnish with lime slice, mint sprig, and pineapple stick.

MANDEVILLE

1½ ozs. light rum
1 oz. dark Jamaica rum
¾ oz. lemon juice
1 teaspoon Pernod
½ oz. cola drink
¼ teaspoon grenadine
1 slice orange

Shake both kinds of rum, lemon juice, Pernod, cola drink, and grenadine well with ice. Strain over rocks in prechilled old-fashioned glass. Add orange slice.

MUSKMELON

1½ ozs. light rum
¼ cup sliced ripe
  cantaloupe meat
⅓ cup crushed ice
½ teaspoon sugar

½ oz. lime juice
½ oz. orange juice
1 cube cantaloupe meat on
  cocktail spear

Put rum, sliced cantaloupe, ice, sugar, lime juice, and orange juice into blender. Blend at low speed 10–15 seconds. Pour into prechilled old-fashioned glass. Add ice cubes or ice slices, if necessary, to fill glass to rim. Garnish with cantaloupe cube.

NAVY GROG

1 oz. dark Jamaica rum
½ oz. light rum
½ oz. lime juice
½ oz. orange juice
½ oz. pineapple juice

½ oz. guava nectar
¼ oz. Falernum
½ cup crushed ice
4 large mint leaves

Put both kinds of rum, lime juice, orange juice, pineapple juice, guava nectar, Falernum, and crushed ice into blender. Blend at low speed 15 seconds. Pour into double old-fashioned glass. Add ice to fill glass to rim. Tear mint leaves partially and float on drink. Serve with straw.

OCHO RIOS

1½ ozs. Jamaica rum
1 oz. guava nectar
½ oz. heavy cream

½ oz. lime juice
½ teaspoon sugar
⅓ cup crushed ice

Put all ingredients into blender. Blend at low speed 10–15 seconds. Pour into prechilled deep-saucer champagne glass. A creamy, rummy drink recommended after a spearfishing expedition.

PAGO PAGO

1½ ozs. golden rum
½ oz. fresh lime juice
½ teaspoon green Chartreuse
¼ teaspoon white crème de cacao
½ oz. pineapple juice

Shake well with ice. Strain into prechilled cocktail glass. Pineapple comes through beautifully.

PENSACOLA

1½ ozs. light rum
½ oz. guava nectar
½ oz. orange juice
½ oz. lemon juice
⅓ cup crushed ice

Put all ingredients into blender. Blend 10–15 seconds at low speed. Pour into prechilled deep-saucer champagne glass.

PINK CREOLE

1½ ozs. golden rum
½ oz. lime juice
1 teaspoon heavy cream
1 teaspoon grenadine
1 black cherry, soaked in rum

Shake rum, lime juice, cream, and grenadine well with ice. Strain into prechilled cocktail glass. Add cherry.

PINK VERANDA

1 oz. golden rum
½ oz. dark Jamaica rum
1½ ozs. cranberry juice
½ oz. lime juice
1 teaspoon sugar
½ egg white

Shake well with ice. Strain into prechilled old-fashioned glass. Add ice slices or ice cubes, if necessary, to fill glass to rim.

POLYNESIA

1½ ozs. light rum
1 oz. passion-fruit syrup
¼ oz. lime juice
½ egg white
⅓ cup crushed ice

Put all ingredients into blender. Blend 10–15 seconds at low speed. Pour into prechilled deep-saucer champagne glass.

POLYNESIAN PARADISE

1½ ozs. golden rum
1 teaspoon brown sugar
¾ oz. lime juice
½ oz. sweet vermouth
¼ oz. Triple Sec
⅓ cup crushed ice

Put all ingredients into blender. Blend at low speed 10–15 seconds. Pour into prechilled deep-saucer champagne glass. Paradise enow.

PONCE DE LEON

1½ ozs. light rum
½ oz. grapefruit juice
½ oz. mango nectar
1 teaspoon lemon juice

Shake well with ice. Strain into prechilled sugar-frosted cocktail glass.

PORT ANTONIO

1 oz. golden rum
½ oz. dark Jamaica rum
½ oz. lime juice
½ oz. coffee liqueur
1 teaspoon Falernum
1 slice lime

Shake both kinds of rum, lime juice, coffee liqueur, and Falernum well with ice. Strain over rocks in prechilled old-fashioned glass. Add lime slice.

PORT CHARLOTTE

1½ ozs. dark Jamaica rum
½ oz. Rose's lime juice
½ oz. fresh lime juice
2 teaspoons sugar
½ slice orange
1 slice lime

Shake rum, Rose's lime juice, fresh lime juice, and sugar well with ice. Strain over ice in prechilled old-fashioned glass. Garnish with orange and lime slices.

PORT MARIA

1½ ozs. light rum
¾ oz. pineapple juice
½ oz. lemon juice
1 teaspoon Falernum
Grated nutmeg

Shake rum, pineapple juice, lemon juice, and Falernum well with ice. Strain into prechilled cocktail glass. Sprinkle nutmeg on top.

PUERTO RICAN PINK LADY

1¾ ozs. golden rum
¾ oz. lemon juice
½ egg white
1 teaspoon grenadine
⅓ cup crushed ice

Put all ingredients into blender. Blend at low speed 10–15 seconds. Pour into prechilled sugar-rimmed deep-saucer champagne glass.

ROSE HALL

1 oz. dark Jamaica rum
1 oz. orange juice
½ oz. banana liqueur
1 teaspoon lime juice
1 slice lime

Shake rum, orange juice, banana liqueur, and lime juice well with ice. Strain over rocks in prechilled old-fashioned glass. Add lime slice.

RUM AND SHERRY

1½ ozs. light rum
¾ oz. sherry
1 maraschino cherry

Stir rum and sherry well with ice. Strain into prechilled cocktail glass. Add cherry. The felicitous blend of rum and sherry may be made with very dry cocktail sherry, medium amontillado, or rich cream sherry to meet your own choice of dryness or sweetness. All are good.

RUM CASSIS

1 oz. light-bodied rum
1 oz. dry white wine or dry vermouth
2 teaspoons crème de cassis
Chilled club soda
1 slice lime

Pour rum, wine, and crème de cassis over rocks in 8-oz. tall glass or old-fashioned glass. Stir well. Add a splash of soda. Stir lightly. Add lime slice.

RUM DUBONNET

1½ ozs. light rum
¾ oz. red Dubonnet
1 teaspoon lime juice
Lime peel

Shake rum, Dubonnet, and lime juice well with ice. Strain into prechilled cocktail glass. Twist lime peel above drink and drop into glass.

RUM OLD-FASHIONED

½ teaspoon sugar
1 or 2 dashes Angostura bitters
1 teaspoon water
2 ozs. light, golden, or dark Jamaica rum
Lime peel
1 teaspoon 151-proof rum

Mix sugar, bitters, and water in old-fashioned glass until sugar is completely dissolved. Add two ice cubes or several pieces of cracked ice. Add 2 ozs. rum. Stir well. Twist lime peel above drink and drop into glass. Float 151-proof rum on top.

RUM SCREWDRIVER

1½ ozs. light rum
3 ozs. cold fresh orange juice
1 slice orange

Put rum and orange juice (without ice) into blender. Blend 10–15 seconds at low speed. Pour over rocks in old-fashioned glass. Garnish with orange slice. A drink sometimes known as the aunt agatha, though it's the most un–aunt agathaish drink we can imagine. A perfect brunch beginner.

RUM SIDECAR

1½ ozs. golden rum
½ oz. Cointreau or Triple Sec
½ oz. lemon juice
¼ oz. dark Jamaica rum

Shake golden rum, Cointreau, and lemon juice well with ice. Strain into cocktail glass or over rocks. Float dark rum on top.

RUM SOUR

2 ozs. light or golden rum
½ oz. lemon juice
1 teaspoon orange juice
1 teaspoon rock-candy syrup or sugar
½ slice orange

Shake rum, lemon juice, orange juice, and syrup or sugar well with ice. Strain into prechilled whiskey-sour glass. Add orange slice. A teaspoon of 151-proof rum may be floated on the drink for a more rummish accent. For a heavier-bodied but richly mellow rum sour, use dark Jamaica rum.

SAGUENAY

1 oz. light rum
1 oz. dry vermouth
1 teaspoon lemon juice
2 teaspoons crème de cassis

Shake well with ice. Strain over rocks in prechilled old-fashioned glass. Add a splash of club soda if desired.

ST. AUGUSTINE

1½ ozs. light rum
1 oz. grapefruit juice
1 teaspoon Cointreau
Lemon peel

Shake rum, grapefruit juice, and Cointreau well with ice. Strain into prechilled sugar-frosted cocktail glass. Twist lemon peel above drink and drop into glass. Perfect before a pompano dinner.

SAN JUAN

1½ ozs. light rum
1 oz. grapefruit juice
1 teaspoon cream of coconut
2 teaspoons lime juice
⅓ cup crushed ice
2 teaspoons 151-proof rum

Put 1½ ozs. light rum, grapefruit juice, cream of coconut, lime juice, and ice into blender. Blend at low speed 10–15 seconds. Pour into prechilled deep-saucer champagne glass. Float 151-proof rum on top.

SCORPION

2 ozs. light rum
2 ozs. orange juice
½ oz. lemon juice
1 oz. California brandy
½ oz. orzata
⅓ cup crushed ice
1 slice orange

Put rum, orange juice, lemon juice, brandy, orzata, and ice into blender. Blend at low speed 10–15 seconds. Pour into prechilled double old-fashioned glass with enough ice cubes to fill glass to rim. Add orange slice.

SEPTEMBER MORN

1½ ozs. light rum
½ oz. lime juice
1 teaspoon grenadine
½ egg white

Shake well with ice. Strain into prechilled sugar-frosted cocktail glass. Glass rim may be moistened with grenadine before dipping in sugar.

SESAME

1½ ozs. light rum
½ oz. lime juice
½ oz. sesame-seed syrup
(ajonjoli)

Shake well with ice. Strain into prechilled cocktail glass. Sesame is a versatile seed. It's available in syrup form in stores featuring Caribbean products. A rummy and offbeat drink.

SHARK'S TOOTH

1½ ozs. golden rum
¼ oz. lemon juice
¼ oz. passion-fruit syrup
¼ oz. sweet vermouth
¼ oz. sloe gin
1 dash Angostura bitters
Orange peel
1 maraschino cherry

Shake rum, lemon juice, passion-fruit syrup, vermouth, sloe gin, and bitters well with ice. Strain into prechilled sugar-frosted cocktail glass. Twist orange peel above drink and drop into glass. Add cherry.

SHAW PARK

1 oz. golden rum
½ oz. Cointreau or
   Triple Sec
¼ oz. apricot liqueur
½ oz. lime juice

Shake well with ice. Strain into prechilled cocktail glass or pour over rocks.

SOUTHERN BANANA COMFORT

1 oz. golden rum
1 oz. Southern Comfort
¼ cup sliced banana
½ oz. lime juice
1 teaspoon sugar
⅓ cup crushed ice

Put all ingredients into blender. Blend at low speed 10–15 seconds. Pour into prechilled saucer champagne glass. The best possible way to usher in a platter of fried or barbecued chicken.

STRATOSPHERE

1 oz. rum
½ oz. California brandy
¼ oz. tart cherry liqueur
½ oz. lemon juice
1 teaspoon sugar

Shake well with ice. Strain into prechilled cocktail glass. Pleasant to drink around a cheese fondue.

STRAWBERRY FROZEN DAIQUIRI

1½ ozs. light rum
¼ cup thawed frozen strawberries in syrup
½ oz. lime juice
1 teaspoon sugar
½ oz. heavy cream
½ teaspoon maraschino liqueur
⅓ cup crushed ice

Whirl all ingredients in blender at high speed 10 seconds. Pour into prechilled deep-saucer champagne glass or old-fashioned glass.

TAHITI CLUB

2 ozs. golden rum
½ oz. lime juice
½ oz. pineapple juice
1 teaspoon maraschino liqueur
1 slice orange

Shake rum, lime juice, pineapple juice, and maraschino liqueur well with ice. Strain into prechilled old-fashioned glass. Add cracked ice or ice cubes to fill glass. Add orange slice.

TOBAGO

1 oz. golden rum
1 oz. gin
1 teaspoon 151-proof rum
2 teaspoons lime juice
1 teaspoon guava syrup (not nectar)
⅓ cup crushed ice
Lime peel

Put golden rum, gin, 151-proof rum, lime juice, guava syrup, and ice into blender. Blend at low speed 10–15 seconds. Pour over rocks in prechilled old-fashioned glass. Twist lime peel above drink and drop into glass.

TORRIDORA COCKTAIL

1½ ozs. light rum
½ oz. coffee liqueur
¼ oz. heavy cream
1 teaspoon 151-proof rum

Shake light rum, coffee liqueur, and cream well with ice. Strain into prechilled cocktail glass. Float 151-proof rum on top. In the Caribbean, the dinner hour commences rather late, about nine o'clock in the evening. By this time, the sweetness of the cocktail hour will have passed on, and one will be left with a rummy repose and a fine appetite.

TRADE WINDS

2 ozs. golden rum
½ oz. lime juice
½ oz. plum brandy
1½ teaspoons sugar
⅓ cup crushed ice

Put all ingredients into blender. Blend at low speed 10–15 seconds. Pour into prechilled deep-saucer champagne glass. Potent with plum flavor but not a scalp raiser.

UNISPHERE

1½ ozs. golden rum
1 teaspoon grenadine
½ oz. lime juice
½ teaspoon Benedictine
½ teaspoon Pernod

Shake well with ice. Strain into prechilled cocktail glass. Small amounts of liqueurs come through beautifully without overpowering flavor.

Tequila Cocktails

APRICOT AND TEQUILA SOUR

1½ ozs. tequila
¾ oz. apricot liqueur
½ oz. lemon juice

Shake well with ice. Strain into cocktail glass or over rocks in 8-oz. glass.

BLOODY MARIA

1½ ozs. tequila
2 ozs. ice-cold tomato juice
1 teaspoon lemon juice
1 dash Tabasco sauce
1 dash celery salt
1 slice lemon

Pour tequila, tomato juice, lemon juice, Tabasco, and celery salt into prechilled old-fashioned glass. Add rocks or ice slices to fill glass. Stir very well. Add lemon slice. *Viva Maria!*

BUNNY BONANZA

1½ ozs. tequila
1 oz. apple brandy
½ oz. lemon juice
1 teaspoon sugar
½ teaspoon curaçao
1 slice lemon

Shake tequila, apple brandy, lemon juice, sugar, and curaçao well with ice. Strain into prechilled old-fashioned glass. Add ice to fill glass. Garnish with lemon slice.

CHAPALA

1½ ozs. tequila
½ oz. orange juice
½ oz. lemon juice
1 dash orange-flower water
2 teaspoons grenadine
1 slice orange

Shake tequila, orange juice, lemon juice, orange-flower water, and grenadine well with ice. Strain over rocks in prechilled old-fashioned glass. Add orange slice.

COCONUT TEQUILA

1½ ozs. tequila
½ oz. cream of coconut
½ oz. lemon juice
1 teaspoon maraschino liqueur
½ cup crushed ice

Put all ingredients into blender. Blend 20 seconds at low speed. Pour into prechilled deep-saucer champagne glass. Perfect before a Polynesian brunch.

FROZEN BLACKBERRY TEQUILA

1½ ozs. tequila
1 oz. blackberry liqueur
½ oz. lemon juice
⅓ cup crushed ice
1 slice lemon

Put tequila, blackberry liqueur, lemon juice, and crushed ice into blender. Blend 10–15 seconds at low speed. Pour into prechilled old-fashioned glass. Add rocks to fill glass. Add lemon slice.

FROZEN MATADOR

1½ ozs. tequila
2 ozs. pineapple juice
½ oz. lime juice
⅓ cup crushed ice
1 cocktail pineapple stick

Put tequila, pineapple juice, lime juice, and crushed ice into blender. Blend at low speed 10–15 seconds. Pour into prechilled deep-saucer champagne glass. Add pineapple stick. Or pour over rocks in prechilled old-fashioned glass. Add ice cubes to fill glass. Garnish with pineapple stick.

FROZEN SUNSET

1½ ozs. tequila
½ oz. lime juice
½ oz. grenadine
½ cup crushed ice
1 slice lime

Put tequila, lime juice, grenadine, and ice into blender. Blend at low speed 10–15 seconds. Pour into prechilled old-fashioned glass. Add ice slices or cubes to fill glass. Garnish with lime slice.

MARGARITA

1½ ozs. tequila
½ oz. Cointreau, Triple Sec, or curaçao
½ oz. lemon or lime juice

Shake well with ice. Strain into prechilled salt-rimmed cocktail glass. To prepare glass, rub rim with outside of lemon peel; then dip in salt and shake off excess. Although traditionally the glass for a margarita is salt-rimmed, it may also be sugar-rimmed. A twist of lime or lemon peel may be added, if desired.

MEXICAN CLOVER CLUB

1½ ozs. tequila
¾ oz. lemon juice
½ oz. grenadine
½ oz. heavy sweet cream
½ slightly beaten egg white

Shake all ingredients extremely well with ice. Strain into prechilled cocktail glass.

MEXICAN CONNECTION

1 oz. Amer Picon
1 oz. tequila
Chilled orange juice

Place two large ice cubes in 8-oz. glass. Add Amer Picon and tequila. Stir well. Add orange juice to fill glass. Stir.

MEXICO PACIFICO

1½ ozs. tequila
½ oz. lime juice
1 oz. passion-fruit syrup
⅓ cup crushed ice
1 slice lime

Put tequila, lime juice, passion-fruit syrup, and crushed ice into blender. Blend 10–15 seconds at low speed. Pour into prechilled deep-saucer champagne glass. Add lime slice. *Exótico!*

MIA VIDA

1 oz. tequila
½ oz. Kahlúa
½ oz. crème de cacao
½ oz. heavy cream
Sweet chocolate

Shake tequila, Kahlúa, crème de cacao, and cream well with ice. Strain into prechilled large cocktail glass. Grate chocolate over large holes of metal grater and sprinkle on drink.

MINT TEQUILA

1½ ozs. tequila
6 large mint leaves
½ oz. lemon juice
1 teaspoon sugar
½ cup crushed ice

Put all ingredients into blender. Blend at low speed 15–20 seconds. Pour into prechilled old-fashioned glass. Add a rock or two to fill glass to rim. Lively and minty.

NORTEAMERICANO

1½ ozs. tequila
½ oz. very dry sherry
  (manzanilla, if possible)
Olive or lemon peel

Stir tequila and sherry very well with ice. Strain into prechilled cocktail glass or over rocks. Add olive, or twist lemon peel above drink and drop into glass.

PETROLEO

1½ ozs. tequila
½ oz. lemon juice
½ teaspoon Maggi sauce
1 slice lemon

Shake tequila, lemon juice, and Maggi sauce well with ice. Strain over rocks in old-fashioned glass. Stir well. Add lemon slice.

PINK MARGARITA

1½ ozs. tequila
½ oz. lemon or lime juice
½ oz. raspberry liqueur
1 teaspoon grenadine
½ slightly beaten egg white

Shake all ingredients well with ice. Strain into prechilled cocktail glass.

PRADO

1½ ozs. tequila
¾ oz. lime juice
½ egg white
½ oz. maraschino liqueur
1 teaspoon grenadine
½ slice lemon
1 maraschino cherry

Shake tequila, lime juice, egg white, maraschino liqueur, and grenadine well with ice. Strain into prechilled whiskey-sour glass. Add lemon slice and cherry.

SANGRITA *(makes 2¼ cups)*

12 ozs. tomato juice	2 tablespoons diced onion
4 ozs. orange juice	¼ teaspoon salt
2 ozs. lime juice	1 small hot chili pepper

Mix all ingredients in blender at high speed 10 seconds. Chill several hours and stir well before serving. Sangrita is a Mexican nonalcoholic drink that is served with tequila, each in a separate glass; guests sip sangrita and tequila alternately. To make a bloody-mary-type drink, combine 4 ozs. sangrita and a jigger of tequila, shake well, and serve on the rocks.

SENOR STINGER

1½ ozs. tequila   ¾ oz. peppermint schnapps

Shake extremely well with ice. Strain into prechilled cocktail glass. Serve glass of ice water on the side, or pour stinger over cracked ice in deep-saucer champagne glass. For a somewhat sweeter drink, use white crème de menthe instead of peppermint schnapps.

SLOE TEQUILA

1 oz. tequila	½ cup crushed ice
½ oz. sloe gin	Cucumber peel
½ oz. lime juice	

Put tequila, sloe gin, lime juice, and ice into blender. Blend 10–15 seconds at low speed. Pour into prechilled old-fashioned glass. Add cucumber peel and fill glass with cubed or cracked ice.

SUNRISE

1½ ozs. tequila	1 teaspoon grenadine
½ oz. lime juice	1 wedge lime
4 ozs. chilled orange juice	

Pour tequila, lime juice, and orange juice over rocks in squat or tall 8-oz. glass. There should be enough rocks to fill glass to rim. Stir well. Pour grenadine on top and let guest stir sunrise, or stir grenadine with other ingredients before serving. Fasten wedge of lime to glass. Grenadine up to ½ oz. (3 teaspoons) may be used, but drink tends to become cloying. Slice of lime may be used instead of wedge. Crème de cassis may be used in place of grenadine.

SUNRISE ANISE

1½ ozs. tequila
½ oz. anise
4 ozs. chilled orange juice
1 teaspoon grenadine

Pour tequila, anise, and orange juice over rocks in 8-oz. glass. Stir well. Pour grenadine on top and let guests stir it when served. For a somewhat snappier sunrise, use Pernod instead of anise.

TEQUILA DUBONNET

1 oz. tequila
1 oz. red Dubonnet
1 slice lemon

Pour tequila and Dubonnet into prechilled old-fashioned glass. Add cubed or cracked ice to fill glass. Stir. Garnish with lemon slice.

TEQUILA FRESA

1½ ozs. tequila
¾ oz. strawberry liqueur
½ oz. lime juice
¼ teaspoon orange bitters
1 slice lime
1 fresh strawberry

Shake tequila, strawberry liqueur, lime juice, and bitters well with ice. Strain over rocks in old-fashioned glass. Add lime slice and strawberry.

TEQUILA FROZEN SCREWDRIVER

1½ ozs. tequila
3 ozs. iced orange juice
⅓ cup crushed ice
1 slice orange

Put tequila, orange juice, and crushed ice into blender. Blend at low speed 10–15 seconds. Pour into prechilled old-fashioned glass. Add orange slice.

TEQUILA GUAYABA

1½ ozs. tequila
½ oz. guava syrup
½ oz. orange juice
½ oz. lime juice
Orange peel

Shake tequila, guava syrup, orange juice, and lime juice well with ice. Pour into prechilled old-fashioned glass. Add a rock or two to fill glass. Twist orange peel above drink and drop into glass. Pass a guacamole dip.

TEQUILA OLD-FASHIONED

½ teaspoon sugar
2 dashes Angostura bitters
1 teaspoon water
1½ ozs. tequila
Iced club soda
Lemon peel
1 cocktail pineapple stick

Stir sugar, bitters, and 1 teaspoon water in prechilled old-fashioned glass until sugar is dissolved. Add tequila. Add rocks or cracked ice to glass. Stir well. Add a splash of soda and stir. Twist lemon peel above drink and drop into glass. Garnish with pineapple stick.

TEQUILA SOUR

2 ozs. tequila
½ oz. lemon juice
1 teaspoon sugar
½ slice lemon
1 maraschino cherry

Shake tequila, lemon juice, and sugar well with ice. Strain into prechilled whiskey-sour glass. Add lemon slice and cherry.

TEQUINI

1½ to 2 ozs. tequila Lemon peel
½ oz. dry vermouth 1 cocktail olive (optional)

Stir tequila and vermouth well with ice. Strain into prechilled cocktail glass. Twist lemon peel above drink and drop into glass. A Mexican martini. Olive may be added for a salty accent.

Vodka Cocktails

AQUEDUCT

1½ ozs. vodka
¼ oz. curaçao
¼ oz. apricot liqueur

½ oz. lime juice
Orange peel

Shake vodka, curaçao, apricot liqueur, and lime juice well with ice. Strain into prechilled cocktail glass. Twist orange peel above drink and drop into glass. Make book on this drink without any qualms.

BLACK RUSSIAN

1½ ozs. vodka   ¾ oz. Kahlúa coffee liqueur

Shake well with ice. Strain over rocks in prechilled old-fashioned glass. Serve at poolside during the cocktail hour or by candlelight at the witching hour.

BLOODY MARY

1½ ozs. vodka
3 ozs. tomato juice
½ oz. lemon juice
1 teaspoon catsup
1 dash Worcestershire sauce
1 dash celery salt
1 dash Tabasco sauce

Shake all ingredients well with ice. Strain into tall or squat 8-oz. glass.

BUCKEYE MARTINI

2¼ ozs. vodka
¼ oz. dry vermouth
1 large ripe black olive

Stir vodka and vermouth well with ice. Strain into prechilled cocktail glass. Add olive.

BULLSHOT

4 ozs. beef bouillon
1½ ozs. vodka
1 teaspoon lemon juice
1 dash Tabasco sauce

Pour ingredients over rocks in squat 10-oz. glass. Stir well. Add ice if necessary to fill glass. Sprinkle, if desired, with freshly ground pepper.

CHERRY VODKA

1¼ ozs. 100-proof vodka
½ oz. lime juice
½ oz. Peter Heering or Cherry Karise

Shake well with ice until the shaker is almost too cold to hold. Strain into prechilled cocktail glass.

CHIQUITA

1½ ozs. vodka
½ oz. banana liqueur
¼ cup sliced ripe banana
½ oz. lime juice
1 teaspoon sugar
¼ cup finely crushed ice

Put all ingredients into blender. Spin at low speed for 15 seconds. Pour into deep-saucer champagne glass.

FLYING GRASSHOPPER

1 oz. vodka
½ oz. green crème de menthe
½ oz. white crème de cacao

Stir well with ice. Strain into prechilled cocktail glass. More potent and less rich than the plain grasshopper.

FROZEN APPLE

1½ ozs. vodka
¼ oz. calvados or applejack
½ oz. lime juice
¼ cup diced fresh apple
¼ cup finely crushed ice
½ teaspoon sugar

Put all ingredients into blender. Spin at low speed for 15 seconds. Pour into deep-saucer champagne glass. A north-country version of the frozen daiquiri.

GYPSY

2 ozs. vodka
½ oz. Benedictine
1 teaspoon lemon juice
1 teaspoon orange juice
1 slice orange

Shake vodka, Benedictine, lemon juice, and orange juice well with ice. Strain over rocks in prechilled old-fashioned glass. Add orange slice.

KREMLIN COLONEL

2 ozs. vodka
½ oz. lime juice
1 teaspoon sugar
2 large fresh mint leaves

Shake vodka, lime juice, and sugar well with ice. Strain into prechilled cocktail glass. Tear each mint leaf in half to release aroma and drop into glass.

KRETCHMA

1 oz. vodka
1 oz. crème de cacao
½ oz. lemon juice
½ teaspoon grenadine

Shake well with ice. Strain into prechilled cocktail glass. Serve to girls with a deep addiction to chocolate.

LORENZO

1 oz. vodka
1 oz. Tuaca liqueur
½ oz. lime juice

Shake well with ice. Strain into prechilled sugar-frosted cocktail glass. Rim of glass may be moistened with Tuaca before dipping in sugar. One sip of this and you'll understand why Lorenzo de' Medici was called Il Magnifico.

PEACE FEELER

1 oz. vodka
½ oz. Triple Sec
½ oz. crème de cassis
½ oz. lemon juice
Lemon peel

Shake vodka, Triple Sec, crème de cassis, and lemon juice well with ice. Strain into prechilled cocktail glass. Twist lemon peel above drink and drop into glass.

RED APPLE

1 oz. 100-proof vodka
1 oz. apple juice
½ oz. lemon juice
½ teaspoon grenadine
1 dash orange bitters

Shake well with ice. Strain into prechilled cocktail glass. Not to be confused with a vodka and apple juice, a lowball rather than a cocktail.

RUSSIAN BEAR

1 oz. vodka
½ oz. crème de cacao
½ oz. heavy cream

Shake well with ice. Strain into prechilled cocktail glass.

RUSSIAN ESPRESSO

1½ ozs. vodka
½ oz. espresso-coffee liqueur
½ teaspoon lemon juice
Lemon peel

Pour vodka, coffee liqueur, and lemon juice over rocks in prechilled old-fashioned glass. Stir well. Twist lemon peel above drink and drop into glass. A coexistence cocktail.

SALTY DOG

1½ ozs. vodka
3 ozs. unsweetened grapefruit juice
1 teaspoon lemon juice
Salt

Pour vodka, grapefruit juice, and lemon juice over rocks in old-fashioned glass. Sprinkle with salt. Stir.

SCREWDRIVER

1½ ozs. vodka
4½ ozs. ice-cold orange juice, freshly squeezed
1 teaspoon lemon juice (optional)

Shake extremely well with ice or pour into blender and blend with ice at high speed for 5 seconds. Strain into prechilled tall or squat 10-oz. glass. Lemon juice gives the screwdriver an extra twist.

SOVIET

1½ ozs. vodka
½ oz. amontillado sherry
½ oz. dry vermouth
Lemon peel

Stir vodka, sherry, and vermouth well with ice. Strain over rocks in prechilled old-fashioned glass. Twist lemon peel above drink and drop into glass. Liquid tranquilizer.

SVETLANA

1½ ozs. 100-proof vodka
½ oz. sweet vermouth
¼ oz. kirsch
¼ oz. orange juice
Orange peel

Shake vodka, vermouth, kirsch, and orange juice well with ice. Strain into prechilled cocktail glass. Twist orange peel above drink and drop into glass. Serve biting cold. No *nyets* will be heard.

TOVARICH

1½ ozs. vodka
½ oz. kümmel
½ oz. lime juice
Lime peel

Shake vodka, kümmel, and lime juice well with ice. Strain into prechilled cocktail glass. Twist lime peel above drink and drop into glass.

VODKA FRAISE

¾ oz. vodka
¾ oz. light rum
½ oz. strawberry liqueur
½ oz. lime juice
½ teaspoon grenadine
½ large fresh strawberry

Shake vodka, rum, strawberry liqueur, lime juice, and grenadine well with ice. Strain into prechilled sugar-frosted cocktail glass. Float strawberry on top.

VODKA GIMLET

2 ozs. vodka
½ oz. Rose's lime juice

Stir well with ice. Strain into prechilled cocktail glass.

VODKA GRAND MARNIER

1½ ozs. vodka
½ oz. Grand Marnier
½ oz. lime juice
1 slice orange

Shake vodka, Grand Marnier, and lime juice well with ice. Strain over rocks in prechilled old-fashioned glass. Garnish with orange slice.

VODKA MARTINI

2 ozs. vodka
¼ oz. dry vermouth

Stir well with ice. Strain into prechilled cocktail glass or serve over rocks. Garnish with twist of lemon peel or olive. Lacks the zip of the gin-based martini, but is wonderful midday solace for vodka partisans.

VODKA OLD-FASHIONED

½ teaspoon sugar
2 dashes Angostura bitters
1 teaspoon water
2 ozs. vodka
Lemon peel

Dissolve sugar with bitters and water in old-fashioned glass. Add vodka. Fill glass to rim with cubes, slices, or coarsely cracked pieces of ice. Stir very well. Twist lemon peel above drink and drop into glass.

VODKA SOUR

1¾ ozs. vodka
¾ oz. lemon juice
1 teaspoon sugar
1 slice lemon
1 maraschino cherry

Shake vodka, lemon juice, and sugar well with ice. Strain into prechilled whiskey-sour glass. Garnish with lemon slice and cherry.

VODKA STINGER

1½ ozs. vodka ½ oz. white crème de menthe

Shake extremely well with ice. Pour into prechilled cocktail glass. Drink must be extremely cold. May be pre- or postprandial.

WARSAW

1½ ozs. vodka 1 teaspoon lemon juice
½ oz. blackberry liqueur Lemon peel
½ oz. dry vermouth

Shake vodka, blackberry liqueur, vermouth, and lemon juice well with ice. Strain into prechilled cocktail glass. Twist lemon peel above drink and drop into glass.

Whiskey Cocktails

ALLEGHENY

1 oz. bourbon
1 oz. dry vermouth
¼ oz. blackberry liqueur
¼ oz. lemon juice
1 dash Angostura bitters
Lemon peel

Shake bourbon, vermouth, blackberry liqueur, lemon juice, and bitters well with ice. Strain into prechilled cocktail glass. Twist lemon peel above drink and drop into glass.

AULD SOD

1½ ozs. Irish whiskey
½ oz. Lillet
½ oz. lemon juice
1 teaspoon sugar
Orange peel

Shake whiskey, Lillet, lemon juice, and sugar well with ice. Strain into prechilled cocktail glass. Twist orange peel above drink and drop into glass.

BLACK HAWK

1 oz. blended whiskey
1 oz. sloe gin (creamy cap)
½ oz. lemon juice
1 maraschino cherry
(optional)

Shake whiskey, sloe gin, and lemon juice well with ice. Strain into prechilled cocktail glass. Garnish with cherry.

BOURBONNAISE

1½ ozs. bourbon
½ oz. dry vermouth
¼ oz. crème de cassis
¼ oz. lemon juice

Shake well with ice. Strain over rocks in prechilled old-fashioned glass. A perfect way to introduce a French girl to American bourbon.

CANADIAN APPLE

1½ ozs. Canadian whisky
½ oz. calvados
¼ oz. lemon juice
1 teaspoon sugar
Ground cinnamon
1 slice lemon

Shake whisky, calvados, lemon juice, sugar, and a spray of cinnamon well with ice. Strain over rocks in prechilled old-fashioned glass. Add lemon slice. A delight before a holiday dinner of roast turkey or goose.

CANADIAN CHERRY

1½ ozs. Canadian whisky
½ oz. Peter Heering or
   Cherry Karise
¼ oz. lemon juice
¼ oz. orange juice

Shake well with ice. Strain into prechilled sugar-frosted cocktail glass. Glass rim may be moistened with cherry liqueur before dipping in sugar.

CANADIAN COCKTAIL

1½ ozs. Canadian whisky
½ oz. lemon juice
¼ oz. curaçao
1 teaspoon sugar
2 dashes bitters

Shake well with ice. Strain into prechilled cocktail glass or over rocks in old-fashioned glass.

CANADIAN OLD-FASHIONED

1½ ozs. Canadian whisky
2 dashes Angostura bitters
½ teaspoon curaçao
½ teaspoon lemon juice
Lemon peel
Orange peel

Pour whisky, bitters, curaçao, and lemon juice into prechilled old-fashioned glass. Add rocks. Stir. Twist lemon peel and orange peel above drink and drop into glass. More suave than the conventional old-fashioned made with U.S. blended whiskey.

CANADIAN PINEAPPLE

1½ ozs. Canadian whisky
½ oz. pineapple juice
½ oz. lemon juice
½ teaspoon maraschino liqueur
1 cocktail pineapple stick

Shake whisky, pineapple juice, lemon juice, and maraschino liqueur well with ice. Strain over rocks in prechilled old-fashioned glass. Add pineapple stick.

CHAPEL HILL

1½ ozs. blended whiskey
½ oz. curaçao
½ oz. lemon juice
1 slice cocktail orange in syrup

Shake whiskey, curaçao, and lemon juice well with ice. Strain over rocks in prechilled old-fashioned glass. Garnish with orange slice. Pass freshly toasted, salted pecans.

COMMODORE

1¾ ozs. blended whiskey
2 teaspoons lime juice
1 teaspoon orange juice
1 teaspoon strawberry
 liqueur
1 dash orange bitters

Shake well with ice. Strain into prechilled cocktail glass. A subtle blend of whiskey and fruit flavors that's appreciated at the end of a lazy Sunday sail.

COMMONWEALTH

1¾ ozs. Canadian whisky
¼ oz. lemon juice
½ oz. Van der Hum liqueur
Tangerine peel or orange
 peel

Shake whisky, lemon juice, and Van der Hum well with ice. Strain into prechilled sugar-frosted cocktail glass. Twist tangerine peel above drink and drop into glass. Serve before a dinner of grilled lobster tails.

CREAMY IRISH SCREWDRIVER

1 oz. Irish cream liqueur
1½ ozs. Irish whiskey
4 ozs. orange juice
Freshly grated nutmeg

Shake Irish cream liqueur, Irish whiskey, and orange juice well with ice. Strain into prechilled squat or tall 10-oz. glass. Add ice, if necessary, to fill glass to rim. Sprinkle with nutmeg.

CROTON

1¾ ozs. bourbon or blended
 whiskey
¼ oz. cocktail sherry
Lemon peel

Stir whiskey and sherry well with ice. Strain into prechilled cocktail glass. Twist lemon peel above drink and drop into glass. A patio or terrace cocktail to be served with a bowl of fresh iced shrimp and a tangy cocktail sauce.

CURRIER

1½ ozs. blended whiskey
½ oz. kümmel
¼ oz. fresh lime juice
¼ oz. Rose's lime juice
1 slice lime

Shake whiskey, kümmel, and both kinds of lime juice well with ice. Strain into prechilled cocktail glass. Add lime slice. A cocktail to savor between the fox hunt and breakfast.

DELTA

1½ ozs. blended whiskey
½ oz. Southern Comfort
½ oz. lime juice
½ teaspoon sugar
½ slice orange
1 slice fresh peach

Shake whiskey, Southern Comfort, lime juice, and sugar well with ice. Strain over rocks in prechilled old-fashioned glass. Garnish with orange and peach slices. A drink to accompany Gershwin on the hi-fi.

ERIN AND SHERRY

1 oz. Irish whiskey
1 oz. medium-dry sherry
½ teaspoon sugar
1 dash Angostura bitters
Iced club soda
Lemon peel

Pour sugar, bitters, and a dash of soda into old-fashioned glass. Stir until sugar dissolves. Fill glass three-quarters full with ice. Add sherry, whiskey, and a splash of soda. Stir. Twist lemon peel above drink and drop into glass.

GATOR ALLEY

1½ ozs. blended whiskey
1 oz. banana liqueur
½ oz. lemon juice
2 dashes Angostura bitters
1 slice lemon

Shake whiskey, banana liqueur, lemon juice, and bitters well with ice. Strain into prechilled old-fashioned glass half filled with ice. Add lemon slice.

GLASGOW

1½ ozs. Scotch
¾ oz. lemon juice
¼ oz. dry vermouth
¼ oz. orzata

Shake well with ice. Strain into prechilled cocktail glass. Serve with thin slices of Nova Scotia salmon on hot buttered toast.

HABITANT COCKTAIL

1½ ozs. blended Canadian whisky
1 oz. lemon juice
1 teaspoon maple-sugar syrup
1 slice orange
1 maraschino cherry

Shake whisky, lemon juice, and syrup well with ice. Strain over rocks in prechilled old-fashioned glass. Garnish with orange slice and cherry.

INDIAN RIVER

1½ ozs. blended whiskey
½ oz. unsweetened grapefruit juice
¼ oz. raspberry liqueur
¼ oz. sweet vermouth

Shake well with ice. Strain over rocks in prechilled old-fashioned glass.

IRISH ALMOND

1½ ozs. blended Irish whiskey
½ oz. orange juice
½ oz. lemon juice
2 teaspoons orgeat or orzata (almond syrup)
1 teaspoon toasted almond slices

Shake whiskey, orange juice, lemon juice, and orgeat well with ice. Strain into prechilled whiskey-sour glass. Sprinkle almond slices on top. (To toast almonds, place sliced almonds in shallow pan in oven preheated to 350°. Bake 8 to 10 minutes or until medium brown, stirring occasionally. Sprinkle with salt. Cool.)

JACKSON SQUARE

1½ ozs. bourbon
½ oz. peppermint schnapps
3 dashes Peychaud's bitters
Iced club soda
Lemon peel

Pour bourbon, peppermint schnapps, and bitters over rocks in old-fashioned glass. Stir. Add soda. Stir. Twist lemon peel above drink and drop into glass.

KENTUCKY

1½ ozs. bourbon
½ oz. lemon juice
½ oz. pineapple juice
1 teaspoon maraschino liqueur

Shake well with ice. Strain into prechilled sugar-frosted cocktail glass.

LAWHILL

1¼ ozs. blended whiskey
¾ oz. dry vermouth
¼ teaspoon Pernod
¼ teaspoon maraschino liqueur
½ oz. orange juice
1 dash Angostura bitters

Shake well with ice. Strain into prechilled cocktail glass. A superb cocktail to mix beforehand, strain into a Thermos, and tote along on a picnic.

MANHASSET

1½ ozs. blended whiskey
½ oz. lemon juice
¼ oz. dry vermouth
¼ oz. sweet vermouth
Lemon peel

Shake whiskey, lemon juice, and both kinds of vermouth well with ice. Strain into prechilled cocktail glass. Twist lemon peel above drink and drop into glass.

MANHATTAN

(See page 220 for a separate discussion of this longtime favorite and its variations.)

MAY COCKTAIL

1½ ozs. blended whiskey
¼ oz. kirschwasser
¼ oz. strawberry liqueur
Chilled May wine
1 slice lemon

Shake whiskey, kirschwasser, and strawberry liqueur well with ice. Strain into prechilled old-fashioned glass with a large ice cube. Fill glass with May wine. Stir. Garnish with lemon slice.

NEVINS

1½ ozs. bourbon
½ oz. grapefruit juice
¼ oz. apricot liqueur
¼ oz. lemon juice
1 dash Angostura bitters

Shake well with ice. Strain into prechilled sugar-frosted cocktail glass.

NEW WORLD

1¾ ozs. blended whiskey
½ oz. lime juice
1 teaspoon grenadine
Lime peel

Shake whiskey, lime juice, and grenadine well with ice. Strain into prechilled cocktail glass. Twist lime peel above drink and drop into glass. Drink this one while listening to Dvořák before a midnight supper.

NEW YORKER

1½ ozs. blended whiskey
½ oz. lime juice
1 teaspoon sugar
¼ teaspoon grenadine
Lemon peel
Orange peel

Shake whiskey, lime juice, sugar, and grenadine well with ice. Strain into prechilled sugar-frosted cocktail glass. Twist lemon peel and orange peel above drink and drop into glass. A fruity terrace cocktail appreciated equally under sun or stars.

NEW YORK SOUR

2 ozs. blended whiskey
½ oz. lemon juice
1 teaspoon sugar
Chilled dry red wine
½ slice lemon

Shake whiskey, lemon juice, and sugar well with ice. Strain into prechilled 6-oz. sour glass. Fill glass with dry red wine. Stir. Garnish with lemon slice. A miniature punch in a sour glass.

NIGHT SHADE

1½ ozs. bourbon
½ oz. sweet vermouth
½ oz. orange juice
¼ teaspoon yellow Chartreuse
½ slice orange
½ slice lemon

Shake bourbon, vermouth, orange juice, and Chartreuse well with ice. Strain over rocks in prechilled old-fashioned glass. Add orange and lemon slices. Pass freshly fried, generously salted shrimp chips.

OLD-FASHIONED

½ teaspoon sugar
1 or 2 dashes Angostura
  bitters
1 teaspoon water
1½ to 2 ozs. blended
  whiskey
Lemon peel

Stir sugar, bitters, and water in prechilled old-fashioned glass until sugar dissolves. Fill glass with ice cubes or large pieces of cracked ice. Add whiskey. Stir well. Twist lemon peel above drink and drop into glass. An old-fashioned may be made with U.S. blended whiskey, Canadian, Irish, or Scotch. In smart men's clubs, the words *garnish* and *garbage* were once synonymous; orange and lemon slices, cherries, cocktail sticks, etc., were considered female diversions for filling a glass with fruit instead of the cocktail itself. Over the years, this attitude has been somewhat mitigated. Generally, however, most men and women appreciate the old-fashioned unencumbered with superfluous fruit.

PRINCE EDWARD

1¾ ozs. Scotch
½ oz. Lillet
¼ oz. Drambuie
1 slice cocktail orange in
  syrup

Shake Scotch, Lillet, and Drambuie well with ice. Strain over rocks in prechilled old-fashioned glass. Garnish with orange slice.

QUEBEC

1½ ozs. Canadian whisky
¼ oz. Amer Picon
¼ oz. maraschino liqueur
½ oz. dry vermouth

Shake well with ice. Strain into prechilled sugar-frosted cocktail glass.

ROBBER BARON

1½ ozs. Canadian whisky ½ oz. dry vermouth
1 oz. aquavit Lemon peel

Stir whisky, aquavit, and vermouth well with ice. Strain over ice in prechilled old-fashioned glass. Twist lemon peel above drink and drop into glass.

ROB ROY

1½ to 2 ozs. Scotch 1 dash orange bitters
½ oz. sweet vermouth (optional)

Stir well with ice. Strain into prechilled cocktail glass. The rob roy is, of course, simply a Scotch manhattan, and variations in whisky and vermouth proportions may be made to your own drinking taste. A light rather than a smoky Scotch is preferred by most people. A brandied cherry may be added for a special flourish. For a dry rob roy, use dry vermouth; add a twist of lemon, if desired.

ROB ROY, HOLIDAY STYLE

½ teaspoon Drambuie ¼ oz. sweet vermouth
2 ozs. Scotch 1 maraschino or brandied
¼ oz. dry vermouth cherry

Pour Drambuie into a prechilled cocktail glass and swirl it around to coat bottom and sides of glass. Stir Scotch and both kinds of vermouth well with ice. Strain into glass. Add cherry.

RUSTY NAIL

¾ oz. Scotch ¾ oz. Drambuie

Pour over rocks in prechilled old-fashioned glass. Stir.

SAZERAC

¼ teaspoon abisante,
  anesone, or any other
  absinthe substitute
½ teaspoon sugar
¼ teaspoon bitters
  (Peychaud's, if possible)
1 tablespoon water
2 ozs. blended whiskey or
  bourbon
Lemon peel

Swirl abisante around in prechilled old-fashioned glass until inside is completely coated. Add sugar, bitters, and 1 tablespoon water. Stir until sugar is dissolved. Add a large ice cube and whiskey. Stir well. Twist lemon peel above drink and drop into glass. A New Orleans specialty and a magnificent prebrunch drink.

SAZERAC A LA PLAYBOY

¼ teaspoon Pernod
1 small sugar cube
2 dashes Peychaud's bitters
1 dash Angostura bitters
Water
1½ ozs. straight rye
Lemon peel

Pour Pernod into prechilled old-fashioned glass and roll glass until inside is entirely coated. Add sugar, both kinds of bitters, and enough cold water to barely cover sugar. Muddle until sugar is completely dissolved. Add whiskey and a large ice cube. Stir well. Twist lemon peel above drink and drop into glass.

SCOTCH HOLIDAY SOUR

2 ozs. light Scotch
1 oz. cherry liqueur
½ oz. sweet vermouth
1 oz. lemon juice
½ egg white
1 slice lemon

Shake Scotch, cherry liqueur, vermouth, lemon juice, and egg white well with ice. Strain into prechilled oversize sour glass or into prechilled old-fashioned glass with a large rock. Garnish with lemon slice.

SEABOARD

1 oz. blended whiskey
1 oz. gin
½ oz. lemon juice
1 teaspoon sugar
2 sprigs mint

Shake whiskey, gin, lemon juice, and sugar well with ice. Strain over rocks in prechilled old-fashioned glass. Tear several leaves of each mint sprig before dropping into drink.

THE SHOOT

1 oz. Scotch
1 oz. dry sherry
1 teaspoon lemon juice
1 teaspoon orange juice
½ teaspoon sugar

Shake well with ice. Strain into prechilled cocktail glass. Serve before a dinner of roast pheasant or partridge.

SINGAPORE

1½ ozs. Canadian whisky
¼ oz. sloe gin
¼ oz. Rose's lime juice
½ oz. lemon juice
Cucumber peel

Shake whisky, sloe gin, Rose's lime juice, and lemon juice well with ice. Strain over rocks in prechilled old-fashioned glass. Add cucumber peel.

SOUTHERN GINGER

1½ ozs. 100-proof bourbon
1 oz. ginger ale
¼ oz. lemon juice
½ teaspoon ginger-flavored brandy
Lemon peel

Shake bourbon, ginger ale, lemon juice, and ginger brandy well with ice. Strain into prechilled cocktail glass. Twist lemon peel above drink and drop into glass.

STONYBROOK

1½ ozs. blended whiskey
½ oz. Triple Sec
¼ teaspoon orzata
½ egg white
Lemon peel
Orange peel

Shake whiskey, Triple Sec, orzata, and egg white well with ice. Strain into prechilled cocktail glass. Twist lemon peel and orange peel above drink and drop into glass. A drink to accompany *barquettes* of hot deviled crab meat.

TROIS RIVIERES

1½ ozs. Canadian whisky
½ oz. red Dubonnet
¼ oz. Cointreau
Orange peel

Shake whisky, Dubonnet, and Cointreau well with ice. Strain into prechilled cocktail glass. Twist orange peel above drink and drop into glass. Perfect before a midnight collation.

TWIN HILLS

2 ozs. blended whiskey
¼ oz. lemon juice
¼ oz. lime juice
2 teaspoons Benedictine
1 teaspoon sugar
½ slice lemon
½ slice lime

Shake whiskey, lemon juice, lime juice, Benedictine, and sugar well with ice. Strain into prechilled whiskey-sour glass. Garnish with lemon and lime slices. Offbeat but a very superior sour.

WARD EIGHT

2 ozs. blended U.S. whiskey
   or Canadian whisky
½ oz. lemon juice
1 teaspoon sugar
½ teaspoon grenadine
1 slice lemon

Shake whiskey, lemon juice, sugar, and grenadine well with ice. Strain into tall 8-oz. glass. Add cracked ice or ice slices to fill glass. Stir. Garnish with lemon slice. A pleasant tall cocktail that survived Prohibition.

WHISKEY MAC

1½ ozs. Scotch whisky *1½ ozs. Stone's ginger wine*

Pour whisky and ginger wine over rocks in 8-oz. glass. Stir. In Scotland this drink is usually served at room temperature without ice. Americans prefer the chilled version. May also be served with lemon twist.

WHISKEY SOUR

2 ozs. blended whiskey
¾ oz. lemon juice
1 teaspoon sugar
½ slice lemon
1 maraschino cherry
(optional)

Shake whiskey, lemon juice, and sugar well with ice. Strain into prechilled whiskey-sour glass. Garnish with lemon slice and cherry, if desired. For a more tart drink, reduce amount of sugar. For a more mellow whiskey sour, use ½ oz. lemon juice and ¼ oz. orange juice. Sours made with Canadian or Scotch whisky are pleasing variants, the former having a strong appeal for the distaff side.

WHISKEY TODDY, COLD

½ teaspoon sugar
2 teaspoons water
2 ozs. bourbon or blended whiskey
Lemon peel (optional)

Put sugar and water into prechilled old-fashioned glass. Stir until sugar dissolves. Fill glass with ice cubes or large pieces of cracked ice. Add whiskey. Stir well. Twist lemon peel above drink and drop into glass. Must be stinging cold.

THE MANHATTAN

In the national drink derby, two or three cocktail generations ago, the manhattan and the martini always wound up in a dead heat. At the present time, the manhattan occupies the second spot. Manhattanites, though less demanding than martini fans, have nevertheless stirred up many spirited variations on the whiskey-vermouth theme. In public pouring houses, the usual manhattan is made with 1½ ounces of whiskey. At private bars, a more generous allowance of whiskey is likely. Here's what most manhattanites expect:

MANHATTAN

1½ to 2 ozs. blended whiskey
½ oz. sweet vermouth
1 dash bitters (optional)
1 maraschino cherry

Stir whiskey, vermouth, and bitters well with ice. Strain into prechilled cocktail glass. Add cherry.

Dry Manhattan. Use dry instead of sweet vermouth; a twist of lemon peel or an olive may be substituted for the cherry.

Bourbon Manhattan. Use 86- or 100-proof bourbon instead of blended whiskey; if 100-proof bourbon is used, a little extra stirring is in order.

Canadian Manhattan. Use Canadian instead of U.S. blended whiskey; don't overstir or the delicate flavor of the Canadian spirits will become pallid.

Muscari Manhattan. Use Muscari (an aperitif wine) instead of vermouth.

Wine Cocktails

Wine cocktails are for those who like wine and also enjoy pleasantly odd combinations of cold mixed drinks that help unwind the day and provoke appetites for dinner but who don't want the fast, sometimes staggering jolt of a martini or an old-fashioned. There are bottled wine cocktails now on the market, but making your own is no formidable task, and the results are extremely pleasant unless you're one of those wine zealots who spend more time appraising one wine versus another than they do drinking them.

The wine cocktails that follow are made from red and white dry table wines. California jug wines are perfect for this kind of bartending. Both red and white wines should be well chilled and should be served in stemmed wineglasses holding 8 to 10 ounces each. The kind of wine you use will naturally determine the final results of the mixed drinks. A medium-bodied California mountain Burgundy will become a cocktail with sturdy flavor; a Beaujolais Nouveau used for the same recipe will result in a lighter, fresher-tasting cocktail. Among the whites, any light-bodied dry wine—from an Italian soave to a dry California Chablis—will do beautifully.

BASES FILLED

4 ozs. chilled dry white wine
½ oz. Cointreau or
  Triple Sec
½ oz. cognac
Orange peel

Pour wine, Cointreau, and cognac into large wineglass. Add two ice cubes. Stir well. Twist orange peel above drink and drop into glass.

BERMUDA BLANC

4 ozs. chilled dry white wine
½ oz. light rum
1 teaspoon Rose's lime juice
1 slice lime

Pour wine, rum, and Rose's lime juice into large wineglass. Add two ice cubes. Stir well. Add lime slice.

BRIGHT BERRY

4 ozs. chilled dry red wine
½ oz. strawberry liqueur
1 teaspoon cognac
1 fresh strawberry

Pour wine, strawberry liqueur, and cognac into large wineglass. Add two ice cubes. Stir well. Add strawberry.

COOL JAZZ

1 oz. dry white wine
¾ oz. banana liqueur
½ oz. lime juice
1 slice banana

Shake wine, banana liqueur, and lime juice well with ice. Strain into cocktail glass. Float banana slice on drink.

CRANBERRY EYE

4 ozs. chilled dry red wine
½ oz. cranberry liqueur
½ oz. California brandy
1 slice orange

Pour wine, cranberry liqueur, and brandy into large wineglass. Add two ice cubes. Stir well. Add orange slice.

FRENCH CURVE

4 ozs. chilled dry white wine
1 teaspoon Pernod
1 teaspoon maraschino liqueur
1 slice lemon
½ slice orange

Pour wine, Pernod, and maraschino liqueur into large wineglass. Add two ice cubes. Stir well. Add lemon and orange slices.

ITALIAN PERFUME

4 ozs. chilled dry white wine
½ oz. Italian brandy
1 teaspoon amaretto
1 slice lemon

Pour wine, brandy, and amaretto into large wineglass. Add two ice cubes. Stir well. Add lemon slice.

MONK'S WINE

4 ozs. chilled dry white wine
1 teaspoon green Chartreuse
1 slice lemon

Pour wine and Chartreuse into large wineglass. Add two ice cubes. Stir well. Add lemon slice.

PIKE'S PICON

4 ozs. chilled dry red wine
½ oz. Amer Picon
1 teaspoon grenadine
Orange peel

Pour wine, Amer Picon, and grenadine into large wineglass. Add two ice cubes. Stir well. Twist orange peel above drink and drop into glass.

RED CARPET

1 oz. dry red wine
1 oz. Chambery Fraise
 (strawberry-flavored
 French vermouth)
½ oz. strawberry liqueur
Iced club soda
1 slice lemon

Stir red wine, Chambery Fraise, and strawberry liqueur well with ice. Strain into 6- or 8-oz. wineglass. Add a small splash of soda. Stir. Add lemon slice.

RED KIR

4 ozs. chilled dry red wine
½ oz. crème de cassis
1 slice lemon

Pour wine and crème de cassis into large wineglass. Add two ice cubes. Stir well. Add lemon slice.

RED LIGHT

4 ozs. chilled dry red wine
½ oz. Cordial Médoc
½ oz. Cointreau or
 Triple Sec
1 slice lemon

Pour wine, Cordial Médoc, and Cointreau into large wineglass. Add two ice cubes. Stir well. Add lemon slice.

RED MANHATTAN

1 dash Angostura bitters
1 teaspoon sugar
Iced club soda
4 ozs. chilled dry red wine
½ oz. sweet vermouth
Orange peel

Pour bitters and sugar into large wineglass. Add a small splash of soda. Stir until sugar dissolves. Add wine and vermouth. Add two ice cubes. Stir well. Twist orange peel above drink and drop into glass.

RUBY

2 ozs. red wine
½ oz. maraschino liqueur
½ oz. lemon juice
1 dash Angostura bitters
1 slice lemon

Stir wine, maraschino liqueur, lemon juice, and bitters well with ice. Strain into 6- or 8-oz. wineglass. Add lemon slice.

SOFT TOUCH

1½ ozs. dry white wine
½ beaten egg white
½ oz. heavy sweet cream
½ oz. lemon juice
1½ teaspoons sugar

Shake all ingredients extremely well with ice. Strain into prechilled cocktail glass.

VESUVIO

3 ozs. dry white wine
1 teaspoon apricot liqueur
1 teaspoon amaretto
1 slice cucumber

Stir white wine, apricot liqueur, and amaretto well with ice. Strain into 6- or 8-oz. wineglass. Add cucumber slice.

WINE AND BITTERS

1 teaspoon sugar
2 dashes Angostura bitters
Iced club soda
4 ozs. chilled dry white wine
1 slice lemon
½ slice orange

Pour sugar, bitters, and a small splash of soda into large wineglass. Stir until sugar dissolves. Add wine and two ice cubes. Stir well. Add lemon and orange slices.

Miscellaneous Cocktails

ANDALUSIA

1½ ozs. very dry sherry
½ oz. cognac
½ oz. light rum
1 dash Angostura bitters

Stir well with ice. Strain into prechilled cocktail glass.

BLOODY SAKE

3 ozs. tomato juice
2 ozs. sake
2 teaspoons lemon juice
1 dash Tabasco sauce
1 dash Worcestershire sauce
Salt, celery salt, pepper

Pour tomato juice, sake, lemon juice, Tabasco sauce, and Worcestershire sauce into cocktail shaker with ice. Add a sprinkling of salt, celery salt, and pepper. Shake very well. Strain into 8-oz. glass. Add a sprinkling of freshly ground pepper, if desired.

BRANDIED MADEIRA

1 oz. Madeira
1 oz. brandy
½ oz. dry vermouth
Lemon peel

Stir Madeira, brandy, and vermouth well with ice. Pour over rocks in prechilled old-fashioned glass. Twist lemon peel above drink and drop into glass.

BRANDIED PORT

1 oz. tawny port
1 oz. brandy
½ oz. lemon juice
1 teaspoon maraschino
    liqueur
1 slice orange

Shake port, brandy, lemon juice, and maraschino liqueur well with ice. Strain over rocks in prechilled old-fashioned glass. Add orange slice.

CLARET COCKTAIL

1 oz. dry red wine
1 oz. brandy
¼ oz. curaçao
¼ oz. lemon juice
½ teaspoon anisette
Orange peel

Shake wine, brandy, curaçao, lemon juice, and anisette well with ice. Strain into prechilled cocktail glass. Twist orange peel above drink and drop into glass.

CREAMY ORANGE

1 oz. orange juice
1 oz. cream sherry
½ oz. heavy cream
2 teaspoons brandy

Shake well with ice. Strain into prechilled cocktail glass. A gentle introduction to a brunch omelet.

DUTCH TREAT

1½ ozs. curaçao
1 oz. orange juice
½ oz. lemon juice
½ slice orange

Shake curaçao, orange juice, and lemon juice well with ice. Strain into prechilled cocktail glass. Add orange slice.

EUREKA

1 oz. light rum
1 oz. Lillet
½ oz. apricot liqueur
3 ozs. orange juice
½-inch piece California orange peel, freshly cut

Shake rum, Lillet, apricot liqueur, and orange juice well with ice. Strain over ice in prechilled 8-oz. glass. Light a match. With other hand, bend orange peel sharply and hold flame to it to make a twinkling flare. Drop peel into glass.

FIORD

1 oz. brandy
½ oz. aquavit
½ oz. orange juice
½ oz. lime juice
1 teaspoon grenadine

Shake well with ice. Strain into prechilled cocktail glass.

FLORIDA

1¼ ozs. orange juice
½ oz. gin
¼ oz. kirschwasser
¼ oz. Triple Sec
1 teaspoon lemon juice

Shake well with ice. Strain into prechilled sugar-frosted cocktail glass. A drink with less hard liquor than citrus juice, but one that always clears up the fog.

FROZEN AQUAVIT

1½ ozs. aquavit
½ oz. lime juice
½ egg white
½ cup crushed ice
1 teaspoon sugar
1 teaspoon kirschwasser

Put all ingredients into blender. Blend at low speed 10–15 seconds. Pour into prechilled deep-saucer champagne glass.

FROZEN SHERRY DAIQUIRI

2 ozs. medium-dry sherry
½ oz. lime juice
2 teaspoons sugar
⅓ cup finely crushed ice

Pour all ingredients into blender. Blend at low speed 10–15 seconds. Pour into prechilled deep-saucer champagne glass.

GENEVER COCKTAIL

1½ ozs. Dutch genever gin
½ oz. lime juice
½ oz. orange juice
1 teaspoon sugar
1 dash Angostura bitters

Shake well with ice. Strain over rocks in prechilled old-fashioned glass. Odd but very obliging.

GRAPPA STREGA

1 oz. grappa
1 oz. Strega
¼ oz. lemon juice
¼ oz. orange juice
Lemon peel

Shake grappa, Strega, lemon juice, and orange juice well with ice. Strain into prechilled cocktail glass. Twist lemon peel above drink and drop into glass.

GREAT DANE

1½ ozs. aquavit
¼ oz. dry vermouth
¼ oz. sweet vermouth
2 cocktail onions

Stir aquavit, dry vermouth, and sweet vermouth well with ice. Strain into prechilled cocktail glass with onions, or serve on rocks.

KIR

3½ ozs. ice-cold dry white wine
½ oz. ice-cold crème de cassis

Pour into prechilled 7- or 8-oz. wide-bellied wineglass. Add an ice cube or two, if desired. Proportions may be varied, but the 7-to-1 *vin blanc*–cassis ratio above (actually a variation of the vermouth cassis) is the most commonly accepted version.

MARY KUMMEL

3 ozs. tomato juice
1 oz. kümmel
1 oz. vodka
1 tablespoon lemon juice
1 dash Tabasco sauce
1 dash Worcestershire sauce
Salt, celery salt, pepper

Pour tomato juice, kümmel, vodka, lemon juice, Tabasco sauce, and Worcestershire sauce into cocktail shaker with ice. Add a sprinkling of salt, celery salt, and pepper. Shake very well. Strain into 8-oz. glass. Add a sprinkling of freshly ground pepper, if desired.

MIDNIGHT SUN

1½ ozs. aquavit
½ oz. unsweetened grapefruit juice
½ oz. lemon juice
1 teaspoon sugar
½ teaspoon grenadine
½ slice orange

Shake aquavit, grapefruit juice, lemon juice, sugar, and grenadine well with ice. Strain into prechilled whiskey-sour glass. Add orange slice. Keep herring tidbits within reach.

NORTHERN LIGHTS

1 oz. aquavit
1 oz. light Canadian whisky
1 dash Angostura bitters
½ teaspoon grenadine
Iced club soda
1 slice lemon
½ slice orange

Pour aquavit, Canadian whisky, Angostura bitters, and grenadine into old-fashioned glass three-quarters filled with ice cubes. Stir well. Add splash of soda. Add lemon and orange slices.

OPHELIA

1½ ozs. aquavit
2 ozs. orange juice
½ oz. Rose's lime juice
1 wedge orange

Shake aquavit, orange juice, and Rose's lime juice well with ice. Strain over ice in prechilled old-fashioned glass. Add orange wedge.

PERNOD DRIP

1½ ozs. Pernod
1 cube sugar

The first requirement for this drink is an absinthe drip glass. If you don't own a drip glass, you can use a tea strainer over an old-fashioned glass as a substitute. First pour the Pernod into the glass. Place the strainer on the glass. Put the sugar over the drip section on top of the glass. Pack a mound of crushed or finely cracked ice atop the sugar. When the ice has melted, the drip is ready. Strictly for curio seekers in the spirit world.

PISCO SOUR

1½ ozs. pisco brandy
½ oz. lemon juice
1 tablespoon sugar
1 tablespoon egg white
Angostura bitters

Shake pisco, lemon juice, sugar, and egg white well with ice. Strain into prechilled cocktail glass with sugar-frosted rim. Float a few drops bitters on top. May also be poured into small punch cups.

ROCKY GREEN DRAGON

1 oz. gin
¾ oz. green Chartreuse
¾ oz. cognac

Shake extremely well with ice. Strain over rocks in prechilled old-fashioned glass. A potent dragon to be slowly sipped, not gulped.

SAKE SOUR

2 ozs. sake
½ oz. lemon juice
1½ ozs. orange juice
1 teaspoon sugar
½ slice orange

Shake sake, lemon juice, orange juice, and sugar well with ice. Strain into whiskey-sour glass. Garnish with orange slice.

SAKE STINGER

1 oz. sake
½ oz. white crème de menthe or peppermint schnapps
½ oz. California brandy
Lemon peel

Shake sake, crème de menthe, and brandy well with ice. Strain into cocktail glass. Twist lemon peel above drink and drop into glass.

SEA ROVER

1½ ozs. aquavit
½ oz. strawberry liqueur
½ oz. lime juice
Lime peel

Shake aquavit, strawberry liqueur, and lime juice well with ice. Strain into prechilled cocktail glass. Twist lime peel above drink and drop into glass.

SHERRY GIMLET

2 ozs. very dry sherry
1 oz. gin
1 oz. Rose's lime juice

Stir sherry, gin, and Rose's lime juice well with ice. Strain into 8-oz. glass. Add ice cubes to fill glass. Stir.

SHERRY SOUR

2 ozs. very dry sherry
2 teaspoons sugar
½ oz. lemon juice
1 oz. orange juice
½ slice orange

Shake sherry, sugar, lemon juice, and orange juice well with ice. Strain into whiskey-sour glass. Garnish with orange slice.

SHERRY SPIDER

1½ ozs. medium-dry sherry
2 dashes Angostura bitters
Iced ginger ale or ginger beer

Fill an old-fashioned glass three-quarters full with ice. Add sherry and bitters. Stir well. Add ginger ale or ginger beer. Stir lightly. A mild, pleasant quencher for those who want to sail a clear sea.

SHINTO

2 dashes Angostura bitters
½ teaspoon sugar
Iced club soda
1 oz. sake
1 oz. Suntory whisky
1 slice lemon

Pour bitters, sugar, and splash of soda into old-fashioned glass. Stir until sugar dissolves. Add sake, Suntory whisky, and three large ice cubes. Stir well. Add splash of soda. Stir. Add lemon slice.

SUISSESSE

1½ ozs. Pernod
½ oz. anisette
¼ oz. heavy cream
½ egg white

Shake well with ice. Pour into prechilled cocktail glass. Perfect midnight cocktail that's really more Mediterranean than Swiss.

SWEDISH SIDECAR

1 oz. aquavit
½ oz. Cointreau or
   Triple Sec
½ oz. lemon juice
½ oz. orange juice

Shake aquavit, Cointreau, lemon juice, and orange juice well with ice. Strain into prechilled sugar-frosted cocktail glass.

TOBACCO ROAD

1½ ozs. Southern Comfort
3 ozs. orange juice
¾ oz. lemon juice
1 teaspoon grenadine
1 slice orange

Shake Southern Comfort, orange juice, lemon juice, and grenadine well with ice. Strain over ice in prechilled squat 10-oz. glass. Stir well. Add ice, if necessary, to fill glass. Add orange slice.

YELLOW PLUM

1½ ozs. quetsch, mirabelle,
   or slivovitz
½ oz. lemon juice
½ oz. orange juice
1 teaspoon maraschino
   liqueur
1 teaspoon sugar

Shake well with ice. Strain into prechilled cocktail glass. Tart, triumphant, titillating.

HIGH SPIRITS
Medium-tall and King-size Potables

If the word *highball* is heard less and less frequently these days, the drink itself is called for more and more often. Drinkers everywhere now ask for Scotch and soda, bourbon and water, applejack and ginger ale, and other happy mixtures suited to their own thirst specifications. Although the highball is the easiest drink in the world to define—a small amount of something strong with a larger amount of something weak in a tall glass with ice—it's the one potable for which you seldom see a recipe. As a matter of fact, a host who, in the intimacy of his own digs, strictly follows a highball recipe is inhospitable. It's the one drink guests themselves expect to mix to their own tastes, in the same way that they salt and pepper their food. No two-finger measurements are alike and no two guests will ever say "when" at the same point on the stopwatch. Even at commuter stand-up bars, where whiskey is carefully measured in a standard jigger, the bubbly water usually remains in the hands of the highballer pouring his soda, 7-Up, or tonic water to his own level.

But the highball is only one of countless potables in tall glasses. A tall drink at the end of a long, tiring day can do things no short drink can ever hope to do. A wilted worthy need only look at a lofty drink clinking with ice and miraculous changes take place within him. His collar seems to cling less tenaciously. He begins to talk in more relaxed, civilized tones. And then, as the first sip of a tall drink passes over his tongue and throat, like springwater gurgling into a hot arroyo, he feels the unparalleled pleasure of a long-delayed thrill.

One of the obvious virtues of tall mixed drinks is that they never seem to get in the way of food, or vice versa. A man may hesitate to eat a trout *au bleu* while drinking a manhattan, but he won't hesitate to drink a tall spritzer of Rhine wine and soda before, during, or after the trout. Although Europophilian wine pundits will be horrified at the thought, many a tall cooler at many a fine feast supplants *both* the cocktail and the wine. Ounce for ounce, a tall cooler with club soda is actually no stronger than wine. But, in the final analysis, tall drinks are made not for debating but for happy guzzling.

In preparing tall drinks, whether they be 8, 12, or 20 ounces, the host should follow this modern code for presenting them:

- Use a fine liquor. The flavor of a poor liquor is actually intensified in a tall drink; you have time to scrutinize it more carefully than when you down it in one gulp. This doesn't mean that you must buy a sixteen-year-old bonded whiskey the next time you serve a round of whiskey collinses, but you should seek one of the eminent brands of liquor that is mellow, smooth, and pleasing whether taken straight or in a tall drink.

- Be meticulous about the quality of the iced club soda or the ginger ale. For a small number of highballers, serve splits of soda or ginger ale. Larger bottles of carbonated waters, except for a party, just stand around going quietly flat unless you and your guests are unusually speedy drinkers.

- Add bubblewater just before the drinks are delivered. For optimum sparkle and so that it retains its fizz as long as possible, pour it against the inside of the tilted glass. Be sure the effervescent water is ice-cold.

- Plain tap water, if used, must be clear and clean, without evidence of rust, lime, iron, chlorination, or other urban evils. Use bottled springwater, if necessary, when your guests decline bubbles.

- Use enough liquor in a tall drink: at least 1½ ounces in an 8-ounce glass, and up to 2 ounces or more in 12- to 20-ounce glasses.

• Use thin glassware with heavy bottoms to avoid the well-known sliding drink.

The gin and tonic has not only joined the tall-drink derby but in many circles is way out in front both in summer and winter. Bitter lemon has joined the same fraternity. While the British Empire was shrinking, the British-inspired bubblies became more and more popular.

Among simple highballs, the whiskey highball is the best known, but there's no dogma that interdicts the use of any liquor in a highball, from aquavit to zubrovka. One of the best contemporary highballs is light, dry rum and iced club soda or iced tonic water.

So-called lowballs are served in glasses that actually hold as much as their taller cousins but that are squat in shape rather than long; old-fashioned-type glasses ranging from 7 to 11 ounces are considered lowballs.

Bucks

Bucks are medium-long drinks—served in tall 8-ounce glasses—that always contain ginger ale and fresh lemon or lime juice. Traditionally the fruit was squeezed and dropped into the glass. You'll find you get better bucks if the lemon or lime juice is measured into the glass and the drink then garnished with a slice of fruit as its crowning touch.

APPLE BUCK

1½ ozs. applejack
1 teaspoon ginger-flavored brandy
½ oz. lemon juice
Iced ginger ale
1 chunk preserved ginger in syrup

Shake applejack, ginger brandy, and lemon juice well with ice. Strain into 8-oz. glass half filled with ice. Add ginger ale. Stir. Add preserved ginger.

BRANDY BUCK

1½ ozs. brandy
1 teaspoon crème de menthe
½ oz. lemon juice
Iced ginger ale
Fresh grapes

Shake brandy, crème de menthe, and lemon juice well with ice. Strain into 8-oz. glass half filled with ice. Add ginger ale. Stir. Add three or four seedless grapes or two large pitted black grapes cut in half.

GIN BUCK

1½ ozs. gin
½ oz. lemon juice
Iced ginger ale
1 slice lemon

Shake gin and lemon juice well with ice. Strain into 8-oz. glass half filled with ice. Add ginger ale. Stir. Add lemon slice.

GREEK BUCK

1½ ozs. Metaxa brandy
½ oz. lemon juice
Iced ginger ale
1 teaspoon ouzo
1 slice lemon

Shake Metaxa and lemon juice well with ice. Strain into 8-oz. glass half filled with ice. Add ginger ale. Stir. Float ouzo on top of drink. Add lemon slice.

NEW ORLEANS BUCK

1½ ozs. light rum
½ oz. lime juice
½ oz. orange juice
2 dashes Peychaud's bitters
Iced ginger ale
1 slice lime

Shake rum, lime juice, orange juice, and bitters well with ice. Strain into 8-oz. glass half filled with ice. Add ginger ale. Stir. Add lime slice.

ORANGE BUCK

1½ ozs. gin
1 oz. orange juice
½ oz. lemon juice

Iced ginger ale
1 slice cocktail orange in syrup

Shake gin, orange juice, and lemon juice well with ice. Strain into 8-oz. glass half filled with ice. Add ginger ale. Stir. Add orange slice.

PEACH BUCK

1¼ ozs. vodka
2 teaspoons peach-flavored brandy
½ oz. lemon juice

Iced ginger ale
1 slice lemon
1 slice fresh or brandied peach

Shake vodka, peach-flavored brandy, and lemon juice well with ice. Strain into 8-oz. glass half filled with ice. Add ginger ale. Stir. Garnish with lemon and peach slices.

RUM BUCK

1½ ozs. light rum
½ oz. lime juice
Iced ginger ale

1 slice lime
Toasted slivered almonds

Shake rum and lime juice well with ice. Strain into 8-oz. glass half filled with ice. Add ginger ale. Stir. Add lime slice and about a teaspoon of almonds.

SCOTCH BUCK

1 oz. Scotch
½ oz. ginger-flavored brandy

Iced ginger beer or ginger ale
½ medium-size lime

Fill a tall 8-oz. glass with ice cubes. Add Scotch and ginger-flavored brandy. Stir well. Add ginger beer to fill glass. Stir. Squeeze lime above drink and drop into glass.

Cobblers

Like a fix (see pages 321–24), of which it is a larger version, a cobbler is concocted in the glass and drunk without club soda, quinine water, or any other sparkling diluents. Though the recipes that follow are designed to fill a 12-ounce glass—including the cracked ice that forms the base of each—they can be extended or abbreviated to fit your own glassware. The cracked ice in a filled glass will usually collapse somewhat when stirred with liquor; an ice refill is then necessary.

AMARETTO COBBLER

1½ ozs. gin
2 ozs. orange juice
1 oz. lemon juice
½ oz. amaretto
½ slice orange

Fill a 12-oz. glass with finely cracked ice. Add gin, orange juice, lemon juice, and amaretto. Stir well. Add more ice to fill glass almost to rim. Stir. Add orange slice.

APRICOT COBBLER

1½ ozs. apricot-flavored brandy
1 oz. California brandy
2 ozs. grapefruit juice
1 slice orange

Fill a 12-oz. glass with finely cracked ice. Add apricot-flavored brandy, California brandy, and grapefruit juice. Stir well. Add more ice to fill glass almost to rim. Stir. Add orange slice.

BRANDY COBBLER

1½ ozs. brandy	1 teaspoon sugar
½ oz. curaçao	1 teaspoon kirschwasser
½ oz. lemon juice	1 cocktail pineapple stick

Fill a 12-oz. glass with finely cracked ice. Add brandy, curaçao, lemon juice, sugar, and kirschwasser. Stir well until sugar is dissolved. Add more ice to fill glass to rim. Stir. Garnish with pineapple stick.

CHERRY COBBLER

1½ ozs. gin	1 teaspoon sugar
½ oz. Peter Heering or Cherry Karise	½ oz. lemon juice
	1 slice lemon
½ oz. crème de cassis	1 maraschino cherry

Fill a 12-oz. glass with finely cracked ice. Add gin, Peter Heering, crème de cassis, sugar, and lemon juice. Stir well until sugar dissolves. Add more ice to fill glass to rim. Stir. Add lemon slice and cherry.

CHERRY RUM COBBLER

1½ ozs. light rum	½ oz. lemon juice
1 oz. cherry-flavored brandy	1 slice lemon
½ teaspoon sugar	1 maraschino stem cherry

Fill a tall 12-oz. glass with coarsely cracked ice. (Ice from a "chipper" tray is good for this drink.) Add rum, cherry-flavored brandy, sugar, and lemon juice. Stir very well until sugar dissolves. Add ice, if necessary, to fill glass to rim. Stir. Add lemon slice and cherry.

CLARET COBBLER

4 ozs. dry red wine
½ oz. lemon juice
½ oz. orange juice
½ oz. maraschino liqueur
½ slice orange
½ slice lime

Fill a 12-oz. glass with finely cracked ice. Add wine, lemon juice, orange juice, and maraschino liqueur. Stir well. Add more ice to fill glass to rim. Stir. Garnish with orange and lime slices.

KENTUCKY COBBLER

1½ ozs. Southern Comfort
1 oz. peppermint schnapps
½ oz. lemon juice
1 teaspoon sugar
1 sprig fresh mint

Fill a 12-oz. glass with finely cracked ice. Add Southern Comfort, peppermint schnapps, lemon juice, and sugar. Stir well until sugar dissolves. Add more ice to fill glass to rim. Stir. Add mint sprig.

MOCHA COBBLER

1 oz. coffee liqueur
½ oz. crème de cacao
1 oz. dark Jamaica rum
1 oz. heavy sweet cream

Fill a tall 12-oz. glass with finely cracked ice. Add coffee liqueur, crème de cacao, rum, and cream. Stir well. Add more ice to fill glass to rim. An after-dinner cobbler for those who like their sweets in a tall liquid form.

PORT COBBLER

4 ozs. tawny port
¾ oz. brandy
½ teaspoon sugar
Lemon peel
Orange peel
2 large mint leaves

Fill a 12-oz. glass with finely cracked ice. Add port, brandy, and sugar. Stir well. Add more ice to fill glass to rim. Stir. Twist lemon peel and orange peel above drink and drop into glass. Tear mint lives partially and drop into glass.

SHERRY COBBLER

2½ ozs. sherry
1 oz. brandy
½ oz. orange juice
½ teaspoon sugar
1 slice cocktail orange in syrup

Fill a 12-oz. glass with finely cracked ice. Add sherry, brandy, orange juice, and sugar. Stir well until sugar dissolves. Add more ice to fill glass to rim. Stir. Garnish with orange slice.

WHISKEY COBBLER

2½ ozs. blended whiskey
¾ oz. lemon juice
½ oz. grapefruit juice
1½ teaspoons orgeat or orzata
½ slice orange
1 slice fresh or brandied peach

Fill a 12-oz. glass with finely cracked ice. Add whiskey, lemon juice, grapefruit juice, and orgeat. Stir well. Add more ice to fill glass to rim. Stir. Garnish with orange and peach slices.

Collinses

Among the oldest and best-known tall summer drinks, collinses always start with liquor, lemon juice, and soda and bear a striking resemblance to fizzes (pages 325–34). A tom collins and a gin fizz are for all practical purposes the same drink. A lemon slice is an accepted garnish. Some bartenders dress up the collins with orange slices, cherries, and other bits of fruit, although this practice is frowned upon by veteran benders at the bar.

APPLEJACK COLLINS

2 ozs. applejack
1 teaspoon sugar
1 oz. lemon juice
2 dashes orange bitters
Iced club soda
1 slice lemon

Shake applejack, sugar, lemon juice, and bitters well with ice. Strain into tall 14-oz. glass half filled with ice. Add soda. Stir. Add lemon slice.

B & B COLLINS

2 ozs. cognac
½ oz. lemon juice
1 teaspoon sugar
Iced club soda
½ oz. Benedictine
1 slice lemon

Shake cognac, lemon juice, and sugar well with ice. Strain into tall 14-oz. glass half filled with ice. Add soda. Stir. Float Benedictine on drink. Add lemon slice. California brandy may be used in place of cognac.

BOURBON COLLINS

2 ozs. 100-proof bourbon
2 dashes Peychaud's bitters
½ oz. lemon juice
1 teaspoon sugar
Iced club soda
1 slice lemon

Shake bourbon, bitters, lemon juice, and sugar well with ice. Strain into tall 14-oz. glass half filled with ice. Add soda. Stir. Add lemon slice.

BRANDIED BANANA COLLINS

1½ ozs. brandy
1 oz. banana liqueur
½ oz. lemon juice
Iced club soda
1 slice lemon
1 slice banana

Shake brandy, banana liqueur, and lemon juice well with ice. Strain into tall 14-oz. glass half filled with ice. Add soda. Stir. Add lemon and banana slices.

COEXISTENCE COLLINS

2 ozs. vodka
½ oz. lemon juice
1 teaspoon sugar
1 teaspoon kümmel
Iced club soda
Cucumber peel, 2 inches long, ½ inch wide
Lemon peel

Shake vodka, lemon juice, sugar, and kümmel well with ice. Strain into tall 14-oz. glass half filled with ice. Add soda. Stir. Add cucumber peel. Twist lemon peel above drink and drop into glass.

CUERNAVACA COLLINS

1 oz. tequila
1 oz. gin
1 oz. lime juice
2 teaspoons sugar
Iced club soda
1 slice lime

Shake tequila, gin, lime juice, and sugar well with ice. Strain into tall 14-oz. glass half filled with ice cubes. Add soda to fill glass. Stir lightly. Add lime slice.

DRY SHERRY COLLINS

3 ozs. very dry sherry
1 oz. gin
1 oz. lemon juice
1 teaspoon sugar or more to taste
Iced club soda
1 slice lemon

Shake sherry, gin, lemon juice, and sugar well with ice. Strain into 14-oz. glass half filled with ice cubes. Fill glass with soda. Add lemon slice.

MINT COLLINS

2 ozs. gin
4 large mint leaves
½ oz. lemon juice
1 teaspoon sugar
½ cup crushed ice
Iced club soda
1 slice lemon

Put gin, mint leaves, lemon juice, sugar, and crushed ice into blender. Blend at high speed 15 seconds or until mint leaves are finely chopped. Pour into tall 14-oz. glass. Add soda to fill glass. Stir. Add lemon slice.

PISTACHIO LIME COLLINS

1½ ozs. gin
1 oz. pistachio liqueur
1 oz. lime juice
Iced club soda
1 slice lime

Pour gin, pistachio liqueur, and lime juice over three large ice cubes in tall 12-oz. glass. Stir well. Add soda. Stir. Add lime slice.

PORT COLLINS

*2 ozs. white port, such as
    Porto Branco
1 oz. gin
1 oz. lemon juice
1 teaspoon sugar
Iced club soda
1 slice lemon*

Shake port, gin, lemon juice, and sugar well with ice. Strain into tall 14-oz. glass half filled with ice cubes. Add soda. Stir. Add lemon slice.

TOM COLLINS

*2 to 2½ ozs. gin
1 to 2 teaspoons sugar
½ to 1 oz. lemon juice
Iced club soda
1 slice lemon (optional)
1 slice orange (optional)
1 maraschino cherry
    (optional)*

Shake gin, sugar, and lemon juice well with ice. Strain into tall 14-oz. glass half filled with ice. Add soda. Stir. Add lemon slice and/or orange slice and/or cherry.

JOHN COLLINS

Same drink as tom collins except made with Dutch genever gin.

Coolers—Miscellaneous Tall Drinks

For every taste, for every mood, for every summer day, the following potpourri of coolers and icy tall drinks will be as welcome as the trade winds to becalmed vessels on a sweltering sea.

ALLA SALUTE!

1 oz. Sciarada
1½ ozs. light rum
½ oz. lime juice
3 ozs. pineapple juice
Iced club soda
1 slice lime

Pour Sciarada, rum, lime juice, and pineapple juice into tall 12-oz. glass filled with rocks. Stir well. Add soda to fill glass. Stir. Add lime slice.

ALMOND EYE

1 oz. gin
1 oz. California brandy
½ oz. amaretto
1 oz. lemon juice
1 teaspoon grenadine
Iced club soda

Shake gin, brandy, amaretto, lemon juice, and grenadine well with ice. Strain into 8-oz. glass. Add two ice cubes. Add splash of soda. Stir.

ALOHA

1 oz. light rum
½ oz. Midori liqueur
½ oz. lime juice
½ oz. dry vermouth
1-inch cube papaya

Shake rum, Midori liqueur, lime juice, and vermouth well with ice. Strain over rocks in 8-oz. glass. Fasten papaya on cocktail spear and place over rim of glass.

AMER PICON COOLER

1½ ozs. Amer Picon
1 oz. gin
½ oz. cherry liqueur
½ oz. lemon juice
1 teaspoon sugar
Iced club soda

Shake Amer Picon, gin, cherry liqueur, lemon juice, and sugar well with ice. Strain into tall 14-oz. glass half filled with ice. Add soda. Stir.

APPLE BRANDY COOLER

2 ozs. brandy
1 oz. light rum
3 ozs. apple juice
½ oz. lime juice
1 teaspoon dark Jamaica rum
1 slice lime

Shake brandy, light rum, apple juice, and lime juice well with ice. Strain into tall 14-oz. glass. Add ice to fill glass. Stir. Float dark rum on drink. Add lime slice.

APPLE KNOCKER

2½ ozs. applejack
½ oz. sweet vermouth
3 ozs. orange juice
½ oz. lemon juice
1½ teaspoons sugar
½ cup crushed ice

Put all ingredients into blender. Blend at high speed 15–20 seconds. Pour into tall 14-oz. glass. Let drink settle a moment. Add ice cubes to fill glass. Stir.

BARBADOS PLANTER'S PUNCH

2 ozs. Barbados Mount Gay rum
½ oz. heavy dark rum
1 oz. lime juice
2 teaspoons sugar
3 dashes Angostura bitters
Freshly ground nutmeg
1 slice lime

Shake both kinds of rum, lime juice, sugar, and bitters well with ice. Strain into tall 12-oz. glass three-quarters filled with coarsely cracked ice. Stir well. Add ice, if necessary, to fill glass to rim. Sprinkle with nutmeg. Add lime slice.

BATTERING RAM

1 oz. light rum
1 oz. dark Jamaica rum
4 ozs. orange juice
½ oz. Wild Turkey liqueur
½ oz. lime juice
Iced tonic water
1 slice lime

Shake light rum, dark rum, orange juice, Wild Turkey liqueur, and lime juice well with ice. Strain into tall 14-oz. glass half filled with ice cubes. Fill glass with tonic water. Stir. Add lime slice.

BEAUJOLAIS CUP

6 ozs. chilled Beaujolais
½ oz. California brandy
½ oz. maraschino liqueur
2½ ozs. chilled orange juice
Chilled club soda
1 slice orange

Pour Beaujolais, brandy, maraschino liqueur, and orange juice into tall 14-oz. glass half filled with ice. Stir well. Add a splash of soda. Stir lightly. Add orange slice.

BEER BUSTER

1½ ozs. ice-cold 100-proof vodka
Ice-cold beer or ale
2 dashes Tabasco sauce

Pour vodka, beer, and Tabasco sauce into prechilled tall 14-oz. glass or beer mug. Stir lightly. A drink for those who like to key up with beer rather than with cocktails before dinner; for football fans hoarse from cheering; for men who like a long, cold drink with their bubbling-hot Welsh rabbit; and for cheese connoisseurs with a thirst.

BELFRY BAT

1 oz. Sciarada
1 oz. dark Jamaica rum
2 ozs. papaya nectar
2 dashes Angostura bitters
Iced club soda
1 slice lemon

Pour Sciarada, rum, papaya nectar, and bitters into tall 14-oz. glass three-quarters filled with ice cubes. Stir well. Add club soda to fill glass. Stir. Add lemon slice.

BITTER BANANA COOLER

1½ ozs. light rum
¼ cup sliced banana
¼ cup pineapple juice
½ oz. lime juice
2 dashes Peychaud's bitters
½ cup crushed ice
Iced bitter-lemon soda

Put rum, sliced banana, pineapple juice, lime juice, bitters, and crushed ice into blender. Blend 10–15 seconds at high speed. Pour into tall 14-oz. glass. Let foamy cap of drink settle somewhat. Add two ice cubes. Fill glass with bitter-lemon soda. A tall drink in the frozen-daiquiri tradition.

BITTER BOURBON LEMONADE

2 ozs. bourbon
1 oz. lemon juice
½ oz. lime juice
1 teaspoon grenadine
1 teaspoon sugar
Iced bitter-lemon soda
1 slice lemon

Shake bourbon, lemon juice, lime juice, grenadine, and sugar well with ice. Strain into tall 14-oz. glass. Add two ice cubes. Fill glass with bitter-lemon soda. Garnish with lemon slice. A bittersweet pleasure.

BITTER BRANDY AND SHERRY

1 oz. brandy
1 oz. oloroso (cream) sherry
½ oz. cherry liqueur
1 teaspoon lemon juice
Iced bitter-lemon soda
1 slice lemon

Shake brandy, sherry, cherry liqueur, and lemon juice well with ice. Strain into tall 14-oz. glass with two large ice cubes. Add soda. Stir. Add lemon slice.

BITTER-LEMON BRACER

2 ozs. vodka
2 ozs. orange juice
½ oz. lemon juice
Iced bitter-lemon soda
1-inch piece orange peel
1-inch piece lemon peel
1 slice orange

Fill 14-oz. glass with ice cubes. Add vodka, orange juice, and lemon juice. Fill with bitter lemon and stir very well. Twist orange and lemon peels over drink and drop into glass. For a drier bracer, use tonic water instead of bitter lemon. Cut orange slice and fasten onto rim of glass.

BITTER-LEMON COOLER

1½ ozs. dry vermouth
1 oz. gin
1 teaspoon strawberry syrup
1 teaspoon lemon juice
Iced bitter-lemon soda
Lemon peel

Shake vermouth, gin, strawberry syrup, and lemon juice well with ice. Strain into tall 14-oz. glass containing two large ice cubes. Add bitter-lemon soda. Stir. Twist lemon peel above drink and drop into glass.

BITTER-ORANGE COOLER

3 ozs. sweet vermouth
2 dashes Angostura bitters
2½ ozs. orange juice
½ oz. lemon juice
½ oz. cherry-flavored brandy
Orange soda
1 slice orange

Shake vermouth, Angostura bitters, orange juice, lemon juice, and cherry-flavored brandy well with ice. Strain into tall 14-oz. glass half filled with ice cubes. Add soda. Stir. Garnish with orange slice.

BITTER PERNOD

1 oz. Pernod
1 oz. vodka
1 oz. lemon juice
Iced bitter-lemon soda
1 slice lemon

Fill tall 14-oz. glass with rocks. Add Pernod, vodka, and lemon juice. Stir very well. Fill with bitter-lemon soda. Add lemon slice.

BITTER PLANTER'S PUNCH

2 ozs. golden rum
1 teaspoon sugar
1 teaspoon grenadine
½ oz. lemon juice
Iced bitter-lemon soda
1 slice lemon

Shake rum, sugar, grenadine, and lemon juice extremely well with ice. Strain into tall 14-oz. glass three-quarters filled with ice cubes. Stir well. Fill glass with bitter-lemon soda. Stir lightly. Add lemon slice.

BLENDED COMFORT

2 ozs. blended whiskey
½ oz. Southern Comfort
¼ cup thawed frozen peaches
½ oz. dry vermouth
1½ ozs. lemon juice
1 oz. orange juice
½ cup crushed ice
1 slice lemon
1 slice cocktail orange in syrup

Put whiskey, Southern Comfort, peaches, vermouth, lemon juice, orange juice, and crushed ice into blender. Blend 10–15 seconds. Pour into tall 14-oz. glass. Add ice to fill glass. Garnish with lemon and orange slices.

BORDER CROSSING

1½ ozs. tequila
½ oz. cranberry liqueur
½ oz. lime juice
1 teaspoon sugar
1 slice lime

Shake tequila, cranberry liqueur, lime juice, and sugar well with ice. Strain over rocks in 8-oz. tall glass. Add lime slice.

BOURBON AND MADEIRA JULEP

1½ ozs. bourbon
1½ ozs. Madeira or amontillado sherry
¼ oz. lemon juice
Sugar (optional)
1 cocktail-pineapple stick
4 sprigs mint

Fill double old-fashioned glass with coarsely cracked ice. Add bourbon, Madeira, and lemon juice. Stir well. Add sugar if desired. Add more ice if necessary to fill glass to rim. Garnish with pineapple stick and mint.

BOURBON MILK PUNCH

2 ozs. bourbon
1 teaspoon sugar
8 ozs. (1 measuring cup) milk
Freshly grated nutmeg

Shake bourbon, sugar, and milk well with ice. Strain into 12-oz. glass. Sprinkle with nutmeg.

BOURBON RUMBO

1 teaspoon sugar
1 dash Angostura bitters
Chilled club soda
¾ oz. bourbon
¾ oz. golden rum
½ oz. sweet vermouth
1 slice cocktail orange in syrup, drained

Pour sugar, bitters, and a small splash of soda into tall 8-oz. glass. Stir until sugar dissolves. Add bourbon, rum, vermouth, and several ice cubes. Stir well. Add a splash of soda. Stir. Add orange slice.

BRANDIED PEACH SLING

1¾ ozs. brandy
½ oz. peach-flavored
  brandy
¾ oz. lemon juice
1 teaspoon sugar

Iced club soda
1 slice brandied or thawed
  frozen peach
Lemon peel

Shake brandy, peach-flavored brandy, lemon juice, and sugar well with ice. Strain into tall 14-oz. glass half filled with ice. Add soda. Stir. Add peach slice. Twist lemon peel above drink and drop into glass.

BRIGHTON PUNCH

1 oz. bourbon
1 oz. cognac
¾ oz. Benedictine
1 oz. orange juice

½ oz. lemon juice
1 oz. iced club soda
½ slice orange
1 slice lemon

Shake bourbon, cognac, Benedictine, orange juice, and lemon juice well with ice. Strain into tall 14-oz. glass. Add soda and enough ice to fill glass. Stir. Garnish with orange and lemon slices. An individual punch brewed outside a punch bowl.

BUENAS TARDES

1½ ozs. tequila
5 ozs. chilled apple juice

1 oz. lemon juice
1 slice lemon

Pour tequila, apple juice, and lemon juice into tall 12-oz. glass. Add ice cubes to fill glass. Stir well. Add lemon slice.

BUNNY MOTHER

1¼ ozs. vodka
1 oz. orange juice
1 oz. lemon juice
1 teaspoon sugar
¼ oz. grenadine
¼ oz. Cointreau
½ slice orange
1 maraschino cherry

Shake vodka, orange juice, lemon juice, sugar, and grenadine well with ice. Strain into prechilled 12-oz. mug. Add coarsely cracked ice to fill mug to ½ inch from top. Float Cointreau on top. Garnish with orange slice and cherry.

BYRRH CASSIS COOLER

2 ozs. Byrrh
½ oz. crème de cassis
Iced club soda
1 slice lemon

Put ice cubes up to the rim in a tall 14-oz. glass. Add Byrrh and crème de cassis. Add soda. Stir. Garnish with lemon slice. Quickens the appetite even though slightly sweet. Nice to hold in your hands when the *blanquette de veau* is simmering in the kitchen.

CABALLO

6 ozs. ice-cold grapefruit juice
1½ ozs. tequila
1 oz. amaretto

Pour into tall 14-oz. glass three-quarters filled with ice cubes. Stir well. Add ice cubes if necessary to fill glass to rim. Stir.

CALYPSO COOLER

2½ ozs. light rum
1 oz. frozen concentrated pineapple juice, thawed but not diluted
½ oz. lime juice
1 teaspoon sugar
Iced club soda
1 thin slice fresh pineapple
1 slice lime

Shake rum, pineapple juice, lime juice, and sugar well with ice. Strain into tall 14-oz. glass. Add a splash of soda and enough ice to fill glass. Stir. Garnish with pineapple and lime slices.

CARIBBEAN COFFEE

1 oz. light rum
½ oz. crème de cacao
6 ozs. cold strong coffee,
    sweetened to taste
1 oz. heavy sweet cream
Dollop of whipped cream

Pour rum, crème de cacao, and coffee into tall 12-oz. glass three-quarters filled with ice cubes. Add heavy cream. Stir well. Add dollop of whipped cream.

CARIBBEAN MULE

1½ ozs. light rum
½ oz. dark Jamaica rum
½ oz. lime juice
¼ oz. Triple Sec
¼ oz. maraschino liqueur
Iced ginger beer or
    ginger ale
1 slice lime
1 sprig mint

Shake both kinds of rum, lime juice, Triple Sec, and maraschino well with ice. Strain into tall 12-oz. glass half filled with ice cubes. Add ginger beer to almost fill glass. Stir lightly. Garnish with lime slice and mint.

CARIBBEAN SLING

2 ozs. light rum
½ oz. lime juice
½ oz. lemon juice
½ oz. Triple Sec
1 teaspoon sugar
Iced club soda
1 piece cucumber rind,
    ½ inch wide, 4 inches
    long

Shake rum, lime juice, lemon juice, Triple Sec, and sugar very well with ice. Strain into tall 14-oz. glass half filled with ice cubes. Stir well. Add soda to fill glass. Place cucumber rind in glass.

CARTHUSIAN COOLER

1 oz. yellow Chartreuse
1 oz. bourbon
Iced club soda

Put three large ice cubes into a tall 14-oz. glass. Add Chartreuse and bourbon. Fill glass with soda. Stir.

CHABLIS COOLER

½ oz. grenadine
½ oz. lemon juice
¼ teaspoon vanilla extract
1 oz. vodka
Iced Chablis

Sugar-frost a tall 14-oz. glass. Pour grenadine, lemon juice, vanilla extract, and vodka into glass. Stir well. Add three large ice cubes. Fill glass to rim with Chablis. Stir.

CHARTREUSE COOLER

2 ozs. yellow Chartreuse
3 ozs. orange juice
1 oz. lemon juice
Iced bitter-lemon soda
1 slice orange

Shake Chartreuse, orange juice, and lemon juice well with ice. Strain into tall 14-oz. glass half filled with ice. Fill glass with bitter-lemon soda. Add orange slice.

CHERRY ISLE

1 oz. aquavit
1 oz. Peter Heering liqueur
Iced tonic water
1 slice lime

Pour aquavit and Peter Heering into 10-oz. glass half filled with rocks. Stir well. Add tonic water. Stir. Add lime slice.

CHERRY PLANTER'S PUNCH

1 oz. kirschwasser
½ oz. dark Jamaica rum
½ oz. lime juice
2 dashes Angostura bitters
1 teaspoon sugar
Freshly grated nutmeg
1 slice lime
½ slice orange

Shake kirschwasser, rum, lime juice, bitters, and sugar extremely well with ice. Strain over rocks in 8-oz. glass. Add ice, if necessary, to fill glass to rim. Stir well. Sprinkle with nutmeg. Garnish with lime and orange slices.

CHERRY RUM COLA

1½ ozs. golden rum
¾ oz. Peter Heering liqueur
1 teaspoon lemon juice
Iced cola
1 slice lemon

Fill a 12-oz. glass three-quarters full with ice cubes. Add rum, Peter Heering liqueur, and lemon juice. Stir very well. Add cola to fill glass to rim. Add lemon slice.

CHICO

1 oz. tequila
1 oz. blackberry-flavored brandy
½ oz. lemon juice
1 teaspoon sugar
Iced club soda
1 slice lemon

Shake tequila, blackberry-flavored brandy, lemon juice, and sugar well with ice. Strain into tall 14-oz. glass half filled with ice cubes. Stir. Add club soda to fill glass. Stir. Add lemon slice.

CLARET COOLER

4 ozs. chilled dry red wine
½ oz. brandy
1 oz. orange juice
½ oz. lemon juice
3 ozs. iced club soda
Orange rind, 3 inches long, ½ inch wide
1 slice lemon

Pour wine, brandy, orange juice, lemon juice, and soda into tall 14-oz. glass. Add ice cubes or cracked ice to fill glass. Stir. Place orange rind in drink. Float lemon slice on top.

CLARET RUM COOLER

3 ozs. chilled dry red wine
1 oz. light rum
½ oz. kirschwasser
½ oz. Falernum
3 ozs. iced club soda
1 slice orange
1 large fresh strawberry

Pour wine, rum, kirschwasser, Falernum, and soda into tall 14-oz. glass. Add ice cubes or cracked ice to fill glass. Stir. Garnish with orange slice and strawberry.

COCONUT COOLER

1½ ozs. CocoRibe
½ oz. California brandy
1½ ozs. papaya nectar
½ oz. lemon juice
1 slice lemon

Shake CocoRibe, brandy, papaya nectar, and lemon juice well with ice. Strain into tall or squat 8-oz. glass. Add ice cubes to fill glass. Stir. Add lemon slice.

COCONUT COOLER IN SHELL

1 coconut
½ cup crushed ice
1 oz. canned cream of coconut
1½ ozs. light rum
1 oz. heavy cream

Remove end of coconut opposite coconut eyes. The best procedure is to hold the base of the coconut firmly in the left hand. With a very heavy French knife or cleaver, chop top off by striking coconut glancing blows diagonally. Several whacks may be necessary. Avoid spilling coconut juice, if possible. Pour out coconut juice and save it. Into blender, pour ¼ cup coconut juice, ice, cream of coconut, rum, and cream. Blend at high speed 10 seconds. Pour into coconut shell. Place coconut shell in large dish surrounded with finely crushed ice. There will usually be enough juice from one coconut for three or four drinks. Reserve drinks may be made up beforehand, poured into a pitcher, and stored in the refrigerator. Coconut shells may then be refilled when necessary. Byron once said nothing calmed the spirit as much as rum and true religion. The balmy beneficence of the preceding recipe will bear out that astute poet to the fullest.

COCONUT FIZZ

2 ozs. CocoRibe
1 oz. lemon juice
½ slightly beaten egg white
Iced club soda
1 slice lemon

Shake CocoRibe, lemon juice, and egg white extremely well with ice. Strain into tall 12-oz. glass half filled with ice cubes. Fill with club soda. Stir. Add lemon slice.

COCONUT GROVE

1½ ozs. CocoRibe
½ oz. Triple Sec
½ oz. lime juice
Iced club soda
1 slice lime

Shake CocoRibe, Triple Sec, and lime juice well with ice. Strain into 8-oz. glass. Add two ice cubes. Add soda to fill glass. Stir. Add lime slice.

COCORIBE MILK PUNCH

2 ozs. CocoRibe
4 ozs. milk
1 small egg
Ground cinnamon

Shake CocoRibe, milk, and egg extremely well with ice. Strain into 10-oz. glass. Sprinkle with cinnamon.

COFFEE COOLER

4 ozs. cold coffee
1½ ozs. vodka
1 oz. heavy cream
1 oz. coffee liqueur
1 teaspoon sugar
1 small dip coffee ice cream

Shake coffee, vodka, cream, coffee liqueur, and sugar well with ice. Strain into tall 14-oz. glass. Add ice cream. A sweet cooler that serves as both iced coffee and dessert in one glass.

COFFEE EGGNOG

1½ ozs. Canadian whisky
1 oz. coffee liqueur
1 small egg
4 ozs. milk
½ oz. heavy cream
1 teaspoon sugar
½ teaspoon instant coffee
Ground coriander seed

Shake whisky, coffee liqueur, egg, milk, cream, sugar, and instant coffee with ice extremely well—about twice the usual mixing time. Strain into tall 14-oz. glass. Sprinkle with coriander.

COFFEE MILK PUNCH

1 oz. coffee liqueur
1 oz. dark Jamaica rum
1 teaspoon sugar
5 ozs. milk
½ oz. heavy sweet cream
Freshly grated nutmeg

Pour all ingredients except nutmeg into cocktail shaker with ice. Shake extremely well. Strain into 12-oz. glass. Sprinkle with nutmeg.

COFFEE RUM COOLER

1½ oz. dark Jamaica rum
1 oz. coffee liqueur
½ oz. lime juice
Iced club soda
1 slice lime

Shake rum, coffee liqueur, and lime juice well with ice. Strain into tall 14-oz. glass three-quarters filled with ice. Fill glass with club soda. Stir. Add lime slice.

COLD IRISH

1½ ozs. Irish whiskey
2 teaspoons Irish Mist liqueur
Iced coffee soda
Whipped cream
Crème de cacao

Pour whiskey and Irish Mist into tall 14-oz. glass. Add one large ice cube. Fill glass to within 1 inch of top with soda. Stir. Flavor whipped cream with crème de cacao, using ½ oz. crème de cacao for each ½ cup heavy cream used for whipping. Add a large dollop of whipped-cream topping to each drink.

COLD TURKEY

1½ ozs. cream sherry
½ oz. Wild Turkey liqueur
1 oz. orange juice
1 slice orange

Pour sherry, Wild Turkey liqueur, and orange juice over rocks in 8-oz. glass. Stir well. Add orange slice. An after-dinner drink that's not too cloying.

COOL COLONEL

1½ ozs. bourbon
1 oz. Southern Comfort
3 ozs. chilled strong black tea
2 teaspoons lemon juice
2 teaspoons sugar
Iced club soda

Pour bourbon, Southern Comfort, tea, lemon juice, and sugar into tall 14-oz. glass. Stir until sugar dissolves. Add two large ice cubes and a splash of soda. Stir. Breathe deeply. Tilt head. Bend elbow.

COOL GUANABANA

Grenadine
Superfine sugar
1½ ozs. light rum
½ oz. dark Jamaica rum
½ oz. lime juice
4 ozs. iced guanabana nectar
1 slice lime

Dip rim of tall 14-oz. glass in grenadine and then in superfine sugar to frost rim. Fill glass with ice cubes. Add both kinds of rum, lime juice, and guanabana nectar. (Guanabana nectar—made from the pulp of the soursop—is available in gourmet shops and in those featuring Puerto Rican foods.) Stir well. Cut lime slice halfway to center and fasten to rim of glass.

CORDIAL MEDOC CUP

1 oz. Cordial Médoc
½ oz. cognac
1 oz. lemon juice
½ teaspoon sugar
Iced brut champagne
1 slice orange

Shake Cordial Médoc, cognac, lemon juice, and sugar well with ice. Strain into 10-oz. glass with two large ice cubes. Fill glass with champagne. Stir very slightly. Add orange slice. A tall drink for toasting.

CRANBERRY COOLER

1 oz. cranberry liqueur
1 oz. California brandy
½ oz. Triple Sec
Iced tonic water

Fill 14-oz. glass three-fourths of the way with ice. Add cranberry liqueur, brandy, and Triple Sec. Stir well. Fill glass with tonic water. Stir.

CRANBERRY RUM PUNCH

1 oz. light rum
1 oz. dark Jamaica rum
4 ozs. chilled cranberry juice
2 ozs. orange juice
½ oz. lemon juice
1 slice lemon

Shake light rum, dark Jamaica rum, cranberry juice, orange juice, and lemon juice well with ice. Strain into tall 14-oz. glass three-quarters filled with ice cubes. Stir. Add lemon slice.

CRANBOURBON

2 ozs. bourbon
1 dash Angostura bitters
1 teaspoon sugar
½ oz. lemon juice

Iced cranberry-juice
   cocktail
1 long strip cucumber rind

Shake bourbon, bitters, sugar, and lemon juice well with ice. Strain into 12-oz. glass half filled with ice cubes. Add cranberry-juice cocktail to fill glass. Stir. Place cucumber rind in glass.

CREAMY SCREWDRIVER

6 ozs. orange juice
1 small egg yolk or ½ large
   yolk, lightly beaten

2 ozs. vodka
¾ cup finely cracked ice
1 teaspoon sugar

Put all ingredients into well of blender. Blend about 20 seconds. Pour over two or three ice cubes in tall 14-oz. glass. Add more ice cubes, if necessary, to fill glass. A prebrunch potation.

CUBA LIBRE

2 ozs. golden rum
½ lime

Iced cola drink

Half fill a tall 14-oz. glass with coarsely chopped ice or ice cubes. Add rum. Squeeze lime above drink and drop into glass. Fill with cola. Stir well. Heavier rums such as Jamaica or Martinique may be used in place of golden rum or may be mixed half-and-half with it. A teaspoon of 151-proof rum may be floated on top of drink for a rummy bite.

CUCUMBER CHAMPAGNE

Cucumber peel
1 oz. Benedictine
½ oz. lemon juice
8 ozs. iced brut champagne

Prechill a 10-oz. pilsner glass. Wash cucumber, rubbing with a vegetable brush or towel, if necessary, to remove any waxy coating. Cut a long strip of peel, about ½ inch wide, the entire length of the cucumber. Place in glass. Pour Benedictine and lemon juice into glass. Slowly add champagne. Stir very slightly. Let drink set a few minutes for flavors to ripen.

CURAÇAO COOLER

1 oz. blue curaçao
1 oz. vodka
½ oz. lime juice
½ oz. lemon juice
Iced orange juice
Lemon peel
Lime peel
Orange peel

Shake curaçao, vodka, lime juice, and lemon juice well with ice. Strain into tall 14-oz. glass. Add two large ice cubes. Fill glass with orange juice. Stir well. Twist each of the peels above the drink and drop into glass. Cool as the blue-green Caribbean itself.

CYNAR CALYPSO

1 oz. Cynar
1 oz. light rum
1 oz. pineapple juice
1 oz. lime juice
1 teaspoon grenadine

Shake extremely well with ice. Pour into tall or squat 10-oz. glass. Add ice cubes to fill glass. Stir well.

CYNAR SCREWDRIVER

1 oz. Cynar
1 oz. vodka
4½ ozs. ice-cold orange juice

Shake ingredients well with ice. Strain into prechilled tall or squat 10-oz. glass.

DEEP END

1 oz. Cordial Médoc
½ oz. gin
2 ozs. chilled papaya nectar
2 ozs. chilled orange juice
Iced club soda
½ slice orange

Pour Cordial Médoc, gin, papaya nectar, and orange juice into tall 14-oz. glass three-quarters filled with ice cubes. Stir well. Add soda to fill glass. Stir. Add orange slice.

DOUBLE DERBY

2½ ozs. bourbon
2 ozs. cold strong black tea
2 ozs. claret
1 oz. red-currant syrup
1 oz. orange juice
½ oz. lemon juice
1 slice cocktail orange in syrup

Pour bourbon, tea, claret, red-currant syrup, orange juice, and lemon juice into double old-fashioned glass. Add ice cubes to fill to brim. Stir well. Add orange slice. If red-currant syrup is not available, red-currant jelly to which a teaspoon of hot water has been added may be heated over a low flame and stirred constantly until jelly is liquid.

DOWN YONDER

1 oz. bourbon
½ oz. peppermint schnapps
2 ozs. peach nectar
½ oz. lemon juice
1 slice fresh peach

Shake bourbon, peppermint schnapps, peach nectar, and lemon juice well with ice. Strain into 8-oz. glass. Add ice cubes to fill glass. Stir. Fasten peach on cocktail spear and rest on rim of glass.

DRACULA

1½ ozs. light rum
2 dashes Angostura bitters
4 ozs. cranberry-juice cocktail
1 oz. lemon juice
½ teaspoon grenadine

Shake well with ice. Strain into 14-oz. glass. Add ice cubes to fill glass to rim. Stir.

DRY MANHATTAN COOLER

2 ozs. blended whiskey
1 oz. dry vermouth
2 ozs. orange juice
½ oz. lemon juice
½ oz. orgeat or orzata
Iced club soda
1 maraschino cherry

Shake whiskey, vermouth, orange juice, lemon juice, and orgeat well with ice. Strain into tall 14-oz. glass. Add a splash of soda and ice to fill glass. Stir. Add cherry.

EAST-WEST

2 ozs. sake
2 dashes Angostura bitters
Iced cranberry-juice cocktail
1 slice lemon

Place three large ice cubes in 8-oz. glass. Add sake and bitters. Fill glass with cranberry-juice cocktail. Stir well. Add lemon slice.

EAU DE VIE CAMPARI

½ oz. framboise
½ oz. kirschwasser
1 oz. Campari
½ oz. lemon juice
½ teaspoon grenadine
Iced club soda
Orange peel

Pour framboise, kirschwasser, Campari, lemon juice, and grenadine into mixing glass with ice. Stir very well. Strain into 8-oz. glass with one or two ice cubes. Add a splash of soda. Stir lightly. Twist orange peel above drink and drop into glass.

EGGNOG FRAMBOISE

4 ozs. milk
1 small egg
1 oz. framboise
½ oz. cognac
½ oz. dark Jamaica rum
2 level teaspoons sugar
Freshly grated nutmeg

Shake milk, egg, framboise, cognac, rum, and sugar extremely well with ice. Strain into 10-oz. glass. Sprinkle with nutmeg.

ELEPHANT'S EYE

1 oz. dark Jamaica rum
1 oz. sweet vermouth
½ oz. Triple Sec
½ oz. lime juice
Iced tonic water
1 slice lime

Shake rum, sweet vermouth, Triple Sec, and lime juice well with ice. Strain into tall 14-oz. glass half filled with ice cubes. Add tonic water to fill glass. Stir. Add lime slice.

ENGLISH MULE

3 ozs. ice-cold green-ginger wine
1½ ozs. gin
2½ ozs. ice-cold orange juice
Iced club soda
1 piece preserved ginger in syrup

Put three ice cubes into tall 14-oz. glass. Pour wine, gin, and orange juice into glass. Stir well. Fill glass with soda. Stir slightly. Fasten preserved ginger, well drained, onto cocktail spear. Fit spear into straw in glass.

FINLANDIA

1 oz. aquavit
½ oz. Vaklova liqueur
Chilled orange juice

Pour aquavit and Vaklova into 10-oz. glass half filled with ice cubes. Stir well. Add orange juice to fill glass. Stir well.

FRENCH COLONIAL

1½ ozs. golden rum
½ oz. crème de cassis
½ oz. Cointreau
½ oz. lemon juice
Iced tonic water
1 slice lemon

Shake rum, crème de cassis, Cointreau, and lemon juice well with ice. Strain into tall 14-oz. glass three-quarters filled with ice cubes. Add tonic water. Stir. Add lemon slice.

FRENCH FOAM

1 teaspoon sugar
1 dash Angostura bitters
1 teaspoon brandy
1 teaspoon kirschwasser
1 split ice-cold brut champagne
Lemon sherbet

Put sugar, bitters, brandy, and kirschwasser into 10-oz. pilsner glass. Stir with a tall stirring rod until sugar dissolves. Fill glass three-quarters full with champagne. Float a small scoop of sherbet on top. The scoop should contain no more than 2 liquid ounces (a parfait scoop). If such a scoop is not available, use a tablespoon to add the small amount of sherbet.

FRENCH 75

1½ ozs. cognac
1 oz. lemon juice
1 teaspoon sugar
Iced brut champagne

Shake cognac, lemon juice, and sugar well with cracked ice. Strain into 10-oz. glass with two large ice cubes. Fill to rim with champagne. Stir very slightly. Gin is sometimes substituted for cognac, making a champagne collins out of this tall classic.

GASPE

2 ozs. very dry sherry
1 oz. Canadian whisky
½ oz. Vaklova liqueur
Lemon peel

Stir sherry, whisky, and Vaklova liqueur well with ice. Strain over rocks in 8-oz. glass. Twist lemon peel above drink and drop into glass.

GEORGIA RUM COOLER

2½ ozs. light rum
1 teaspoon salted peanuts
½ oz. lemon juice
1 teaspoon grenadine
1 teaspoon Falernum
½ cup crushed ice
Iced club soda
Ground cinnamon

Put rum, peanuts, lemon juice, grenadine, Falernum, and crushed ice into blender. Blend at high speed 30 seconds. Pour into tall 14-oz. glass. Let froth on drink settle. Add two ice cubes and a splash of soda. Stir. Sprinkle lightly with cinnamon. Pass a platter of cold country ham, sliced paper-thin.

GIN AND GINGER COOLER

1 oz. gin
1 oz. ginger-flavored brandy
½ oz. lemon juice
1 teaspoon sugar
4 ozs. ginger beer or ginger ale
1 slice lemon
1 small chunk preserved ginger in syrup

Shake gin, ginger-flavored brandy, lemon juice, and sugar well with ice. Strain into tall 12-oz. glass half filled with ice. Stir. Add ginger beer. Stir. Add ice, if necessary, to fill glass. Stir. Garnish with lemon slice and preserved ginger.

GIN SWIZZLE

2 ozs. gin	½ oz. lime juice
½ teaspoon Angostura bitters	1 teaspoon sugar
	Iced club soda

Shake gin, bitters, lime juice, and sugar well with ice. Strain into tall 14-oz. glass half filled with ice. Add soda. Stir. A patriarchal drink invented when swizzle sticks were smart. Toothsome tipple now best handled in cocktail shaker and tall glass.

GOLD COASTER

1 oz. dry vermouth	1 teaspoon maraschino liqueur
1 oz. California brandy	
½ oz. lemon juice	1 slice fresh pineapple
2 ozs. pineapple juice	

Shake vermouth, brandy, lemon juice, pineapple juice, and maraschino liqueur well with ice. Strain into 10-oz. glass. Add ice cubes to fill glass. Stir. Fasten pineapple on cocktail spear and place on rim of glass.

GRANADA

1 oz. very dry (fino) sherry	Iced tonic water
1 oz. brandy	1 slice orange
½ oz. curaçao	

Shake sherry, brandy, and curaçao well with ice. Strain into tall 14-oz. glass. Add two large ice cubes. Add tonic water. Stir. Add orange slice.

GRAPEFRUIT COOLER

2 ozs. blended whiskey
4 ozs. unsweetened grape-
    fruit juice
½ oz. red-currant syrup
1 teaspoon lemon juice
½ slice orange
½ slice lemon

Shake whiskey, grapefruit juice, red-currant syrup, and lemon juice well with ice. Strain into tall 14-oz. glass. Add ice to fill glass. Stir. Garnish with orange and lemon slices.

GRAPEFRUIT NOG

½ cup unsweetened grape-
    fruit juice
1 oz. lemon juice
1 tablespoon honey
1½ ozs. brandy
1 small egg
½ cup crushed ice

Put all ingredients into blender. Blend 20 seconds. Pour into double old-fashioned glass or tall 14-oz. glass. Add ice cubes to fill glass.

GRINGO

1½ ozs. tequila
4 ozs. Clamato juice
1 teaspoon catsup
1 teaspoon lemon juice
½ teaspoon horseradish
Tabasco sauce
Worcestershire sauce
Freshly ground black
    pepper

Pour tequila, Clamato, catsup, lemon juice, and horseradish into cocktail shaker. Add a dash or two each of Tabasco and Worcestershire. Shake very well with ice. Strain into old-fashioned glass. Sprinkle with ground black pepper.

GUANABANA COOLER

2 ozs. light rum
4 ozs. chilled guanabana
  nectar
1 oz. chilled orange juice

Chilled club soda
½ slice orange
1 slice lime

Pour rum, guanabana nectar, and orange juice into tall 14-oz. glass three-quarters filled with ice cubes. Stir well. Add soda to fill glass to rim. Add orange and lime slices.

GUAVA COOLER

1½ ozs. rum
1½ ozs. guava nectar
½ teaspoon sugar
½ oz. maraschino liqueur
½ oz. lemon juice

½ oz. pineapple juice
Iced club soda
1 canned guava shell
½ slice lemon

Shake rum, guava nectar, sugar, maraschino liqueur, lemon juice, and pineapple juice well with ice. Strain into tall 14-oz. glass half filled with ice. Add soda. Stir. Garnish with guava shell and lemon slice. Wonderful cooler before or with a jambalaya feast.

HARVEY WALLBANGER

1½ ozs. vodka
4½ ozs. ice-cold orange
  juice

¾ oz. Galliano

Put three large ice cubes into tall or squat 10-oz. glass. Add vodka and orange juice. Stir well. Float Galliano on top. Or shake vodka, Galliano, and orange juice with ice and strain into glass. Add ice cubes to fill glass. Stir.

HIGH POCKET

2 ozs. dry vermouth
½ oz. cherry-flavored
  brandy

½ oz. California brandy
½ oz. lemon juice
Iced apricot nectar

Be sure apricot nectar is well chilled beforehand. Shake vermouth, cherry-flavored brandy, California brandy, and lemon juice well with ice. Strain into tall 14-oz. glass half filled with ice cubes. Add apricot nectar to fill glass. Stir.

HONEYDEW COOLER

1/3 cup diced ripe honeydew melon
1 1/2 ozs. gin
1/4 teaspoon Pernod
1 tablespoon heavy cream
3/4 oz. lemon juice
1/2 teaspoon sugar
1/2 cup crushed ice
Iced club soda

Put honeydew, gin, Pernod, cream, lemon juice, sugar, and crushed ice into blender. Blend at low speed 15–20 seconds. Pour into tall 14-oz. glass. When foam settles, add a splash of soda and enough ice to fill glass to rim, if necessary.

HONKY TONIC

1 oz. Sciarada
1 oz. gin
1/2 oz. lemon juice
Iced tonic water
1 slice lemon

Pour Sciarada, gin, and lemon juice into tall 12-oz. glass half filled with ice cubes. Stir well. Fill with tonic water. Stir. Add lemon slice.

HORSE'S NECK WITH GIN

Peel of whole lemon
2 ozs. gin
1/2 oz. lemon juice
Iced ginger ale

To peel lemon, start at stem end, using a sharp paring knife, and cut peel about 1/2 inch wide in a continuous strip until lemon is completely peeled. Place peel in a 14-oz. highball glass so that the top of peel overlaps rim of glass, with the rest spiraling down into glass. Fill glass with coarsely cracked ice. Pour gin and lemon juice into glass. Fill with ginger ale. Stir.

ICED RUM COFFEE

1½ ozs. light rum
1 teaspoon dark Jamaica rum
6 ozs. iced double-strength coffee
Sugar
2 tablespoons sweetened whipped cream

Pour rums and coffee into tall 14-oz. glass. Add ice to fill glass. Add sugar to taste. Top with whipped cream.

ICED RUM TEA

1½ ozs. light rum
½ oz. 151-proof rum
6 ozs. iced strong black tea
1 teaspoon sugar
1 teaspoon Falernum
1 teaspoon lemon juice
1 slice lemon
2 large mint leaves

Pour rums, tea, sugar, Falernum, and lemon juice into tall 14-oz. glass. Add ice to fill glass. Stir. Garnish with lemon slice and mint leaves partially torn. To prevent tea clouding, let it cool to room temperature before combining with ice.

INDEPENDENCE SWIZZLE

2 ozs. dark Trinidad rum
3 dashes Angostura bitters
1 teaspoon honey
1 teaspoon sugar
½ oz. lime juice
1 slice lime

In tall 14-oz. glass, stir rum, bitters, honey, sugar, and lime juice until honey is blended with other ingredients. Add finely cracked ice to fill glass. Twirl with a swizzle stick if you have one, or stir and churn with a barspoon or iced-tea spoon. As drink is stirred, ice will melt. Add more ice as necessary to fill glass to rim, swizzling or stirring until ice and liquids reach top of glass. Add lime slice. A drink used to celebrate the independence of Trinidad and Tobago.

IRISH EGGNOG

1½ ozs. Irish cream liqueur
1 oz. Irish whiskey
1 small egg
4 ozs. milk
1 oz. heavy sweet cream
1 teaspoon sugar
Freshly ground nutmeg

Shake all ingredients except nutmeg extremely well with ice. Strain into tall 12-oz. glass. Sprinkle with nutmeg.

IRISH MILK-AND-MAPLE PUNCH

2 ozs. blended Irish whiskey
8 ozs. milk
1 tablespoon maple syrup
Freshly grated nutmeg

Shake whiskey, milk, and maple syrup very well with ice. Strain into tall 14-oz. glass. Sprinkle with nutmeg.

JAMAICA ELEGANCE

1½ ozs. golden Jamaica rum
½ oz. brandy
½ oz. pineapple juice
1 oz. lime juice
1 teaspoon simple syrup or rock-candy syrup
1 slice lime

Shake rum, brandy, pineapple juice, lime juice, and syrup well with ice. Strain into prechilled tall 12-oz. glass. Add ice to fill glass. Add lime slice.

JAMAICA GINGER

1½ ozs. light rum
½ oz. dark Jamaica rum
½ oz. 151-proof rum
½ oz. Falernum
½ oz. lime juice
Iced ginger beer
½ slice pineapple in crème de menthe
1 cube preserved ginger in syrup

Shake the three kinds of rum, Falernum, and lime juice well with ice. Strain into tall 14-oz. glass half filled with ice. Fill glass with ginger beer. Stir. Garnish with pineapple and ginger.

JOCOSE JULEP

2½ ozs. bourbon
½ oz. green crème de menthe
6 mint leaves
1 teaspoon sugar
1 oz. lime juice
Iced club soda
3 tall mint sprigs

Put into blender, without ice, bourbon, crème de menthe, 6 mint leaves, sugar, and lime juice. Blend 10–15 seconds or until mint is very finely chopped. Pour into tall 14-oz. glass half filled with ice. Add soda. Stir. Insert mint sprigs. Serve to nearest belle.

KERRY COOLER

2 ozs. Irish whiskey
1½ ozs. Madeira or sherry
1 oz. orgeat
1 oz. lemon juice
Iced club soda
1 slice lemon

Into tall 14-oz. glass, pour whiskey, Madeira, orgeat, and lemon juice. Stir well. Add three large ice cubes. Fill glass with soda. Stir. Float lemon slice on top.

KIRSCH CUBA LIBRE

1½ ozs. kirschwasser
½ lime
Iced cola drink

Put three large ice cubes into a tall 14-oz. glass. Add kirschwasser. Squeeze lime above drink and drop into glass. Fill with cola. Stir.

LAIT DE VIE

2 ozs. cognac or California brandy
4 ozs. milk
½ oz. heavy cream
½ oz. grenadine
Freshly grated nutmeg

Shake cognac, milk, cream, and grenadine with ice. Strain into tall 14-oz. glass filled with ice cubes. Stir. Sprinkle with nutmeg.

LATIN DOG

½ oz. Sciarada
½ oz. Pernod

Chilled grapefruit juice

Fill 8-oz. glass with ice cubes. Add Sciarada, Pernod, and enough grapefruit juice to fill glass. Stir well. Very pleasant brunch drink.

LEMON RUM COOLER

2 ozs. light rum
1 teaspoon 151-proof rum
2 ozs. pineapple juice
½ oz. lemon juice

½ oz. Falernum
Iced bitter-lemon soda
1 slice lemon

Shake both kinds of rum, pineapple juice, lemon juice, and Falernum well with ice. Strain into tall 14-oz. glass. Add two ice cubes. Fill glass with bitter-lemon soda. Add lemon slice.

LONG SUIT

2 ozs. Southern Comfort
3 ozs. grapefruit juice
2 dashes Angostura bitters

Chilled tonic water
1 slice lemon

Pour Southern Comfort, grapefruit juice, and bitters into tall 14-oz. glass three-quarters filled with ice. Stir well. Add tonic water to fill glass. Stir again. Add lemon slice.

MADAMA ROSA

1½ ozs. light rum
½ oz. cherry-flavored
  brandy

2 ozs. orange juice
½ oz. lime juice
Iced tonic water

Shake rum, cherry-flavored brandy, orange juice, and lime juice well with ice. Strain into tall 12-oz. glass. Add two large ice cubes. Fill with tonic water. Stir.

MANGO COOLER

3 ozs. ice-cold mango nectar
1½ ozs. vodka
½ oz. ice-cold lemon juice
1½ ozs. ice-cold orange juice
½ oz. Cointreau
1 slice orange
1 slice mango, if in season

Into tall 14-oz. glass, pour mango nectar, vodka, lemon juice, orange juice, and Cointreau. Add ice to fill glass. Stir well. Garnish with orange and mango slices. A fruity libation to serve before an Oriental or Polynesian menu.

MELBA TONIC

1½ ozs. vodka
½ oz. peach liqueur
½ oz. raspberry liqueur
½ oz. lemon juice
1 teaspoon sugar
Chilled tonic water

Shake vodka, peach liqueur, raspberry liqueur, lemon juice, and sugar well with ice. Strain into tall 12-oz. glass half filled with ice cubes. Add tonic water to fill glass. Stir.

MEXICAN MILK PUNCH

1 oz. tequila
1 oz. dark rum
4 ozs. milk
1 oz. heavy cream
1 small egg
2 teaspoons sugar
Freshly ground nutmeg

Shake all ingredients except nutmeg extremely well with ice. Strain into tall 12-oz. glass. Sprinkle with nutmeg.

MEXICAN MULE

1½ ozs. tequila
Iced ginger beer
½ lime

Place three large ice cubes in tall 12-oz. glass or 12-oz. mug. Add tequila. Fill glass with ginger beer. Stir. Squeeze lime over drink and drop into glass.

MINT JULEP

12 mint leaves on stem
1 teaspoon sugar
2 teaspoons water

2½ ozs. 86- or 100-proof
   bourbon
6 mint leaves on stem

Tear the 12 mint leaves partially while leaving them on stem. Place in tall 12-oz. glass or silver julep mug with sugar and water. Muddle or stir until sugar is completely dissolved. Fill glass with finely cracked ice. Add bourbon. Stir. Ice will dissolve partially. Add more ice to fill glass to rim, again stirring. Tear the 6 mint leaves partially to release aroma and insert into ice with leaves on top. Serve with or without straw.

MINT JULEP, DRY, PARTY STYLE
(Serves 8)

1 25.4 oz. bottle bourbon
1 pint finely chopped mint
   leaves

8 sprigs mint

Steep mint leaves in bourbon for 1 hour at room temperature. Fill eight tall 14-oz. glasses with finely cracked ice. Strain bourbon and pour into glasses, allowing 3 ozs. minted bourbon per glass. Stir. Add more ice to fill glass to rim. Tear a few leaves of each of the mint sprigs and fit a sprig into each glass. If your party is late getting started, store prepared juleps in freezer. A few sips of this unsweetened julep should turn the longest of hot summer days into the coolest.

MINT SPRITZER

6 ozs. chilled Rhine wine
2 large sprigs of mint

1 oz. white crème de menthe
Chilled club soda

Place mint sprigs in tall 12-oz. glass. Rub sprigs against glass with back of spoon to muddle mint, releasing flavor. Add four ice cubes. Add wine, crème de menthe, and enough soda to almost fill glass to rim. Stir.

MISTY IRISH

1 oz. blended Irish whiskey
½ oz. Irish Mist liqueur
1 oz. orange juice
½ oz. lemon juice
1 teaspoon sugar
½ cup crushed ice
1 brandied cherry

Pour whiskey, Irish Mist, orange juice, lemon juice, sugar, and ice into blender. Blend at high speed 10 seconds. Pour into old-fashioned glass. Add ice cubes to fill glass to rim. Add brandied cherry.

MOBILE MULE

2 ozs. light rum
½ lime
Iced ginger beer

Pour rum into tall 12- or 14-oz. glass or copper mug with ice cubes or cracked ice. Squeeze lime above drink and drop into glass. Fill with ginger beer. Stir. A switch on the vodka-inspired moscow mule.

MOCHA COOLER

6 ozs. cold freshly brewed strong coffee
1 oz. light rum
½ oz. Galliano
1 teaspoon sugar or more to taste
Heavy cream

Pour coffee, rum, Galliano, and sugar into tall 12-oz. glass. Stir well until sugar dissolves. Add ice to nearly fill glass and stir well again. Float heavy cream on top by pouring it over the back of a spoon so that cream flows to rim of glass.

MOLOKAI

1 oz. sake
1 oz. cranberry liqueur
2 ozs. orange juice
1 slice orange

Pour sake, cranberry liqueur, and orange juice into 8-oz. glass. Add ice cubes to fill glass. Stir very well. Add orange slice.

MOSCOW MULE

1½ to 2 ozs. vodka
½ lime
Iced ginger beer

Pour vodka into tall 12- or 14-oz. glass or copper mug with ice cubes or cracked ice. Squeeze lime above drink and drop into glass. Fill with ginger beer. Stir. A variation of the moscow mule includes a long spiral of lemon peel in the mug.

MUSCARI COOLER

1½ ozs. gin
1 oz. Muscari
1 oz. lemon juice
1 teaspoon sugar
Iced club soda
1 slice lemon

Shake gin, Muscari, lemon juice, and sugar well with ice. Pour into tall 14-oz. glass half filled with rocks. Add club soda. Stir. Add lemon slice.

NECTARINE COOLER

2 ozs. vodka
3 ozs. iced orange juice
¼ cup cold sliced ripe nectarine
1 teaspoon sugar
⅓ cup crushed ice
Iced club soda
1 slice fresh nectarine
1 slice lemon

Put vodka, orange juice, nectarine, sugar, and crushed ice into blender. Blend at low speed 15–20 seconds. Pour into tall 14-oz. glass. Add a splash of soda and enough ice to fill glass. Stir. Garnish with nectarine and lemon slices.

OAHU GIN SLING

2 ozs. gin
½ oz. crème de cassis
½ oz. Benedictine
1 oz. lime juice
1 teaspoon sugar
Iced club soda
Lime-rind spiral

To make lime-rind spiral, cut continuous strip of lime peel from stem end to bottom of fruit. Place peel in tall 14-oz. glass, hooking it to rim. Shake gin, crème de cassis, Benedictine, lime juice, and sugar well with ice. Strain into glass and add ice cubes until three-quarters full. Fill glass with soda. Stir.

OLD-FASHIONED ARTICHOKE

1 oz. gin
½ oz. dry vermouth
½ oz. Cynar
Iced club soda
1 slice lemon

Pour gin, vermouth, and Cynar over rocks in old-fashioned glass. Stir well. Add splash of soda. Add lemon slice.

OLD-FASHIONED RUM AND MUSCARI

1 oz. light rum
1 oz. Muscari
2 or 3 dashes Angostura
    bitters
Iced club soda
Lemon peel

Pour rum, Muscari, and bitters into old-fashioned glass. Fill glass with rocks. Stir well. Add splash of soda. Twist lemon peel above drink and drop into glass.

ORANGEADE WITH PEPPERMINT SCHNAPPS

6 ozs. chilled fresh orange
    juice
1½ ozs. peppermint
    schnapps
Ice water
½ slice orange

Pour orange juice and peppermint schnapps into tall 14-oz. glass half filled with ice. Add enough ice water to fill glass almost to rim. Stir well. Add orange slice.

ORANGE COOLER IN SHELL

1 extra-large California orange	½ oz. lime juice
1 oz. 151-proof rum	1 teaspoon sugar
½ oz. curaçao	1 slice cocktail orange in syrup

Cut a cap off top of orange about ½ inch from top. With a sharp grapefruit knife, gouge out the meat, leaving orange shell intact. Squeeze enough juice from meat to make 1½ ozs. Shake orange juice, rum, curaçao, lime juice, and sugar well with ice. Strain into orange shell. Place orange shell in a bowl or soup dish about 7 inches in diameter. Pack finely crushed ice around orange. Fasten orange slice onto cocktail spear and place across orange cup. Serve with a short colored straw. A show-off concoction for drink hobbyists and rum specialists.

ORANGE OASIS

4 ozs. ice-cold fresh orange juice	½ oz. cherry liqueur
	Iced ginger ale
1½ ozs. gin	1 slice orange

Pour orange juice, gin, and cherry liqueur into tall 14-oz. glass. Add ice cubes or ice slices to rim of glass. Add ginger ale. Stir. Garnish with orange slice.

PALMETTO COOLER

2 ozs. bourbon	3 dashes Angostura bitters
½ oz. apricot liqueur	Iced club soda
½ oz. sweet vermouth	Fresh mint

Fill a tall 14-oz. glass with ice cubes. Add bourbon, apricot liqueur, vermouth, and bitters. Stir well. Fill glass almost to top with club soda and stir lightly. Place generous bouquet of mint sprigs in glass. Tear a few leaves to release aroma.

PANAMA COOLER

2 ozs. iced Rhine wine
2 ozs. iced very dry sherry
1 oz. orange juice
1 teaspoon lime juice
½ oz. maraschino liqueur
1 dash Angostura bitters
1 oz. iced club soda
1 slice lemon

Shake Rhine wine, sherry, orange juice, lime juice, maraschino liqueur, and bitters well with ice. Strain into tall 14-oz. glass. Add soda. Fill glass with ice. Stir. Add lemon slice.

PASSION FRUIT COOLER

4 ozs. passion-fruit nectar
   (not syrup)
1½ ozs. light rum
1 oz. gin
½ oz. lemon juice
1 oz. orange juice
2 sprigs mint

Shake passion-fruit nectar, rum, gin, lemon juice, and orange juice well with ice. Strain into tall 14-oz. glass. Add enough coarsely cracked ice or ice cubes to fill glass. Decorate with mint after partially tearing several leaves to release fragrance.

PERNOD AND PEPPERMINT

1 oz. Pernod
1 oz. peppermint schnapps
1 oz. lime juice
Iced club soda
1 slice lime

Fill tall 14-oz. glass with ice cubes. Add Pernod, peppermint schnapps, and lime juice. Stir well. Fill with club soda. Add lime slice.

PILE DRIVER

4 ozs. orange juice
1 oz. vodka
1 oz. apricot liqueur
½ oz. lemon juice

Shake all ingredients very well with ice. Strain into tall 12-oz. glass half filled with ice. Stir. Add ice, if necessary, to fill glass to rim.

PIMM'S CUP

1½ ozs. Pimm's No. 1 Cup
Iced 7-Up or lemon soda
1 slice lemon
Cucumber peel

Pour Pimm's Cup into 8- or 10-oz. glass or Pimm's glass tankard with ice. Fill with 7-Up. Add lemon slice and cucumber peel. Stir. The old English gin sling is bottled as Pimm's No. 1 Cup, made with a gin base and fruit flavors. Other prepared Pimm's Cups are bottled with other liquor bases, but the No. 1 is the best known in the States.

PINA COLADA

1½ ozs. light rum
1 oz. coconut cream
3 ozs. pineapple juice

Pour rum, coconut cream and pineapple juice into blender. Add two ice cubes. Blend 15–20 seconds or until ice cubes are crushed. Pour over rocks in 8-oz. tall glass. Stir.

PINEAPPLE MINT COOLER

2 ozs. gin
½ oz. white crème de menthe
3 ozs. pineapple juice
1 oz. lemon juice
Iced club soda
1 cocktail pineapple stick
1 green cocktail cherry

Shake gin, crème de menthe, pineapple juice, and lemon juice well with ice. Strain into tall 14-oz. glass. Add a splash of soda and enough ice to fill glass. Stir. Garnish with pineapple stick and cherry.

PINK LEMONADE A LA PLAYBOY

5 ozs. chilled rosé wine
2 ozs. chilled lemon juice
2 ozs. chilled orange juice
½ oz. kirschwasser
2 teaspoons sugar
1 slice lemon
1 maraschino cherry

Into tall 14-oz. glass, pour wine, lemon juice, orange juice, kirschwasser, and sugar. Stir well until sugar dissolves. Add two large ice cubes and enough ice-cold water (not club soda) to fill glass. Stir. Garnish with lemon slice and cherry.

PINK RUM AND TONIC

2½ ozs. light rum
½ oz. lime juice
1 teaspoon grenadine
Iced tonic water
1 slice lime

Shake rum, lime juice, and grenadine well with ice. Strain into tall 14-oz. glass half filled with ice. Add tonic water. Stir. Add lime slice. Curiously refreshing yo-ho-ho.

PINKY

2 ozs. ruby port
1 oz. strawberry liqueur
½ oz. heavy cream
1 large fresh strawberry

Shake port, strawberry liqueur, and cream well with ice. Strain over rocks in 8-oz. glass. Fasten strawberry on cocktail spear and place over rim of glass.

PLANTER'S PUNCH

1½ ozs. dark Jamaica rum
3 ozs. orange juice
½ oz. lemon juice
1 teaspoon sugar
¼ teaspoon grenadine
½ slice orange
1 slice lemon

Shake rum, orange juice, lemon juice, sugar, and grenadine well with ice. Strain over rocks in tall 10-oz. glass. Stir well. Add ice, if necessary, to fill glass. Garnish with orange and lemon slices.

PLANTER'S PUNCH WITH FALERNUM

2 ozs. dark Jamaica rum
1 dash Angostura bitters
½ oz. Falernum
1 teaspoon sugar
½ oz. lime juice
Iced club soda
1 slice orange
1 maraschino cherry

Shake rum, bitters, Falernum, sugar, and lime juice extremely well with ice. Strain into tall 14-oz. glass three-quarters filled with ice cubes. Stir. Add club soda to fill glass. Garnish with orange slice and cherry.

PLAYBOY COOLER

1¼ ozs. golden Jamaica rum
1¼ ozs. Jamaica coffee liqueur
3 ozs. pineapple juice
2 teaspoons lemon juice
Cola drink
1 slice pineapple

Shake rum, coffee liqueur, pineapple juice, and lemon juice well with ice. Strain into prechilled tall 14-oz. glass. Add ice to fill glass to 1 inch from top. Add cola. Garnish with pineapple slice.

PLUM AND TONIC

¾ oz. mirabelle or quetsch
1 oz. gin
½ oz. lemon juice
Iced tonic water
1 slice lemon

Pour mirabelle, gin, and lemon juice over three large ice cubes in tall 10-oz. glass. Add tonic water to fill glass. Stir lightly. Add lemon slice.

PORTAMENTO

2 ozs. tawny port
1 oz. bourbon
2 dashes Peychaud's or
    Angostura bitters
½ egg white
1 teaspoon lemon juice
1 slice lemon

Shake port, bourbon, bitters, egg white, and lemon juice extremely well with ice. Strain over rocks in 8-oz. old-fashioned glass. Add lemon slice.

PORT AND COGNAC MILK PUNCH

2 ozs. white port, such as
    Porto Branco
1½ ozs. cognac
4 ozs. (½ measuring cup)
    milk
1 small egg
Freshly grated nutmeg

Shake port, cognac, milk, and egg extremely well with ice. Strain into 12-oz. glass. Sprinkle with nutmeg.

PORT ARMS

3 ozs. California port
1 oz. California brandy
1 oz. orange juice
½ oz. lemon juice
1 teaspoon Triple Sec
Iced club soda
½ slice orange
1 slice lemon

Shake port, brandy, orange juice, lemon juice, and Triple Sec well with ice. Strain into tall 14-oz. glass half filled with ice cubes. Add soda. Stir. Add orange and lemon slices.

PORT CASSIS

2½ ozs. chilled white port,
    such as Porto Branco
½ oz. crème de cassis
½ oz. lemon juice
Iced club soda
1 slice lemon

Pour port, crème de cassis, and lemon juice over rocks in 8-oz. glass. Stir well. Add splash of soda. Add lemon slice.

PORTCULLIS

2 ozs. ruby port
1 oz. cherry-flavored brandy
4 ozs. cranberry-juice cocktail
1 oz. lemon juice
1 slice lemon

Pour port, cherry-flavored brandy, cranberry-juice cocktail, and lemon juice into tall 14-oz. glass half filled with ice cubes. Stir well. Add ice cubes to fill glass. Stir well. Add lemon slice.

PUNTA GORDA

1½ ozs. dark Jamaica rum
½ oz. sloe gin
4 ozs. pineapple juice
½ oz. lime juice
1 teaspoon grenadine

Shake all ingredients well with ice. Pour into tall 12-oz. glass half filled with ice. Stir. Add ice, if necessary, to fill glass to rim.

PUNT E LEMON

3 ozs. Punt e Mes
Iced bitter-lemon soda
1 wedge old-fashioned-cocktail orange in syrup

Pour Punt e Mes into tall 12-oz. glass three-quarters filled with ice cubes. Add bitter lemon to almost fill glass. Stir very well. Pierce orange wedge with cocktail spear and rest across top of glass.

QUADRUPLE PINEAPPLE
(4 single or 2 double drinks)

1 large chilled pineapple
½ cup pineapple sherbet
6 ozs. light rum
3 ozs. orange juice
1½ ozs. lime juice
½ oz. maraschino liqueur

The pineapple should measure at least 7 inches from base to top of fruit, not including stem. Cut a cap off pineapple about ½ inch from top. To remove meat from pineapple, cut a deep circle around edge of pineapple about ½ inch from rim, leaving a large cylinder of fruit, which must then be gouged out. A very sharp boning knife is a good instrument for the job. Cut wedges of fruit loose by slicing diagonally toward rim of fruit. Use a grapefruit knife or large *parisienne*-potato cutter to remove small pieces of fruit. Do not pierce shell of fruit or it will not hold liquid. The cavity of the pineapple should be large enough to hold 2 measuring cups of liquid. Test it for size. Cut hard core of fruit away and discard it. Cut enough tender pineapple meat to make ½ cup fruit in small dice. Into well of blender, put the ½ cup diced pineapple, sherbet, rum, orange juice, lime juice, and maraschino liqueur. Blend 5 seconds. Pour into pineapple shell. Place pineapple in deep dish or bowl surrounded with finely crushed ice. Place two or four colored straws in drink, allowing for two or four pineapple sippers. An elaborate production, beloved by rum barons. A second round may be prepared beforehand from the same pineapple and blended just before refilling pineapple.

RANCHO CONTENTO

1½ ozs. tequila
4 ozs. orange juice
¼ oz. dry vermouth
¼ oz. sweet vermouth
1 slice orange

Shake tequila, orange juice, and both kinds of vermouth well with ice. Strain into 10-oz. glass. Add two large ice cubes and orange slice.

RASPBERRY CLARET CUP

4 ozs. dry red wine
1 oz. brandy
1 oz. Himbeergeist (dry white raspberry brandy)
¾ oz. raspberry syrup
1 oz. lemon juice
Iced club soda
2 or 3 fresh or frozen whole raspberries

Be sure wine and brandies are ice-cold before mixing drink. Put three ice cubes into tall 14-oz. collins glass. Pour wine, brandy, Himbeergeist, raspberry syrup, and lemon juice into glass. Stir until all ingredients are very well blended. Fill glass with soda. Stir slightly. Float raspberries on top.

RED BAIT

1 oz. sloe gin
½ oz. dark Jamaica rum
2 ozs. chilled guava nectar
½ oz. lime juice
Iced tonic water
1 slice lime

Pour sloe gin, rum, guava nectar, and lime juice into tall 14-oz. glass three-quarters filled with ice cubes. Stir well. Add tonic water to fill glass. Stir. Add lime slice.

RED DANE

1½ ozs. aquavit
2 ozs. cranberry-juice cocktail
½ oz. lime juice
1 teaspoon sugar
1 slice lemon

Shake aquavit, cranberry-juice cocktail, lime juice, and sugar well with ice. Strain into 8-oz. glass with rocks. Stir. Add lemon slice.

RED PERIL

1 oz. sloe gin
½ oz. vodka
2 ozs. chilled papaya nectar
½ oz. lime juice
Iced club soda
1 slice lime

Pour sloe gin, vodka, papaya nectar, and lime juice into tall 14-oz. glass three-quarters filled with ice cubes. Stir well. Add soda to fill glass. Stir. Add lime slice.

RHENISH RASPBERRY

2 ozs. Riesling wine
1 oz. vodka
¼ cup frozen raspberries
　in syrup, thawed
2 teaspoons grenadine
½ oz. lemon juice
½ cup crushed ice
Iced club soda

Put raspberries with their syrup, Riesling, vodka, grenadine, lemon juice, and ice into blender. Blend at high speed 10 seconds. Pour into tall 14-oz. glass. Add a splash of soda. Add ice, if necessary, to fill glass to brim. Stir lightly.

ROCK AND RYE COOLER

1½ ozs. vodka
1 oz. rock and rye
½ oz. lime juice
Iced bitter-lemon soda
1 slice lime

Shake vodka, rock and rye, and lime juice well with ice. Strain into tall 14-oz. glass half filled with ice. Add bitter-lemon soda. Stir. Add lime slice.

ROMAN COOLER

1½ ozs. gin
½ oz. Punt e Mes
½ oz. lemon juice
1 teaspoon sugar
Iced club soda
Lemon peel

Shake gin, Punt e Mes, lemon juice, and sugar well with ice. Strain into tall 14-oz. glass. Add soda and ice to fill glass. Twist lemon peel above drink and drop into glass.

ROMAN FRULLATI

3 ozs. gin
¼ cup diced Delicious
　apple, with skin
¼ cup diced ripe pear,
　with skin
¼ cup frozen sliced
　peaches, thawed
1 oz. maraschino liqueur
1 oz. orzata or orgeat
½ cup crushed ice

Put all ingredients into blender. Blend at high speed 20 seconds. Pour into tall 14-oz. glass. Add ice, if necessary, to fill glass to rim.

RUM AND COCONUT COOLER

2½ ozs. light rum
1 oz. cream of coconut
½ oz. lemon juice
Iced club soda
1 slice lemon
1 maraschino cherry

Shake rum, cream of coconut, and lemon juice well with ice. Strain into tall 14-oz. glass half filled with ice. Add a splash of soda. Garnish with lemon slice and cherry.

RUM AND PINEAPPLE COOLER

2½ ozs. light rum
2 ozs. pineapple juice
½ oz. lemon juice
1 teaspoon 151-proof rum
1 teaspoon sugar
1 dash Angostura bitters
Iced club soda
1 pineapple chunk
1 papaya chunk in syrup

Shake rum, pineapple juice, lemon juice, 151-proof rum, sugar, and bitters well with ice. Strain into tall 14-oz. glass. Add a splash of soda and enough ice to fill glass. Garnish with pineapple and papaya chunks fastened onto a cocktail spear.

RUM CITRUS COOLER

2 ozs. light rum
1 oz. orange juice
½ oz. lime juice
½ oz. Cointreau
1 teaspoon sugar
Iced 7-Up
1 slice lime
½ slice lemon

Shake rum, orange juice, lime juice, Cointreau, and sugar well with ice. Strain into tall 14-oz. glass half filled with ice. Add 7-Up. Stir. Garnish with lime and lemon slices. Solace or celebration after eighteen holes on the fairway.

RUM CURAÇAO COOLER

1 oz. dark Jamaica rum
1 oz. curaçao
½ oz. lime juice
Iced club soda
1 slice lime
½ slice orange

Shake rum, curaçao, and lime juice with ice. Strain into tall 12-oz. glass. Add soda and ice to fill glass. Garnish with lime and orange slices.

RUM ROYALE

1 oz. light rum
2 ozs. sauterne wine
1½ ozs. lemon juice
2 ozs. pineapple juice
1 teaspoon sugar
1 dash Peychaud's bitters
1 cube pineapple
1 maraschino cherry

Shake rum, sauterne, lemon juice, pineapple juice, sugar, and bitters well with ice. Strain into prechilled tall 14-oz. glass. Add ice to fill glass. Affix pineapple cube and cherry to cocktail spear and rest on rim of glass.

ST.-CROIX COOLER

Peel of ½ large orange
2 ozs. light rum
½ oz. dark Jamaica rum
1 oz. brandy
1 tablespoon brown sugar
2½ ozs. orange juice
1½ ozs. lemon juice
1 dash orange-flower water
Iced club soda

Cut orange peel from stem end in one continuing spiral about ½ inch wide. Place peel in tall 14-oz. glass, permitting one end to overhang rim. Shake both kinds of rum, brandy, brown sugar, orange juice, lemon juice, and orange-flower water well with ice. Strain into glass. Fill glass to rim with coarsely cracked ice or ice cubes. Add a splash of soda. Stir. A rich tropical cooler that will easily outlast two ordinary cocktails.

SAKE CASSIS

1 oz. sake
1 oz. vodka
½ oz. crème de cassis
Iced club soda
1 slice lemon

Pour sake, vodka, and crème de cassis over rocks in 10-oz. glass. Stir well. Add a splash of soda. Stir. Add lemon slice.

SAKE SUNRISE

1 oz. sake
1 oz. California brandy
Chilled grapefruit juice
1 teaspoon grenadine

Place four ice cubes in squat or tall 10-oz. glass. Add sake, brandy, and enough grapefruit juice to almost fill glass. Stir well. Pour grenadine on top of drink. Guests stir drink to blend grenadine with other ingredients.

SAN JUAN SLING

¾ oz. light rum
¾ oz. cherry liqueur
¾ oz. Benedictine
½ oz. lime juice
Iced club soda
Lime peel

Shake rum, cherry liqueur, Benedictine, and lime juice well with ice. Strain into tall 14-oz. glass half filled with ice. Add soda. Twist lime peel above drink and drop into glass.

SARASOTA

2 ozs. cream sherry
3 ozs. papaya nectar
1 oz. light rum
½ oz. lime juice
1 slice lime

Shake sherry, papaya nectar, rum, and lime juice well with ice. Strain into tall 14-oz. glass three-quarters filled with ice cubes. Add lime slice.

SCOTCH APPLE

1½ ozs. Scotch
½ oz. apple brandy
4 ozs. apple juice
½ oz. orange juice
½ oz. lemon juice
Orange peel
Lemon peel

Shake Scotch, apple brandy, apple juice, orange juice, and lemon juice well with ice. Strain into tall 12-oz. glass half filled with ice cubes. Stir well. Add ice, if necessary, to fill glass to rim. Twist orange and lemon peels above drink and drop into glass.

SCOTCH HORSE'S NECK

Peel of whole lemon, in one spiral
3 ozs. Scotch
½ oz. sweet vermouth
½ oz. dry vermouth

Place lemon peel in tall 14-oz. glass with one end of peel overhanging rim. Add Scotch and both kinds of vermouth. Fill glass with cracked ice. Stir. Add more ice, if necessary, to fill glass. Every horse's neck is improved if it ages about 10 minutes before sipping.

SCOTCH SOLACE

2½ ozs. Scotch
½ oz. honey
½ oz. Triple Sec
4 ozs. milk
1 oz. heavy cream
⅛ teaspoon freshly grated orange rind

Pour Scotch, honey, and Triple Sec into 14-oz. glass. Stir until honey is thoroughly blended. Add milk, cream, and orange rind. Add ice cubes to fill glass to brim. Stir well. Cold, creamy, and soothing.

SCREWDRIVER WITH SHERRY

½ cup orange juice
2 ozs. oloroso sherry
1 oz. vodka
½ cup crushed ice

Put all ingredients into blender. Blend 20 seconds. Pour into double old-fashioned or tall 14-oz. glass. Add ice cubes to fill glass. An outsize screwdriver especially suited for the brunchboard.

SHOO-IN

1 oz. California brandy
½ oz. dark Jamaica rum
1 oz. light rum
½ oz. maraschino liqueur
2 ozs. chilled grapefruit juice
2 ozs. chilled pineapple juice

Pour all ingredients into tall 14-oz. glass half filled with ice cubes. Stir well. Add ice cubes, if necessary, to fill glass. Stir.

SHORE LEAVE

1 oz. sloe gin
1 oz. light rum
½ oz. lime juice
Iced tonic water
1 slice lime

Shake sloe gin, rum, and lime juice well with ice. Strain into tall 12-oz. glass three-quarters filled with ice cubes. Fill glass with tonic water. Stir. Add lime slice.

SIMPATICO

2 ozs. peppermint schnapps
1 oz. white rum
Iced bitter-lemon soda
1 slice lemon

Pour peppermint schnapps and white rum into tall 14-oz. glass three-quarters filled with ice cubes. Stir well. Add bitter lemon to fill glass. Stir. Add lemon slice.

SINGAPORE GIN SLING

1½ ozs. gin
1 oz. cherry-flavored brandy
1 oz. lime juice
Iced club soda
1 slice lime

Shake gin, cherry-flavored brandy, and lime juice well with ice. Strain into tall 14-oz. glass half filled with ice cubes. Fill glass with soda. Add lime slice.

SKI JUMPER

1½ ozs. aquavit
1 teaspoon kümmel liqueur
1 teaspoon lemon juice
Iced bitter-lemon soda
1 slice lemon

Pour aquavit, kümmel, and lemon juice into tall or squat 10-oz. glass three-quarters filled with ice cubes. Stir well. Fill glass with bitter lemon. Stir. Add lemon slice.

SLOE AND BITTER

1 oz. sloe gin
1 oz. tequila
½ oz. lemon juice
Iced bitter-lemon soda
1 slice lemon

Shake sloe gin, tequila, and lemon juice well with ice. Strain into tall 12-oz. glass three-quarters filled with ice cubes. Fill glass with bitter lemon. Stir. Add lemon slice.

SLOE CRANBERRY COOLER

2½ ozs. ice-cold sloe gin
6 ozs. ice-cold cranberry juice
1¼ ozs. lemon juice
1 slice lemon

Pour sloe gin, cranberry juice, and lemon juice into tall 14-oz. glass. Add ice cubes to fill glass. Stir well. Add lemon slice.

SLOE DOG

1 oz. sloe gin
½ oz. gin
2 ozs. grapefruit juice
1 slice lime

Shake sloe gin, gin, and grapefruit juice well with ice. Strain over rocks in 8-oz. glass. Add lime slice.

SLOE DOWN

1½ ozs. sloe gin
½ oz. gin
½ oz. kirschwasser
4 ozs. orange juice
½ oz. lime juice
Iced club soda
1 slice lime

Shake sloe gin, gin, kirschwasser, orange juice, and lime juice well with ice. Strain into tall 14-oz. glass half filled with ice. Add soda. Stir. Add lime slice.

SLOE SWEDE

1½ ozs. aquavit
½ oz. sloe gin
½ slightly beaten egg white
1 teaspoon sugar
¾ oz. lemon juice
Iced club soda
1 slice lemon

Shake aquavit, sloe gin, egg white, sugar, and lemon juice extremely well with ice. Strain into tall 14-oz. glass three-quarters filled with ice cubes. Stir well. Add soda to fill glass. Stir. Add lemon slice.

SOUTHERN RASPBERRY

¾ oz. framboise
¾ oz. Southern Comfort
½ oz. lemon juice
1 teaspoon sugar
Iced club soda
1 slice lemon

Shake framboise, Southern Comfort, lemon juice, and sugar extremely well with ice. Strain over rocks in tall or squat 8-oz. glass. Add splash of soda. Add ice, if necessary, to fill glass to rim. Stir. Add lemon slice.

STEEPLEJACK

2 ozs. apple brandy
2½ ozs. iced apple juice
2½ ozs. iced club soda
1 teaspoon lime juice
1 slice lime

Pour apple brandy, apple juice, soda, and lime juice into tall 14-oz. glass. Add ice to fill glass. Stir. Add lime slice.

STONE FENCE

1½ ozs. bourbon
Chilled apple juice

Pour bourbon and apple juice over rocks in 10-oz. glass. Stir well. Add ice cubes, if necessary, to fill glass.

STRAWBERRY BLONDE

3 fresh strawberries
1 oz. strawberry liqueur
6 ozs. well-chilled Rhine wine
½ oz. kirschwasser
Iced club soda
1 slice lime

Marinate strawberries in strawberry liqueur for 1 hour. Fasten strawberries onto cocktail spear. Pour Rhine wine, strawberry liqueur, and kirschwasser into tall 14-oz. glass. Add a splash of soda and ice to fill glass. Stir. Add lime slice. Place speared strawberries over rim of glass.

STRAWBERRY CREAM COOLER

1½ ozs. gin
¼ cup frozen sliced strawberries (fruit and syrup), thawed
1 oz. lemon juice
2 tablespoons heavy sweet cream
1 teaspoon sugar
Iced club soda

Put gin, strawberries, lemon juice, cream, and sugar into blender. Blend 10–15 seconds at high speed. Pour into tall 14-oz. glass. Add a splash of soda and enough ice to fill glass. Stir.

STRAWBERRY VERMOUTH COOLER

2½ ozs. dry vermouth
¼ cup fresh strawberries,
    hulled and sliced
1 oz. gin
2 teaspoons strawberry
    syrup
½ cup crushed ice
Iced club soda
1 slice lemon

Put vermouth, strawberries, gin, strawberry syrup, and ice into blender. Blend 10–15 seconds at low speed. Pour into tall 14-oz. glass containing two ice cubes. Add a splash of soda. Stir. Garnish with lemon slice.

STRAWBERRY VIN BLANC

4 ozs. chilled dry white
    wine, Graves if possible
1 oz. strawberry liqueur
Iced club soda
1 slice lemon
1 fresh large strawberry

Pour wine and strawberry liqueur over two large ice cubes in tall 12-oz. glass. Stir. Add soda to fill glass. Garnish with lemon slice and strawberry.

STRAWBERRY WHITE PORT

4 ozs. imported white port
Iced tonic water
½ oz. strawberry liqueur
1 slice lemon
1 large fresh strawberry,
    with long stem if
    possible

Be sure port is a dry imported wine, such as Sandeman's extra-dry Porto Branco. Fill tall 14-oz. glass with ice cubes. Add port. Fill glass to within ½ inch of rim with tonic water. Float strawberry liqueur on top by pouring it over the back of a spoon held against the inside of the glass.

Place lemon slice so that it rests on top of ice cubes. Place strawberry on lemon slice.

SUMMER LIGHT

2 ozs. dry vermouth *Iced bitter-lemon soda*
3 ozs. dry white wine

Pour vermouth and wine into tall 14-oz. glass half filled with ice cubes. Fill glass with bitter lemon. Stir.

SURF RIDER

2 ozs. sake *3 ozs. pineapple juice*
1 oz. light rum *Iced bitter-lemon soda*

Shake sake, rum, and pineapple juice well with ice. Strain into tall 14-oz. glass half filled with ice cubes. Fill glass with bitter lemon.

TALL ANNIE

1 oz. anisette *Iced tonic water*
1 oz. gin *½ small lime*

Fill tall 12-oz. glass three-quarters full with ice. Add anisette, gin, and enough tonic to fill glass almost to rim. Stir well. Squeeze lime above drink and drop into glass.

TALL BLONDE

1 oz. aquavit *Iced bitter-lemon soda*
½ oz. apricot liqueur *1 slice lemon*

Pour aquavit and apricot liqueur into tall 12-oz. glass three-quarters filled with ice cubes. Stir well. Add iced bitter lemon to fill glass. Stir. Add lemon slice.

TALL DUTCH EGGNOG

1½ ozs. Advokaat liqueur	6 ozs. milk
1½ ozs. light rum	1 teaspoon sugar
½ oz. 151-proof rum	½ cup finely cracked ice
1 oz. orange juice	Ground cinnamon

Put Advokaat, both kinds of rum, orange juice, milk, sugar, and ice into blender. Blend at high speed 10 seconds. Pour into tall 14-oz. glass. Sprinkle with cinnamon. The Dutch way of getting the new year rolling as merrily as possible.

TALL HAOLE

2½ ozs. CocoRibe	1 oz. lemon juice
3 ozs. orange juice	Iced club soda
2 ozs. apricot nectar	½ slice orange

Shake CocoRibe, orange juice, apricot nectar, and lemon juice well with ice. Strain into tall 14-oz. glass half filled with ice cubes. Add soda to fill glass. Stir. Add orange slice.

TALL ISLANDER

2 ozs. light rum	1 teaspoon sugar syrup
3 ozs. pineapple juice	Iced club soda
1 oz. lime juice	1 slice lime
1 teaspoon dark Jamaica rum	

Shake light rum, pineapple juice, lime juice, dark rum, and syrup well with ice. Strain into tall 14-oz. glass. Add a splash of soda and enough ice to fill glass. Stir. Add lime slice. Bound to make natives unrestless; equally at home in a high-rise or down among the sheltering palms.

TALL LIMONE

1 oz. Sciarada
1 oz. gin
½ oz. lemon juice
Iced bitter-lemon soda
1 slice lemon

Pour Sciarada, gin, and lemon juice into a tall 12-oz. glass three-quarters filled with ice cubes. Stir well. Fill glass with bitter lemon. Stir. Add lemon slice.

TALL MARGARITA

1½ ozs. tequila
½ oz. Cointreau or Triple Sec
¾ oz. lemon juice
Iced bitter-lemon soda
1 slice lemon

Shake tequila, Cointreau, and lemon juice well with ice. Strain into 12-oz. glass three-quarters filled with ice cubes. Fill glass with bitter lemon. Stir. Add lemon slice.

TALL MIDORI

1 oz. Midori
1 oz. dark Jamaica rum
½ oz. lime juice
Iced tonic water

Pour Midori, rum, and lime juice into a tall 14-oz. glass three-quarters filled with ice cubes. Stir well. Fill with tonic water.

TALL MUSCARI

1½ ozs. Muscari
1 oz. vodka
3 ozs. orange juice
Iced tonic water

Pour Muscari, vodka, and orange juice into tall 14-oz. glass three-quarters filled with ice cubes. Stir well. Fill glass to top with tonic water.

TALL ORDER

3 ozs. dry vermouth
4 ozs. chilled strawberry
    nectar

Iced club soda

Pour vermouth and strawberry nectar into tall 14-oz. glass three-quarters filled with ice cubes. Stir very well. Fill glass with soda. Stir lightly.

TALL SACK

3 ozs. cream sherry
2 ozs. apricot nectar
3 ozs. orange juice
½ oz. lemon juice
½ slice orange

Shake sherry, apricot nectar, orange juice, and lemon juice well with ice. Strain into tall 14-oz. glass. Add ice cubes to fill glass. Stir. Add orange slice.

TALL SARDINIAN

1 oz. Cynar
1 oz. vodka
2 ozs. orange juice
Iced tonic water
1 slice orange

Put four large ice cubes into tall 14-oz. glass. Add Cynar, vodka, and orange juice. Stir well. Fill with tonic water. Add orange slice.

TALL SUNRISE

2 ozs. tequila
½ oz. lime juice
½ oz. curaçao
1 teaspoon crème de cassis
Iced club soda
1 slice lime

Shake tequila, lime juice, curaçao and crème de cassis well with ice. Strain into tall 14-oz. glass half filled with ice. Fill glass with soda. Stir. Garnish with lime slice. One to contemplate while waiting for the hot chili.

TALL TAWNY

3 ozs. tawny port
1 oz. white rum
2 ozs. papaya nectar
2 ozs. chilled orange juice
Iced club soda
1-inch square of papaya

Pour port, rum, papaya nectar, and orange juice into tall 14-oz. glass half filled with ice cubes. Add soda. Stir. Fasten papaya onto cocktail spear and place over rim of glass.

TAMARIND COOLER

3 ozs. chilled tamarind nectar
2 ozs. chilled mango nectar
1 oz. chilled orange juice
1 oz. chilled pineapple juice
1½ ozs. light rum
½ oz. 151-proof rum
1 slice lemon
2 large sprigs mint

Pour all ingredients except lemon slice and mint into tall 14-oz. glass. Add ice cubes to fill glass. Stir well. Add lemon slice and mint. (Note: nectars such as tamarind, mango, guanabana, etc., are available in shops featuring Puerto Rican specialties.)

TEE OFF

1 oz. California brandy
½ oz. peppermint schnapps
2 ozs. chilled pineapple juice
2 ozs. chilled orange juice

Shake brandy, peppermint schnapps, pineapple juice, and orange juice well with ice. Strain over rocks in 10-oz. glass. Stir.

TEQUILA COLADA

1½ ozs. tequila
4 ozs. pineapple juice
1 oz. cream of coconut
½ cup crushed ice

Pour tequila, pineapple juice, cream of coconut, and crushed ice into blender. Blend at high speed 10 seconds. Pour into tall or squat 12-oz. glass.

TEQUILA COOLER

1½ ozs. tequila
2 ozs. Stone's ginger wine
2 ozs. orange juice
½ oz. lime juice
Iced tonic water
1 slice lime
½ slice orange

Pour tequila, ginger wine, orange juice, and lime juice into tall 14-oz. glass three-quarters filled with ice cubes. Stir very well. Add tonic water to fill glass. Add lime and orange slices.

TEQUILA MIEL

1½ ozs. tequila
½ oz. honey liqueur
4 ozs. grapefruit juice

Shake well with ice. Strain over rocks in squat or tall 10-oz. glass.

TIGER TAIL

4 ozs. ice-cold fresh orange juice
1 oz. Pernod
1 slice lime

Pour orange juice and Pernod into tall 12- or 14-oz. glass. Add cracked ice to fill glass. Stir. Add lime slice. Magnificent breakfast first course.

VAMPIRO

1½ ozs. tequila
3 ozs. sangrita *(page 193)*
3½ ozs. grapefruit juice
¼ teaspoon lime juice

Shake tequila, *sangrita*, grapefruit juice, and lime juice well with ice. Strain into tall 12-oz. glass. Add ice cubes to fill glass to rim. Stir. The reigning queen of tall tequila drinks in Guadalajara.

VERMOUTH AND GINGER

1 oz. dry vermouth
1 oz. ginger-flavored brandy
Iced ginger ale
1 slice lemon

Pour vermouth and ginger-flavored brandy into 8-oz. glass with several ice cubes. Stir well. Add ginger ale. Stir. Add lemon slice.

VERMOUTH COOLER

2 ozs. sweet vermouth
1 oz. vodka
½ oz. lemon juice
1 teaspoon sugar
Iced club soda
1 slice lemon

Shake vermouth, vodka, lemon juice, and sugar well with ice. Strain into tall 14-oz. glass half filled with ice. Add soda. Stir. Add lemon slice.

VILLA NOVA

1½ ozs. ruby port
1 oz. California or Spanish brandy
Angostura bitters
Iced club soda
Lemon peel

Pour port, brandy, and several dashes bitters over rocks in old-fashioned glass. Stir well. Add splash of soda. Stir. Twist lemon peel above drink and drop into glass.

VOLUPTUOSO

1 oz. tequila
1½ ozs. banana liqueur
⅓ cup sliced ripe banana
1 cup crushed ice
1 teaspoon sugar
½ oz. lemon juice

Put all ingredients into blender. Blend 10 seconds at high speed. Pour into tall 12-oz. glass.

WATERMELON CASSIS

2 ozs. gin
½ cup diced watermelon, seeds removed
½ oz. crème de cassis
¾ oz. lemon juice
½ cup crushed ice
Iced club soda
1 slice lemon

Put gin, watermelon, crème de cassis, lemon juice, and crushed ice into blender. Blend at low speed 10–15 seconds. Pour into tall 14-oz. glass. Let drink settle for a few moments. Add two ice cubes and a splash of soda. Add lemon slice.

WATERMELON COOLER

½ cup diced watermelon, sans seeds
2¼ ozs. light rum
½ oz. lime juice
¼ oz. maraschino liqueur
1 teaspoon sugar
½ cup crushed ice
1 slice lime

Put watermelon, rum, lime juice, maraschino liqueur, sugar, and ice into blender. Blend 10–15 seconds at low speed. Pour into tall 14-oz. glass. When foam subsides, add ice to fill glass. Stir. Add lime slice.

WHITE WINE COOLER

6 ozs. chilled dry white wine
½ oz. brandy
2 dashes orange bitters
1 teaspoon kümmel
2 teaspoons sugar
½ oz. lemon juice
Iced club soda
Cucumber peel, 2 inches long, ½ inch wide

Put wine, brandy, bitters, kümmel, sugar, and lemon juice into tall 14-oz. glass. Stir until sugar dissolves. Add splash of soda and enough ice to fill glass. Stir. Add cucumber peel.

YUCATAN TONIC

1½ ozs. tequila
½ oz. crème de cassis
½ lime
Iced tonic water

Fill a tall 10-oz. glass with ice cubes. Add tequila and crème de cassis. Stir well. Squeeze lime over drink and drop into glass. Stir. Fill with tonic water.

PICNIC COOLERS

The following nine drinks are planned for serving from the tailgate, whether it's a day in the dunes, at the dockside, or near a shady grove. All nine are designed for picnic jugs. Soda, rocks, etc., should be taken in insulated containers.

BITTER BOURBON
(6 drinks)

7½ ozs. bourbon
5 ozs. orange juice
1½ ozs. peppermint schnapps
1 teaspoon Angostura bitters
Iced tonic water

Shake bourbon, orange juice, peppermint schnapps, and bitters well with ice. Strain into prechilled picnic jug. Serve over rocks in 10-oz. glass. Add tonic water.

BLACK CURRANT COOLER
(6 drinks)

9 ozs. blended whiskey
3 ozs. crème de cassis
7 ozs. lemon juice
7 ozs. orange juice
Iced club soda

Combine—but do not mix with ice—whiskey, crème de cassis, lemon juice, and orange juice. Chill in refrigerator. Pour into prechilled picnic jug. Serve over rocks in 10-oz. glass. Add splash of soda.

CARTHUSIAN CUP
(6 drinks)

1 fifth iced dry white wine
6 ozs. chilled orange juice
3 ozs. chilled yellow
    Chartreuse

Iced club soda
6 slices orange

Pour orange juice and Chartreuse into prechilled picnic jug. Carry iced dry white wine in another insulated container. Pour 1½ ozs. orange juice–Chartreuse mixture into 12-oz. glass. Add 4 ozs. wine and about 2 ozs. soda. Add ice cubes to fill each glass. Stir lightly. Add orange slice.

CELTIC CUP
(6 drinks)

9 ozs. Scotch
1½ ozs. cherry-flavored
    brandy

1½ ozs. sweet vermouth
1½ ozs. lemon juice
Iced club soda

Shake Scotch, cherry-flavored brandy, vermouth, and lemon juice well with ice. Strain into prechilled picnic jug. Serve over rocks in 10-oz. glass. Add splash of soda.

ICED COFFEE OPORTO
(6 drinks)

12 ozs. tawny port
6 ozs. brandy

24 ozs. (1½ pints) strong
    black coffee, sweetened
    to taste
Heavy sweet cream

Combine port, brandy, and coffee, and chill in refrigerator. Do not shake with ice. Pour into prechilled picnic jug. At picnic site, divide among six tall 12-oz. glasses, allowing about 7 ozs. for each glass. Add ice cubes to fill glasses. Top with sweet cream and stir. A tall potable that, for some picnickers, takes the place of dessert.

PEACH CUP WITH CHABLIS
(6 drinks)

10-oz. package frozen peaches in syrup
2 ozs. California brandy
3 ozs. lemon juice
1 fifth iced Chablis
Iced club soda

Be sure you have an outsize picnic jug to hold all ingredients. Thaw peaches slightly. Put peaches together with their syrup, brandy, and lemon juice into blender. Blend until smooth. Pour into prechilled picnic jug. Add Chablis. At picnic site, divide contents of jug among six 12-oz. highball glasses. Add several ice cubes to each glass. Add soda. Stir lightly.

RUM AND SOURSOP
(6 drinks)

9 ozs. light rum
6 ozs. lime juice
2 7-oz. cans guanabana nectar
Iced club soda
6 slices lime

Combine rum, lime juice, and guanabana nectar (made from the pulp of the soursop—a delightful tropical fruit—and available in specialty food shops). Chill in refrigerator, but do not shake with ice. Pour into prechilled picnic jug. At picnic site, pour into tall 10-oz. glasses, allowing about 5 ozs. of the chilled mixture for each drink. Add two large ice cubes to each and a splash of soda. Stir. Add lime slice.

RUMBO
(6 drinks)

7 ozs. golden rum
1½ ozs. banana liqueur
3 ozs. lime juice
1½ ozs. orange juice
1½ ozs. guava syrup
6 slices lime

Shake rum, banana liqueur, lime juice, orange juice, and guava syrup well with ice. Strain into prechilled picnic jug. Serve over rocks as a cocktail rather than as a long drink. Garnish with lime slice.

TALL FRENCH GIMLET
(6 drinks)

9 ozs. gin
1½ ozs. Rose's lime juice
1½ ozs. Amer Picon
1½ teaspoons grenadine
Iced tonic water

Shake gin, lime juice, Amer Picon, and grenadine well with ice. Strain into prechilled picnic jug. At picnic site, divide gimlets among six 10-oz. glasses, allowing about 3 ozs. to each glass. Add ice cubes and tonic water. Stir lightly.

Daisies

The daisy, which originated in the mauve decade, is a medium-tall drink served, if possible, in knob glassware, a silver mug, or any vessel that conveys a feeling of sumptuousness. An amalgam of spirits and fruit juice, it is invariably sweetened with a red agent such as grenadine or raspberry syrup and usually topped with a float of some compatible liqueur—a last-minute touch that adds to its subtlety and good humor.

APPLEJACK DAISY

1½ ozs. applejack
½ oz. lime juice
1 teaspoon raspberry syrup
Iced club soda
1 teaspoon ginger-flavored brandy
1 slice lime

Shake applejack, lime juice, and raspberry syrup well with ice. Strain into tall 8-oz. glass half filled with ice. Add soda. Stir. Float ginger-flavored brandy on drink. Add lime slice.

BOURBON DAISY

1½ ozs. bourbon
½ oz. lemon juice
1 teaspoon grenadine
Iced club soda
1 teaspoon Southern
   Comfort
½ slice orange
1 cocktail pineapple stick

Shake bourbon, lemon juice, and grenadine well with ice. Strain into tall 8-oz. glass half filled with ice. Add soda. Stir. Float Southern Comfort on drink. Garnish with orange slice and pineapple stick.

CANADIAN DAISY

1½ ozs. Canadian whisky
½ oz. lemon juice
1 teaspoon raspberry syrup
Iced club soda
1 teaspoon Metaxa brandy
2 fresh or thawed frozen
   raspberries

Shake whisky, lemon juice, and raspberry syrup well with ice. Strain into tall 8-oz. glass half filled with ice. Add soda. Stir. Float Metaxa on drink. Add raspberries.

GIN DAISY

1½ ozs. gin
½ oz. lemon juice
1½ teaspoons raspberry
   syrup
Iced club soda
1 slice lemon
2 sprigs mint

Shake gin, lemon juice, and raspberry syrup well with ice. Strain into tall 8-oz. glass half filled with ice. Add soda. Garnish with lemon slice and mint sprigs.

HAWAIIAN DAISY

1½ ozs. light rum
½ oz. pineapple juice
1 teaspoon lime juice
1 teaspoon grenadine
Iced club soda
1 teaspoon 151-proof rum
1 papaya chunk in syrup

Shake light rum, pineapple juice, lime juice, and grenadine well with ice. Strain into tall 8-oz. glass half filled with ice.

Add soda. Stir. Float 151-proof rum on drink. Add papaya chunk.

WHISKEY DAISY

1½ ozs. blended whiskey
1 teaspoon red-currant
 syrup
½ oz. lemon juice
Iced club soda
1 teaspoon yellow
 Chartreuse
1 slice lemon

Shake whiskey, red-currant syrup, and lemon juice well with ice. Strain into tall 8-oz. glass half filled with ice. Add club soda. Stir. Float Chartreuse on drink. Add lemon slice.

Fixes

Fixes are medium-tall drinks in which the ingredients are "fixed" in the glass itself, which is then packed with crushed or finely cracked ice. As with the cobbler, no club soda or other extender is added, and shaking or straining is unnecessary. The simple fix of liquor, sugar, ice, and a slice of lemon is an heirloom from Victorian drinking days. Modern variations make gloriously refreshing summer libations.

APPLE GINGER FIX

½ teaspoon sugar
1 teaspoon water
1 oz. applejack
1 oz. ginger-flavored brandy
½ oz. lemon juice
1 slice lemon

Dissolve sugar in 1 teaspoon water in an 8-oz. glass. Add applejack, ginger-flavored brandy, and lemon juice. Fill glass with crushed ice. Stir well. Add more ice to fill glass to rim. Stir. Garnish with lemon slice.

BOURBON SLOE-GIN FIX

½ teaspoon sugar
1 teaspoon water
1½ ozs. bourbon
½ oz. sloe gin
½ oz. lemon juice
1 slice lemon
1 slice fresh or brandied peach

Dissolve sugar in 1 teaspoon water in an 8-oz. glass. Add bourbon, sloe gin, and lemon juice. Fill glass with crushed ice. Stir well. Add more ice to fill glass to rim. Stir. Garnish with lemon and peach slices.

BRANDY BERRY FIX

1 teaspoon sugar
2 teaspoons water
2 ozs. brandy
1 teaspoon strawberry liqueur
½ oz. lemon juice
1 slice lemon
1 large strawberry

Dissolve sugar in 2 teaspoons water in an 8-oz. glass. Add brandy, strawberry liqueur, and lemon juice. Fill glass with crushed ice. Stir well. Add more ice to fill glass to rim. Stir. Garnish with lemon slice and strawberry.

CANADIAN BLACKBERRY FIX

1½ ozs. Canadian whisky
½ oz. blackberry-flavored brandy
½ teaspoon sugar
½ oz. lemon juice
1 slice lemon
1 fresh blackberry, if available

Pour whisky, blackberry-flavored brandy, sugar, and lemon juice into tall 8-oz. glass. Stir very well until sugar dissolves. Fill glass with coarsely cracked ice or ice from an ice-tray chipper and stir well. Add ice, if necessary, to fill glass to rim. Stir. Garnish with lemon slice and blackberry.

CHERRY RUM FIX

1 teaspoon sugar
2 teaspoons water
1½ ozs. light rum
½ oz. Peter Heering or
    Cherry Karise
½ oz. lemon juice
1 slice lemon
1 brandied cherry

Dissolve sugar in 2 teaspoons water in an 8-oz. glass. Add rum, Peter Heering, and lemon juice. Fill glass with crushed ice. Stir well. Add more ice to fill glass to rim. Stir. Garnish with lemon slice and cherry.

DERBY RUM FIX

1 teaspoon sugar
2 teaspoons water
2 ozs. light rum
½ oz. lime juice
1 oz. orange juice
1 slice cocktail orange in
    syrup
1 maraschino cherry

Dissolve sugar in 2 teaspoons water in an 8-oz. glass. Add rum, lime juice, and orange juice. Fill glass with crushed ice. Stir well. Add more ice to fill glass to rim. Stir. Garnish with orange slice and cherry.

GIN MINT FIX

1 teaspoon sugar
2 teaspoons water
2 ozs. gin
½ oz. lemon juice
1 teaspoon white crème de
    menthe
2 large mint leaves

Dissolve sugar in 2 teaspoons water in an 8-oz. glass. Add gin, lemon juice, and crème de menthe. Fill glass with crushed ice. Stir well. Add more ice to fill glass to rim. Stir. Tear mint leaves slightly and float on drink.

IRISH FIX

1 teaspoon sugar
2 teaspoons water
2 ozs. Irish whiskey
½ oz. lemon juice
½ slice orange
½ slice lemon
2 teaspoons Irish Mist

Dissolve sugar in 2 teaspoons water in an 8-oz. glass. Add whiskey and lemon juice. Fill glass with crushed ice. Stir well. Add more ice to fill glass to rim. Stir. Garnish with orange and lemon slices. Float Irish Mist on top.

SCOTCH ORANGE FIX

1 teaspoon sugar
2 teaspoons water
3-inch piece orange peel, in one spiral
2 ozs. Scotch
½ oz. lemon juice
1 teaspoon curaçao

Dissolve sugar in 2 teaspoons water in an 8-oz. glass. Place orange peel in glass. Add Scotch and lemon juice. Fill glass with crushed ice. Stir well. Add more ice to fill glass to rim. Stir. Float curaçao on drink.

WHISKEY OUZO FIX

1 teaspoon sugar
2 teaspoons water
2 ozs. blended whiskey
½ oz. lemon juice
1 teaspoon ouzo
Lemon peel

Dissolve sugar in 2 teaspoons water in an 8-oz. glass. Add whiskey and lemon juice. Fill glass with crushed ice. Stir well. Add more ice to fill glass to rim. Stir. Float ouzo on top of drink. Twist lemon peel above drink and drop into glass.

Fizzes

Fizzes are effervescent cooling agents all built on lemon or lime juice and iced club soda. They're designed here for tall 14-ounce glasses, but they can easily be stretched into 16-, 18-, or 20-ounce portions for further appeasement of parched throats.

APRICOT ANISE FIZZ

1¾ ozs. gin	½ oz. lemon juice
½ oz. apricot-flavored brandy	Iced club soda
	½ brandied or fresh apricot
¼ oz. anisette	Lemon peel

Shake gin, apricot-flavored brandy, anisette, and lemon juice well with ice. Strain into tall 14-oz. glass half filled with ice. Fill glass with soda. Stir. Add brandied apricot. Twist lemon peel above drink and drop into glass.

AQUAVIT FIZZ

2½ ozs. aquavit
½ oz. lemon juice
1 teaspoon sugar
½ egg white
1 teaspoon Peter Heering or
   Cherry Karise
Iced club soda
Lemon peel
1 brandied cherry

Shake aquavit, lemon juice, sugar, egg white, and Peter Heering well with ice. Strain into tall 14-oz. glass half filled with ice. Fill glass with soda. Stir. Twist lemon peel above drink and drop into glass. Add brandied cherry.

BAYARD FIZZ

2 ozs. gin
½ oz. lemon juice
2 teaspoons maraschino
   liqueur
1 teaspoon raspberry syrup
Iced club soda
1 slice lemon
2 fresh or thawed frozen
   raspberries

Shake gin, lemon juice, maraschino liqueur, and raspberry syrup well with ice. Strain into tall 14-oz. glass half filled with ice. Fill glass with soda. Stir. Add lemon slice and raspberries.

BLUEBERRY RUM FIZZ

2½ ozs. light rum
1 teaspoon Triple Sec
½ oz. blueberry syrup
¾ oz. lemon juice
Iced club soda
1 slice lemon
3 large fresh blueberries

Shake rum, Triple Sec, blueberry syrup, and lemon juice well with ice. Strain into tall 14-oz. glass half filled with ice. Fill glass with soda. Stir. Add lemon slice and blueberries.

BRANDIED PEACH FIZZ

2 ozs. brandy
½ oz. peach-flavored
   brandy
½ oz. lemon juice
1 teaspoon sugar
1 teaspoon banana liqueur
Iced club soda
1 slice fresh or brandied
   peach

Shake brandy, peach-flavored brandy, lemon juice, sugar, and banana liqueur well with ice. Strain into tall 14-oz. glass half filled with ice. Fill glass with soda. Stir. Garnish with peach slice.

BRANDY MINT FIZZ

2 ozs. brandy
2 teaspoons white crème de
   menthe
1 teaspoon crème de cacao
½ oz. lemon juice
½ teaspoon sugar
Iced club soda
2 large fresh mint leaves

Shake brandy, crème de menthe, crème de cacao, lemon juice, and sugar well with ice. Strain into tall 14-oz. glass half filled with ice. Fill glass with soda. Stir. Tear mint leaves partially and place on top of drink.

CALVADOS FIZZ

2 ozs. calvados
½ oz. lemon juice
1 teaspoon sugar
½ egg white
1 teaspoon heavy cream
Iced club soda
1 slice lime
1 maraschino cherry

Shake calvados, lemon juice, sugar, egg white, and cream well with ice. Strain into tall 14-oz. glass half filled with ice. Fill glass with soda. Stir. Add lime slice and cherry. A fine wintertime fizz while waiting for the roast suckling pig.

CRANBERRY FIZZ

1 oz. cranberry liqueur
1 oz. vodka
¾ oz. lemon juice
½ egg white
1 teaspoon sugar
Iced club soda
1 slice lemon

Shake cranberry liqueur, vodka, lemon juice, egg white, and sugar well with ice. Strain into tall 14-oz. glass half filled with ice. Fill glass with soda. Stir. Add lemon slice.

DANISH GIN FIZZ

1½ ozs. gin
½ oz. Peter Heering or
   Cherry Karise
¼ oz. kirschwasser
½ oz. lime juice
1 teaspoon sugar
Iced club soda
1 slice lime
1 maraschino cherry

Shake gin, Peter Heering, kirschwasser, lime juice, and sugar well with ice. Strain into tall 14-oz. glass half filled with ice. Fill glass with soda. Stir. Add lime slice and cherry. A single round will pave the way for a Danish open-sandwich party.

DUBONNET FIZZ

1 oz. red Dubonnet
1 oz. cherry-flavored
   brandy
1 oz. orange juice
½ oz. lemon juice
1 teaspoon kirschwasser
Iced club soda
1 slice lemon
1 fresh or canned pitted
   black cherry

Shake Dubonnet, cherry-flavored brandy, orange juice, lemon juice, and kirschwasser well with ice. Strain into tall 14-oz. glass half filled with ice. Fill glass with soda. Stir. Add lemon slice and cherry.

FERN GULLY FIZZ

1 oz. dark Jamaica rum
1 oz. light rum
1 oz. pineapple juice
¾ oz. lime juice
1 teaspoon sugar

Iced club soda
1 slice or chunk fresh
   pineapple
1 slice lime

Shake both kinds of rum, pineapple juice, lime juice, and sugar well with ice. Strain into tall 14-oz. glass half filled with ice. Fill glass with soda. Stir. Garnish with pineapple and lime slices.

FRAISE FIZZ

1½ ozs. gin
1 oz. Chambery Fraise
½ oz. lemon juice
1 teaspoon sugar

Iced club soda
Lemon peel
1 large strawberry, sliced in
   half

Shake gin, Chambery Fraise, lemon juice, and sugar well with ice. Strain into tall 14-oz. glass half filled with ice. Fill glass with soda. Stir. Twist lemon peel above drink and drop into glass. Add strawberry. Perfect as an aperitif.

GIN FIZZ

2 ozs. gin
½ oz. lemon juice
1 teaspoon sugar

Iced club soda
1 slice lemon

Shake gin, lemon juice, and sugar well with ice. Strain into tall 14-oz. glass half filled with ice. Fill glass with soda. Stir. Add lemon slice. Brandy, whiskey, rum, or vodka may be used in place of the gin. A 10- or 12-oz. glass may be used instead of the 14-oz., but any diminution in its size only shortens the pleasure of the long, lazy drink implied by a fizz.

GOLDEN GIN FIZZ

2¼ ozs. gin
1 oz. lemon juice
1 egg yolk
2 teaspoons sugar
Iced club soda
1 slice lemon
Freshly ground nutmeg
   (optional)

Shake gin, lemon juice, egg yolk, and sugar well with ice. Strain into tall 14-oz. glass half filled with ice. Fill glass with soda. Stir. Add lemon slice. Sprinkle with nutmeg, if desired.

JAPANESE FIZZ

2¼ ozs. blended whiskey
¾ oz. port
½ oz. lemon juice
1 teaspoon sugar
Iced club soda
Orange peel
1 cocktail pineapple stick

Shake whiskey, port, lemon juice, and sugar well with ice. Strain into tall 14-oz. glass half filled with ice. Fill glass with soda. Stir. Twist orange peel above drink and drop into glass. Add pineapple stick.

MORNING-GLORY FIZZ

2 ozs. Scotch
1 teaspoon Pernod
½ oz. lemon juice
1 teaspoon sugar
½ egg white
1 dash Peychaud's bitters
Iced club soda
1 slice lemon

Shake Scotch, Pernod, lemon juice, sugar, egg white, and bitters well with ice. Strain into tall 14-oz. glass half filled with ice. Fill glass with soda. Stir. Add lemon slice. A drink for the elite of the fizz fraternity.

NEW ORLEANS GIN FIZZ

2½ ozs. gin
1 oz. lemon juice
½ egg white
1 teaspoon heavy cream
¼ teaspoon orange-flower
   water
2 teaspoons sugar
Iced club soda
1 slice lemon

Shake gin, lemon juice, egg white, cream, orange-flower water, and sugar well with ice. Strain into tall 14-oz. glass half filled with ice. Fill glass with soda. Stir. Garnish with lemon slice. A variation of the Ramos gin fizz.

ORANGE FIZZ

2 ozs. gin
1½ ozs. orange juice
½ oz. lemon juice
2 teaspoons Triple Sec
1 teaspoon sugar
2 dashes orange bitters
Iced club soda
1 slice orange

Shake gin, orange juice, lemon juice, Triple Sec, sugar, and bitters well with ice. Strain into tall 14-oz. glass half filled with ice. Fill glass with soda. Stir. Add orange slice.

OSTEND FIZZ

1½ ozs. kirschwasser
½ oz. crème de cassis
½ oz. lemon juice
1 teaspoon sugar
Iced club soda
1 slice lemon

Shake kirschwasser, crème de cassis, lemon juice, and sugar well with ice. Strain into tall 14-oz. glass half filled with ice. Fill glass with soda. Stir. Add lemon slice. Splendid with a summer smorgasbord.

PEACHBLOW FIZZ

2 ozs. gin
½ oz. strawberry liqueur
½ oz. lemon juice
½ teaspoon sugar
1 teaspoon heavy cream
Iced club soda
1 slice lemon
1 large fresh strawberry

Shake gin, strawberry liqueur, lemon juice, sugar, and cream well with ice. Strain into tall 14-oz. glass half filled with ice. Fill glass with soda. Stir. Garnish with lemon slice and strawberry. A classic old fizz—and a semantic mystery, since there's no peach in the recipe—but a joy for parched throats.

PEPPERMINT SCHNAPPS FIZZ

1 oz. peppermint schnapps
1½ ozs. gin
1 teaspoon sugar
1 oz. lemon juice
Iced club soda
1 slice lemon
1 sprig mint

Shake peppermint schnapps, gin, sugar, and lemon juice well with ice. Strain into tall 14-oz. glass half filled with ice. Add soda. Stir. Add lemon slice and mint sprig.

RAMOS GIN FIZZ

2 ozs. gin
1 egg white
½ oz. heavy cream
2 teaspoons sugar
½ oz. lemon juice
¼ oz. lime juice
½ teaspoon orange-flower water
1 cup crushed ice
Iced club soda

Put gin, egg white, cream, sugar, lemon juice, lime juice, orange-flower water, and crushed ice into blender. Blend at high speed 5 seconds. Pour into tall 14-oz. glass. Add enough club soda to fill glass. Stir. In the old days, no New Orleans bartender would think of serving a Ramos gin fizz if the drink hadn't been shaken at least 5 minutes. The electric blender does a better job in 5 seconds.

ROYAL GIN FIZZ

2¼ ozs. gin
1 oz. lemon juice
1 whole egg
2 teaspoons sugar
Iced club soda
1 slice lemon

Shake gin, lemon juice, egg, and sugar well with ice. Strain into tall 14-oz. glass half filled with ice. Fill glass with soda. Stir. Add lemon slice.

RUM COCONUT FIZZ

2¼ ozs. light rum
½ oz. cream of coconut
½ oz. lime juice
Iced club soda
1 slice lime

Shake rum, cream of coconut, and lime juice well with ice. Strain into tall 14-oz. glass half filled with ice. Fill glass with soda. Stir. Add lime slice. Sip while the teriyaki is browning over the charcoal.

RUM PINEAPPLE FIZZ

2 ozs. golden rum
½ oz. 151-proof rum
⅓ cup fresh pineapple, small dice
½ egg white
2 teaspoons sugar
½ oz. lemon juice
½ oz. lime juice
½ cup crushed ice
Iced club soda
1 slice lime

Put both kinds of rum, pineapple, egg white, sugar, lemon juice, lime juice, and ice into blender. Blend at low speed 10–15 seconds. Pour into tall 14-oz. glass. Add ice cubes to almost fill glass. Add a splash of soda and lime slice.

SLOE GIN FIZZ

1 oz. sloe gin (creamy cap)
1 oz. gin
¾ oz. lemon juice
Iced club soda
1 slice lemon

Shake sloe gin, gin, and lemon juice well with ice. Strain into tall 14-oz. glass half filled with ice. Fill glass with soda. Stir. Add lemon slice.

TEQUILA FIZZ

2 ozs. tequila
1½ ozs. lemon juice
2 teaspoons sugar
2 dashes Angostura bitters
1 small egg
Iced club soda
Salt

Shake tequila, lemon juice, sugar, bitters, and egg well with ice. Strain into tall 14-oz. glass half filled with ice. Fill glass with soda. Stir. Sprinkle very lightly with salt.

WHISKEY CURAÇAO FIZZ

2 ozs. blended whiskey
½ oz. curaçao
1 teaspoon sugar
1 oz. lemon juice
Iced club soda
½ slice orange

Shake whiskey, curaçao, sugar, and lemon juice well with ice. Strain into tall 14-oz. glass half filled with ice. Fill glass with soda. Stir. Add orange slice.

Rickeys

The first time you try a rickey, your reaction may be the same kind of shudder you get with the first taste of Campari or Greek olives. But the instant shock of pleasure to a heat-weary body will draw you back again and again. Rickeys are made without sugar.

The word *rickey* evokes an immediate association with gin. But the gin rickey—though it's a justifiably renowned classic among warm-weather coolers—is only one among a multitude of these refreshingly effervescent lime libations. Other rickeys can be made by substituting other liquors for gin. Bourbon, blended whiskey, Canadian whisky, Scotch, apple brandy, vodka, and rum all make interesting and refreshing rickeys. But more imaginative rickeys may be created, too, as witnessed by these tried and tested formulas.

APPLE RUM RICKEY

¾ oz. applejack
¾ oz. light rum
¼ large lime

Iced club soda
Orange peel

Put three ice cubes into an 8-oz. glass. Add applejack and rum. Squeeze lime above drink and drop into glass. Add soda. Stir. Twist orange peel above drink and drop into glass.

AQUAVIT RICKEY

1½ ozs. aquavit
1 teaspoon extra-dry kümmel
¼ large lime
Iced club soda

Put three ice cubes into an 8-oz. glass. Add aquavit and kümmel. Squeeze lime above drink and drop into glass. Add soda. Stir.

FINO RICKEY

¾ oz. very dry (fino) sherry
¾ oz. gin
¼ large lime
Iced club soda

Put three ice cubes into an 8-oz. glass. Add sherry and gin. Squeeze lime above drink and drop into glass. Add soda. Stir. Serve with something salty, such as a bowl of assorted stuffed olives or anchovy canapés.

GIN RICKEY

1½ ozs. gin
¼ large lime
Iced club soda

Put three ice cubes into an 8-oz. glass. Add gin. Squeeze lime above drink and drop into glass. Add soda. Stir.

KIRSCH RICKEY

1½ ozs. kirschwasser
¼ large lime
Iced club soda
2 large fresh or canned pitted black cherries

Put three ice cubes into an 8-oz. glass. Add kirschwasser. Squeeze lime above drink and drop into glass. Add soda. Stir. Cut fresh cherries in half, remove pits, and fasten halves to cocktail spear; or fasten canned cherries to spear. Place spear across glass.

OUZO COGNAC RICKEY

1 oz. ouzo	¼ large lime
1 oz. cognac	Iced club soda

Put three ice cubes into an 8-oz. glass. Add ouzo and cognac. Squeeze lime above drink and drop into glass. Add soda. Stir. Ouzo has a delightful but forceful flavor, and cognac is one of the few liquors that can stand up to it and live compatibly with it in the same drinking glass. A plate of freshly toasted, salted almonds on the side really brings the ouzo-cognac combination into proper perspective.

PEAR RICKEY

1½ ozs. dry pear brandy	Iced club soda
(Birnebrande)	2 wedges fresh ripe pear
¼ large lime	

Put three ice cubes into an 8-oz. glass. Add pear brandy. Squeeze lime above drink and drop into glass. Add soda. Stir. Fasten the pear slices to a cocktail spear and place across rim of glass. Munch pear piecemeal while you drink.

PLUM RICKEY

1½ ozs. plum brandy	¼ large lime
(quetsch, mirabelle,	Iced club soda
or slivovitz)	3 wedges fresh ripe plum

Put three ice cubes into an 8-oz. glass. Add plum brandy. Squeeze lime above drink and drop into glass. Add soda. Stir. Fasten the plum slices to a cocktail spear and place across the rim of glass.

RASPBERRY RICKEY

1½ ozs. Himbeergeist
¼ large lime
Iced club soda
3 fresh or thawed frozen raspberries

Put three ice cubes into an 8-oz. glass. Add Himbeergeist. Squeeze lime above drink and drop into glass. Add soda. Stir. Float frozen raspberries on drink or fasten fresh raspberries to cocktail spear as garnish.

TEQUILA RICKEY

1½ ozs. tequila
¼ large lime
Iced club soda
Salt
1 sliced cocktail orange in syrup

Put three ice cubes into an 8-oz. glass. Add tequila. Squeeze lime above drink and drop into glass. Add soda. Stir. Sprinkle lightly with salt. Fasten orange slice to cocktail spear. Munch it before or after each swallow.

Sangarees

Sangarees are slightly sweet lowball drinks on the rocks. Unlike an old-fashioned, the sangaree contains no bitters. Each drink receives a benediction of freshly grated nutmeg and should be very well stirred for proper dilution.

APPLE GINGER SANGAREE

1½ ozs. apple brandy
½ oz. green-ginger wine
1 slice lemon
Freshly grated nutmeg

Pour apple brandy and ginger wine over rocks in old-fashioned glass. Stir. Add lemon slice. Sprinkle lightly with nutmeg.

BRANDY SANGAREE

½ teaspoon sugar
Iced club soda
2 ozs. brandy
1 teaspoon Madeira
Orange peel
Freshly grated nutmeg

Stir sugar and 1 tablespoon soda in prechilled old-fashioned glass until sugar dissolves. Add brandy and Madeira. Add ice to rim of glass. Stir. Add a splash of soda. Stir. Twist orange peel above drink and drop into glass. Sprinkle lightly with nutmeg.

CRANBERRY SANGAREE

1 oz. cranberry liqueur	Orange peel
1 oz. U.S. blended whiskey	Freshly grated nutmeg

Fill old-fashioned glass with ice cubes. Pour cranberry liqueur and whiskey into glass. Stir well. Sprinkle with nutmeg. Twist orange peel over glass and drop into drink.

IRISH CANADIAN SANGAREE

1¼ ozs. Canadian whisky	1 teaspoon lemon juice
½ oz. Irish Mist liqueur	Freshly grated nutmeg
1 teaspoon orange juice	

Pour whisky, Irish Mist, orange juice, and lemon juice into prechilled old-fashioned glass. Stir. Add ice to rim of glass. Stir. Sprinkle lightly with nutmeg.

SANGAREE COMFORT

1 oz. bourbon	½ teaspoon sugar
1 oz. Southern Comfort	Iced club soda
1 teaspoon lemon juice	Freshly grated nutmeg
1 teaspoon peach-flavored brandy	

Stir bourbon, Southern Comfort, lemon juice, peach-flavored brandy, and sugar in prechilled old-fashioned glass. Add ice to rim of glass. Add splash of soda. Stir. Sprinkle lightly with nutmeg.

SCOTCH SANGAREE

½ teaspoon honey
Iced club soda
2 ozs. Scotch

Lemon peel
Freshly grated nutmeg

Stir honey, 1 tablespoon soda, and Scotch in prechilled old-fashioned glass until honey dissolves. Add ice to rim of glass. Add a splash of soda. Stir. Twist lemon peel above drink and drop into glass. Sprinkle lightly with nutmeg.

ODDBALLS

This chapter contains drinks that, like some of those who drink them, refuse to be classified in conventional categories. But each of the offbeat offerings that follow has a special appeal that sets it apart as a perfect potation to please that special someone or to make a fête more festive: the creamy smoothness of a sherry flip sipped next to a blazing fire; the reviving effects of an eye-opening pick-me-up the mornin' after a long night; the crowning touch that a mist adds to any dinner. The only thing these drinks have in common—with those we've already discussed as well as with one another—is their excellence as libations for discriminating drinkers.

Flips

Flips, like pousse-cafés and frappés, prove that good liquids often come in small glasses. A flip is simply a liquor or wine with egg and sugar, shaken to a gay froth. Flips are rich; too much egg makes them overrich. Thus, for each drink it's best to use a small pullet-size egg, or one large egg for two flips. A classic brandy flip, for instance, is made like this: 2 ounces brandy, 1 small egg, 1 teaspoon sugar are shaken with plenty of ice, strained into a Delmonico glass, then lightly topped with freshly grated nutmeg. Following the same pattern, standard flips are made by substituting whiskey, gin, rum, applejack, port, sherry, or Madeira for the brandy.

The following snug comforts are for winter holidays, mornings after, and long, carefree brunches near a glowing fireplace.

BRANDIED APRICOT FLIP

1 oz. brandy
1 oz. apricot-flavored brandy
1 small egg
1 teaspoon sugar
Grated nutmeg

Shake brandy, apricot-flavored brandy, egg, and sugar well with ice. Strain into prechilled Delmonico glass. Sprinkle with nutmeg.

CARAWAY FLIP

1½ ozs. aquavit
½ oz. lemon juice
½ oz. orange juice
1 small egg
2 teaspoons sugar
Grated nutmeg

Shake aquavit, lemon juice, orange juice, egg, and sugar extremely well with ice. Strain into 6-oz. glass. Sprinkle with nutmeg.

COFFEE FLIP

1 oz. cognac
1 oz. tawny port
1 small egg
1 teaspoon sugar
Grated nutmeg

Shake cognac, port, egg, and sugar well with ice. Strain into prechilled Delmonico glass. Sprinkle with nutmeg.

CRANBERRY FLIP

1 oz. cranberry liqueur
1 oz. California brandy
1 small egg
Grated nutmeg

Shake cranberry liqueur, brandy, and egg extremely well with ice. Strain into prechilled Delmonico glass. Sprinkle with nutmeg.

MADEIRA MINT FLIP

1½ ozs. Madeira
1 oz. chocolate-mint liqueur
1 small egg
1 teaspoon sugar
Grated nutmeg

Shake Madeira, chocolate-mint liqueur, egg, and sugar well with ice. Strain into prechilled Delmonico glass. Sprinkle with nutmeg.

PERNOD FLIP

1 oz. Pernod
½ oz. Cointreau
2 teaspoons lemon juice
1 small egg
1 teaspoon sugar
Grated nutmeg

Shake Pernod, Cointreau, lemon juice, egg, and sugar well with ice. Strain into prechilled Delmonico glass. Sprinkle with nutmeg.

SPICED APPLE FLIP
(2 drinks)

3 ozs. applejack
1 egg
1 tablespoon sugar
2 teaspoons lemon juice
⅛ teaspoon ground cloves
⅛ teaspoon ground cinnamon
Grated nutmeg

Shake applejack, egg, sugar, lemon juice, cloves, and cinnamon with ice. Strain into prechilled whiskey-sour glasses. Sprinkle with nutmeg.

STRAWBERRY RUM FLIP

1 oz. strawberry liqueur
1 oz. light rum
1 teaspoon lemon juice
1 small egg
1 teaspoon sugar
Grated nutmeg

Shake strawberry liqueur, rum, lemon juice, egg, and sugar well with ice. Strain into prechilled Delmonico glass. Sprinkle with nutmeg.

STREGA FLIP

1 oz. Strega
1 oz. brandy
½ oz. orange juice
1 teaspoon lemon juice
1 small egg
1 teaspoon sugar
Grated nutmeg

Shake Strega, brandy, orange juice, lemon juice, egg, and sugar well with ice. Strain into prechilled Delmonico glass. Sprinkle with nutmeg.

TOKAY FLIP

2½ ozs. imported Tokay
   wine (Tokaji Aszu)
1 teaspoon sugar

1 small egg
Grated nutmeg

Shake Tokay, sugar, and egg well with ice. Strain into pre-chilled Delmonico glass. Sprinkle with nutmeg. It may cause another Hungarian revolution to suggest that the magnificent imported Tokay be turned into a flip. Actually the wine turns into sweet bliss.

Mists

A mist is simply straight liquor poured over crushed ice. The normal proportions are 1½ ounces of liquor poured into an 8-ounce old-fashioned glass filled with crushed ice. Sometimes a twist of lemon is added. Mists are cousins of frappés, which are sweet liqueurs poured over crushed ice. Actually, the large amount of fine ice in a mist doesn't befog the liquor's intrinsic flavor; the quality of a fine whiskey in a mist will seem more vivid than the same shot bolted straight down. We now draw the veil from ten of the best-known mists.

Brandy Mist. The triumphant flavor of cognac makes the non-Cognac brandies seem pallid by comparison. (In mixed drinks the story may be different.) Metaxa, the Greek semisweet brandy, creates a velvety, tremulous mist.

Scotch Mist. Best when made with a full-bodied twelve-year-old Highland dew. When it comes to mists, some of the lighter Scotches turn into ordinary fog.

Vodka Mist. Ice and vodka emerge as just ice and vodka, nothing more; but an added dram of dry vermouth (a mere teaspoon or so) and a twist of lemon turn the mist into an instant vodka martini. Zubrovka vodka makes a subtle mist.

Kirschwasser Mist. A happy, silvery mist with a hauntingly dry aftertaste of cherries.

Bourbon Mist. Either 86 or 100 proof is fine, but more important than proof is a quality aged bourbon with a smooth, ripe flavor. Half bourbon and half Southern Comfort create a heavenly mist.

Rye Mist. One of the best ways of appreciating genuine straight rye.

Blended U.S. Whiskey Mist. As in bourbon, smoothness shows up in the very first sip. A slice of lemon is a pleasant garnish.

Canadian Mist. Use top Canadian whisky, but increase portion to 1¾ ounces to keep the cool north-country flavor from dissipating too soon.

Gin Mist. It's surprising how close a gin mist is to the modern martini. Add a tiny splash of dry vermouth for a martini mist. A good way to introduce Dutch genever gin to someone who's never tasted it is via the mist.

Rum Mist. The potent flavors of Martinique and Jamaica rums emerge beautifully in mists. Light rum is extremely pleasant with a slice of lime or a small gardenia as garnish. For a more rummy accent, float a teaspoon of 151-proof rum on a light-rum mist.

Pick-Me-Ups

The ancient Egyptians thought that boiled cabbage would prevent a big head after an all-night drinking session. A ground swallow's beak blended with myrrh was recommended by the Assyrians. In South America, the Warau Indian women took care of their overindulgent males by deftly tying them like mummies in hammocks until their hangovers passed. In this country the "hair of the dog"—the very thing that caused you to see double—may be the shot in the arm that will straighten your sight. For generations, experienced barmen, especially in men's clubs, where hangover victims can be observed and treated at close range, have vouched for the hair-of-the-dog therapy. Naturally, the danger of taking a swig of liquor the morning after is that the stimulus and relief it brings may provide just enough narcosis to set you right back on the rocky road to ruin. Nevertheless, the effect of a small amount of liquor, especially if combined with citrus juice or tomato juice, seems in many cases to have an extremely salutary effect. The following are from PLAYBOY's repertory of classic and modern pick-me-ups.

CANADIAN STAVE

2 ozs. Canadian whisky
1 oz. red Dubonnet
½ egg white
¼ teaspoon Angostura bitters
2 teaspoons lemon juice
2 dashes Tabasco sauce

Shake all ingredients well with ice. Strain into prechilled old-fashioned glass. Add ice cubes to fill glass. Stir well.

CLAM JUICE COCKTAIL

4 ozs. clam juice
½ oz. catsup
¼ oz. lemon juice
1 dash Worcestershire sauce
Salt and pepper
Celery salt

Shake clam juice, catsup, lemon juice, Worcestershire sauce, salt, and pepper well with ice. Strain into prechilled Delmonico glass. Sprinkle with celery salt. Nonalcoholic but a wonderful bracer.

COGNAC COUPLING

2 ozs. cognac
1 oz. tawny port
½ oz. Pernod
1 teaspoon lemon juice
½ teaspoon Peychaud's bitters

Shake well with ice. Strain into prechilled old-fashioned glass. Add ice cubes to fill glass. Stir well.

FRENCH PICK-ME-UP

1½ ozs. Pernod
1 oz. cognac
1 small egg
½ oz. lemon juice
2 teaspoons sugar
Freshly grated nutmeg

Shake Pernod, cognac, egg, lemon juice, and sugar extremely well with ice. Strain into 8-oz. glass. Sprinkle with nutmeg. Fine tranquilizer for the moaning after.

GIN BRACER

2 ozs. gin
½ oz. catsup
½ oz. lemon juice
1 dash Tabasco sauce
1 dash celery salt
¼ teaspoon Worcestershire sauce
1 cup crushed ice

Put all ingredients into blender. Blend at low speed 15–20 seconds. Pour into tall 10-oz. glass. Add ice cubes to fill glass.

MORNING FIZZ

2 ozs. blended whiskey
½ egg white
½ oz. lemon juice
1 teaspoon sugar
½ teaspoon Pernod
Iced club soda

Shake whiskey, egg white, lemon juice, sugar, and Pernod well with ice. Strain into tall 8-oz. glass. Add a splash of soda and enough ice to fill glass. Stir.

ORANGE WAKE-UP

4 ozs. cold freshly squeezed orange juice
½ oz. cognac
½ oz. light rum
½ oz. sweet vermouth
1 slice orange

Pour all liquid ingredients into a squat 8-oz. glass. Add ice cubes to fill glass almost to rim. Stir well. Add orange slice.

POLYNESIAN PICK-ME-UP

½ cup pineapple juice
1½ ozs. vodka
½ teaspoon curry powder
½ teaspoon lemon juice
1 tablespoon heavy sweet cream
2 dashes Tabasco sauce
½ cup crushed ice
Cayenne pepper

Put pineapple juice, vodka, curry powder, lemon juice, cream, Tabasco sauce, and crushed ice into blender. Blend

10 seconds at high speed. Pour into prechilled old-fashioned glass. Dust very lightly with cayenne.

PRAIRIE OYSTER

1½ ozs. cognac
2 teaspoons cider vinegar
½ oz. Worcestershire sauce
1 teaspoon catsup
½ teaspoon Angostura
 bitters
1 egg yolk
Cayenne pepper

Shake cognac, vinegar, Worcestershire sauce, catsup, and bitters well with ice. Strain into prechilled old-fashioned glass. Add an ice cube or two to fill glass almost to rim. Place egg yolk on top of drink without breaking it. Sprinkle yolk lightly with cayenne. This oldest and most stunning of all morning-after drinks should be swallowed in one long, determined gulp. Grit your teeth. Then open your eyes very slowly.

RUDDY MARY

1½ ozs. aquavit
½ cup tomato juice
1 tablespoon heavy sweet
 cream
1 dash Tabasco
½ egg yolk
¼ oz. lemon juice
¼ oz. catsup
½ cup crushed ice

Put all ingredients into blender. Blend at high speed 20 seconds. Pour into old-fashioned glass. When foam settles, add ice to fill glass to rim.

THE BRIMMING BOWL

In the world of entertaining, there is no more delightfully flexible potable than a good punch. This protean party favorite can assume any festive task to which it's put. Made with light Moselle or Rhenish wines, it can beguile your guests with a light, delicate flavor that rests easily on the tongue. Switch to the heavier-duty brandies and rums and it can single-handedly catalyze jolly high spirits and flowing conversation.

Nevertheless, for some time the punch bowl was trotted out only at the year-end saturnalia, when it was filled with a hot wassail or a rich whiskey eggnog, emptied a few times, and then stashed away in dry storage for the next twelve months. But today more and more hosts are reviving the reigns of the four Georges of England, when men like David Garrick and Samuel Johnson vied with each other all year round to invent newer and stronger punch recipes as they ladled their way through clubs and taverns all over England, and when punch bowls in numerous shapes and sizes sparkled invitingly and were the center of conviviality at celebrations of everything from weddings to military triumphs.

Now, as then, there are a few punch recipes in which fruit has to be marinated in liquors for a day or two, but—happily—those are the exceptions. Generally, an hour or so is all you need for ripening the strong and the weak, the tart and the sweet into a really superior punch. And yet, for all its simplicity, the punch bowl, with its gleaming island of ice in a sea of liquor, turns any casual affair into a gala occasion. The mere sight of the brimming bowl seems an irresistible enticement to drinkers of all persuasions, be they light, moderate, or heavy.

Punch is made cold in two ways: by prechilling all the ingredients from the brandy to the bitters, and by placing a floating island of ice in the bowl itself to both cool and properly dilute the liquid—though a few cold punches, such as some of the champagne varieties, aren't diluted with ice but instead are sometimes ice-girt in a surrounding vessel of crushed ice. These days, when the iceman no longer cometh, it's sometimes difficult to buy a really good-sized chunk. However, in our age of the cube, this is no particular problem; in fact, cubes are faster in their chilling effect than a block. But to serious punch makers, they are puny craft alongside the traditional icy blockbuster in the punch bowl. You can make your own by simply freezing water in a metal or plastic container, a deep saucepan, or metal mixing bowl. For each gallon of punch, you'll normally need a chunk of ice made with two quarts of water. After freezing, dip the sides of the bowl in warm water for a few seconds and the ice will slide free. The top may form a slight peak and reveal a crack or two, but the inverted iceberg will be smooth and should float serenely.

The punch recipes that follow each make approximately a gallon of potables, enough for eight bibulous guests at three rounds apiece.

APPLE EGG BOWL

12 eggs
½ cup sugar
1 liter applejack
3 quarts milk
1½ cups heavy sweet cream
1 tablespoon vanilla extract
Ground cinnamon

Pour eggs and sugar into blender, and blend at low speed 2 minutes. Pour into punch bowl. Gradually add applejack and beat with wire whip until well blended. Stir in milk, cream, and vanilla. Let mixture ripen in refrigerator at least 1 hour for flavors to blend. Stir well before serving. Serve in punch cups. Sprinkle with cinnamon.

APPLE GINGER PUNCH

25.4-oz. bottle apple brandy, either calvados or applejack
2 ozs. maraschino liqueur
2 ozs. kirsch
1 quart pineapple-grapefruit juice
25.4-oz. bottle green-ginger wine
1 quart plus 1 pint ginger beer or ginger ale
2 red apples
2 yellow apples

Chill all ingredients. Pour all liquids except ginger beer over large block of ice in punch bowl. Stir well. Let mixture ripen 1 hour in refrigerator. Cut unpeeled apples into wedgelike slices, discarding core. Just before serving, pour ginger beer into bowl. Float apple slices on top.

ARTILLERYMEN'S PUNCH

1 liter 86-proof bourbon
9 ozs. light rum
4 ozs. dark Jamaica rum
6 ozs. apricot-flavored brandy
12 ozs. lemon juice
24 ozs. orange juice
1 quart strong black tea
¼ cup sugar

Pour all ingredients over large block of ice in punch bowl. Stir well to dissolve sugar. Let mixture ripen 1 hour in refrigerator before serving.

BARBADOS BOWL

8 medium-size ripe bananas
1 cup lime juice
1 cup sugar
25.4-oz. bottle light rum
8 ozs. 151-proof rum
1 quart plus 12 ozs. pineapple juice
12 ozs. mango nectar
2 limes, sliced

Chill all ingredients except bananas. Cut 6 bananas into thin slices and place in electric blender with lime juice and sugar. Blend until smooth. Pour over block of ice in punch bowl. Add both kinds of rum, pineapple juice, and mango

BERMUDA BOURBON PUNCH

3 tablespoons jasmine tea
  leaves
3 cups boiling water
25.4-oz. bottle bourbon
8 ozs. Madeira
8 ozs. lemon juice
1½ ozs. Pernod
4 ozs. Falernum
1 quart plus 1 pint ginger
  ale
3 lemons, thinly sliced

Pour boiling water over tea leaves. Steep for 5 minutes; strain, cool to room temperature, and chill in refrigerator. Over large block of ice in punch bowl pour tea, bourbon, Madeira, lemon juice, Pernod, and Falernum. Stir well. Let mixture ripen 1 hour in refrigerator. Add ginger ale and sliced lemons. Add several spiced walnuts (recipe below) to each drink after pouring it into punch cup.

SPICED WALNUTS

1 egg white
2 teaspoons cold water
½ lb. shelled walnut halves
1 cup sugar
1 tablespoon ground
  cinnamon
¼ teaspoon ground cloves
⅛ teaspoon ground nutmeg

Beat egg white until slightly foamy but not stiff. Add the water and mix well. Combine egg white and walnuts in a bowl; stir to coat nuts; drain thoroughly in colander to remove excess egg white. In another bowl, combine sugar, cinnamon, cloves, and nutmeg. Preheat oven to 325° F. Dip walnuts, a few pieces at a time, into sugar mixture (they should be coated thoroughly but should not have thick gobs of sugar adhering to them), place them on a greased baking sheet, and bake 20 minutes, or until medium brown. Remove from baking sheet with spatula, separating them from sugar coating on pan. Cool to room temperature.

BLACK-CHERRY RUM PUNCH

25.4-oz. bottle light rum
4 ozs. 151-proof rum
4 ozs. dark Jamaica rum
2 17-oz. cans pitted black cherries in heavy syrup
8 ozs. fresh lemon juice
4 ozs. fresh orange juice
4 ozs. fresh lime juice
8 ozs. Peter Heering
8 ozs. crème de cassis
2 limes, thinly sliced
1 quart chilled club soda

Put all ingredients except soda into punch bowl. Add block of ice. Stir well. Refrigerate 1 hour. Add soda. Stir well.

BRANDY EGGNOG BOWL

12 eggs
½ cup sugar
25.4-oz. bottle cognac or non-Cognac brandy
4 ozs. Jamaica rum
3 quarts milk
8 ozs. heavy cream
Grated nutmeg

Carefully separate egg yolks from whites. In punch bowl, combine egg yolks and sugar. Beat well with a wire whisk. Gradually add cognac, rum, milk, and cream. Beat well. Taste. Add more sugar if desired. Place the bowl in the refrigerator for at least 2 hours. Just before serving, beat egg whites in a separate bowl or in mixer, in two batches if necessary, until stiff. Fold whites into punch; that is, do not mix them with a round-the-bowl movement but use the wire whisk in a down-over-up stroke until whites are thoroughly blended. Ladle into cups. Sprinkle with nutmeg.

CAPE COD CRANBERRY PUNCH

2 quarts plus 6 ozs. cranberry juice
1 liter 100-proof vodka
6 ozs. cherry liqueur
1 tablespoon orange-flower water
24 ozs. orange juice
1 teaspoon ground cinnamon
½ teaspoon ground allspice
¼ teaspoon ground nutmeg
2 limes, thinly sliced

Chill all liquid ingredients. Mix cinnamon, allspice, and nutmeg with a small amount of vodka until a smooth, lump-free paste is formed. Pour the paste and all other liquids over large block of ice in punch bowl. Stir well. Refrigerate 1 hour before serving. Float lime slices on top of punch.

CHAMPAGNE BLUES

25.4-oz. bottle blue curaçao
8 ozs. lemon juice
4 25.4-oz. bottles dry champagne
Peel of 2 lemons

Chill all ingredients. Cut lemon peel into strips 1½ to 2 inches long and ¼ inch wide. Pour curaçao and lemon juice into glass punch bowl. Stir well. Add champagne and stir lightly. Float lemon peel, yellow side up, in bowl. Do not use ice in bowl. It may be surrounded by cracked ice, if desired, by placing glass bowl in vessel of larger diameter.

CHAMPAGNE PUNCH WITH KIRSCH

4 25.4-oz. bottles iced brut champagne
5 ozs. iced kirsch liqueur (not dry kirschwasser)
5 ozs. iced oloroso (cream) sherry
4 ozs. iced lemon juice
16 ozs. iced orange juice

Pour all ingredients into prechilled punch bowl. Stir lightly. Bowl may be surrounded by ice in larger bowl, or punch may be made in pitchers surrounded by ice.

CHAMPAGNE PUNCH WITH MARASCHINO

6 ozs. maraschino liqueur
6 ozs. cognac
1 teaspoon orange bitters
2 oranges, thinly sliced
1 lemon, thinly sliced
4 25.4-oz. bottles iced brut champagne

Put maraschino, cognac, orange bitters, and sliced fruit into punch bowl. Let mixture brew about 1 hour in refrigerator. Place large chunk of ice in bowl. Pour champagne over ice. Stir lightly.

CHAMPAGNE SHERBET PUNCH

2 quarts lemon sherbet or lemon ice, frozen very hard

5 25.4-oz. bottles iced brut champagne
1½ teaspoons Angostura bitters

Be sure lemon sherbet has been in freezing section of refrigerator set at the coldest point for at least 1 day. Place lemon sherbet in prechilled punch bowl. Pour champagne over sherbet. Add bitters. Stir. Let mixture ripen in refrigerator for about 15–20 minutes before serving.

EMERALD BOWL

4 25.4-oz. bottles chilled Emerald Riesling
6 ozs. California brandy
6 ozs. apricot-flavored brandy

1½ pints chilled apple juice
16 slices cucumber peel, each 1 inch long and ½ inch wide

Pour Riesling, California brandy, apricot-flavored brandy, and apple juice over large block of ice in punch bowl. Add cucumber peel. Stir. Refrigerate 1 hour.

FISH HOUSE PUNCH I

1½ cups sugar
1 quart cold water (not carbonated water)
25.4-oz. bottle cognac
25.4-oz. bottle golden rum

25.4-oz. bottle Jamaica rum
24 ozs. lemon juice
6 ozs. peach-flavored brandy

A traditionally high-proof punch. Put sugar into punch bowl. Add about 1 cup of the water and stir until sugar is dissolved. Add all other ingredients, including balance of water. Let mixture ripen in refrigerator about 1 hour. Place large chunk of ice in bowl. Ladle punch over ice. Add more cold water if a weaker mixture is desired.

FISH HOUSE PUNCH II

2 12-oz. packages frozen
    sliced peaches, thawed
1 liter golden rum
25.4-oz. bottle cognac
1 pint lemon juice
1 cup sugar
1 quart ice water

Put peaches into blender. Blend 1 minute at high speed. Pour over large block of ice in punch bowl. Add rum, cognac, lemon juice, sugar, and water. Stir well to dissolve sugar. Let punch ripen in refrigerator for about 1 hour before serving. A modern version of the colonial recipe fish house punch I.

FLORENTINE PUNCH

2 25.4-oz. bottles coffee-
    cream Marsala wine
2 25.4-oz. bottles Italian
    rosé wine
1 liter brandy
4 ozs. lemon juice
2 oranges

Chill all ingredients. Pour both kinds of wine, brandy, and lemon juice over large block of ice in punch bowl. Stir well. Refrigerate 1 hour. Cut oranges into thin rounds. Slice in half and float atop punch.

GUAVA MILK PUNCH

2½ quarts milk
1 quart (32 ozs.) guava
    nectar
1 cup light cream
25.4-oz. bottle light rum
6 ozs. golden rum
3 ozs. 151-proof rum
¼ cup sugar
12 1-inch pieces lemon peel
12 1-inch pieces orange peel

Pour all ingredients except lemon and orange peel into punch bowl. Stir very well to dissolve sugar. Add large block of ice, lemon peel, and orange peel. Place bowl in refrigerator 1 hour for flavors to ripen. A good low-proof punch to serve the morning after, either before or with brunch; also pleasant on a lazy afternoon on deck.

INTERPLANETARY PUNCH

25.4-oz. bottle light rum
4 ozs. dark Jamaica rum
12 ozs. peppermint schnapps
1 quart mango nectar
12 ozs. (1½ cups) heavy sweet cream
1 quart orange juice
8 large sprigs mint
1 large ripe fresh mango, if available
6 thin slices orange

Prechill all ingredients including liquors. Place large block of ice in punch bowl. Add both kinds of rum, peppermint schnapps, mango nectar, cream, and orange juice. Stir very well. Tear mint leaves from stems. Peel and cut mango into small slices. (Canned mango may be used in place of fresh; canned fruit, however, will not float.) Cut orange rounds into quarters. Float mint leaves and fruit on punch. Refrigerate 1 hour for flavors to ripen.

IRISH APPLE BOWL

25.4-oz. bottle applejack
16 ozs. blended Irish whiskey
10 ozs. Rose's lime juice
4 limes, sliced thin
2 large red Delicious apples
2 quarts plus 1 pint ginger ale

All ingredients, including spirits, should be prechilled. Apples should be cored, but not peeled, and cut into ½-inch dice. Pour applejack, whiskey, and lime juice over large block of ice in punch bowl. Add lime slices and apples. Stir well. Let mixture ripen in refrigerator 1 hour. Pour cold ginger ale into bowl. Stir lightly.

MOSELLE BOWL

1 very ripe medium-size pineapple
½ cup sugar
12 ozs. Grand Marnier
16 ozs. brandy
4 25.4-oz. bottles Moselle wine
1 quart large ripe strawberries

Cut ends off pineapple, remove shell and all "eyes," and cut lengthwise into four pieces. Cut away hard core from each piece; then cut crosswise into thin pieces. Place pineapple, sugar, Grand Marnier, and brandy in salad bowl or mixing bowl. Marinate, covered, in refrigerator at least 24 hours—48 hours if possible. Pour well-chilled wine into punch bowl with large block of ice. Add pineapple mixture and stir well. Let mixture ripen in bowl ½ hour before serving. Cut stems off strawberries. Cut lengthwise in half and float on punch.

MOUNTAIN RED PUNCH

2 1.5-liter bottles chilled California mountain red wine
4 ozs. amaretto
4 ozs. California brandy
4 ozs. cherry-flavored brandy
1 pint ginger ale
2 ozs. julienne almonds, toasted

Pour wine, amaretto, California brandy, and cherry-flavored brandy over large block of ice in punch bowl. Refrigerate 1 hour. Add ginger ale. Stir lightly. Float almonds on top. (Note: Almonds may be toasted by placing in shallow pan in moderate oven for about 10 minutes; avoid scorching.)

ORANGE ALMOND BOWL

6 ozs. slivered almonds
2 tablespoons melted butter
Salt
18 ozs. blended U.S. whiskey
12 ozs. Danish aquavit
1 quart plus 8 ozs. orange juice
8 ozs. sweet vermouth
1 teaspoon orange bitters
Peel of 2 large California oranges
1½ quarts quinine water

Preheat oven to 375° F. Place almonds in shallow pan or pie plate. Pour butter over almonds, mixing well. Place pan in oven and bake until almonds are medium brown, about 8 to 10 minutes, stirring once during baking. Avoid scorching. Sprinkle with salt. Chill almonds and all other ingredients. Pour whiskey, aquavit, orange juice, vermouth, and bitters over large block of ice in punch bowl. Refrigerate mixture for 1 hour. Cut orange peel into narrow strips about 2 inches long. Pour quinine water into bowl. Stir. Float orange peel and almonds on punch.

PHI BETA BLUEBERRY

25.4-oz. bottle 100-proof vodka
16 ozs. Metaxa brandy
16 ozs. bottled blueberry syrup
12 ozs. lemon juice
2 quarts club soda
2 lemons, thinly sliced
1 pint cultivated blueberries

Chill all ingredients. Pour vodka, Metaxa, blueberry syrup, and lemon juice over large block of ice in punch bowl. Let mixture ripen in refrigerator 1 hour before serving. Pour club soda into bowl and stir. Float lemon slices and blueberries on punch.

POLYNESIAN PUNCH BOWL

25.4-oz. bottle light rum
6 ozs. cream of coconut
1 quart plus 1 cup pineapple juice
3 cups orange juice
8 ozs. sloe gin
5 ozs. peppermint schnapps
1 cup lemon juice
12 thin slices very ripe fresh pineapple
12 thin slices orange
1 pint iced club soda

Pour rum, cream of coconut, pineapple juice, orange juice, sloe gin, peppermint schnapps, and lemon juice into punch bowl. Stir well until all ingredients, particularly cream of coconut, are well blended. Add a large block of ice and pineapple and orange slices, and place in refrigerator for about 1 hour for flavors to ripen. Add soda and stir lightly just before serving.

ROSE PUNCH

3 liters chilled rosé wine
8 ozs. cranberry liqueur
4 ozs. California brandy
16 thin slices ripe fresh
  pineapple
1 quart large ripe
  strawberries
1 pint iced club soda

Pour wine, cranberry liqueur, and California brandy over large block of ice in punch bowl. Add pineapple slices and strawberries. Refrigerate 1 hour. Add iced club soda. Stir lightly.

RUM CUP WITH WHITE WINE
(8–10 punch cups)

25.4-oz. bottle light rum
10 ozs. very dry white wine
1 cup (8 ozs.) orange juice
½ cup (4 ozs.) lime juice
2 ozs. orgeat (almond syrup)
2 ozs. Falernum
2 ozs. Triple Sec
6 slices lime
6 large sprigs mint

Pour all ingredients except lime slices and mint into 2-quart pitcher. Add lime slices and mint. Chill 1 to 2 hours. Fill pitcher almost to rim with ice cubes. Stir very well. Pour into punch cups or 6-oz. fruit-juice glasses.

SANGRIA
(6 servings of 6–8 ozs.)

25.4-oz. bottle light dry red
  wine
1 whole orange
1 ripe Elberta peach,
  peeled and sliced
6 slices lemon
1½ ozs. cognac
1 oz. Triple Sec
1 oz. maraschino liqueur
1 tablespoon or more sugar
  to taste
6 ozs. iced club soda

Cut entire peel of orange in a single strip, beginning at stem end and continuing until spiral reaches bottom of fruit. White part should be cut along with outer peel, so that orange fruit is exposed. Leave peel attached to orange bottom, so that fruit may be suspended in pitcher. Pour wine into glass pitcher. Add peach, lemon, cognac; Triple Sec, maraschino liqueur, and sugar. Stir to dissolve sugar. Carefully place orange in pitcher, fastening top end of peel over rim. Let mixture marinate at room temperature at least 1 hour. Add soda and one tray of ice cubes to pitcher. Stir. (Peach may be omitted if not in season.)

WHISKEY PUNCH

3 cups orange juice
1 cup lemon juice
1 cup sugar
2 lemons, thinly sliced
2 liters blended U.S. whiskey
1 quart iced club soda

Put fruit juices and sugar into punch bowl. Stir until sugar dissolves. Add lemon slices. Place a large chunk of ice in bowl. Add whiskey. Refrigerate 1 hour. Add club soda. Stir. Additional club soda may be added, if desired.

WHITE SANGRIA
(6 servings of 6–8 ozs.)

25.4-oz. bottle dry white wine
1 whole orange
2 slices lemon
2 slices lime
1 oz. cognac
2 tablespoons sugar
1 piece stick cinnamon
8 large strawberries, stems removed, halved
6 ozs. iced club soda

Cut entire peel of orange, following procedure for sangria recipe above. Pour wine into glass pitcher. Add lemon, lime, cognac, sugar, cinnamon, and strawberries. Stir to dissolve sugar. Carefully place orange in pitcher, fastening top end of peel over rim. Let mixture marinate at room temperature at least 1 hour. Add soda and one tray of ice cubes to pitcher. Stir.

WHITE WINE PUNCH

3 liters chilled dry white wine
4 ozs. Triple Sec
4 ozs. kirschwasser
4 ozs. California brandy
8 slices orange
8 slices lemon
1 pint iced club soda

Pour wine, Triple Sec, kirschwasser, and brandy over large block of ice in punch bowl. Add orange and lemon slices. Place bowl in refrigerator 1 hour for flavors to blend. Add club soda. Stir lightly.

HOT CHEER

When hot drinks had to wait on icy weather, the ideal accompaniments for a hot-toddy party were a raging blizzard and a roaring fireplace. They're still picturesque backdrops, but nowadays any cool evening in the fall or winter is reason enough for filling the cups to the brim with grogs and nogs—and not just at the hearthside. Almost any casual brisk-weather get-together—a tailgate party at a football or soccer field, a caravan to the ski country—is perfect for tapping the cordial pleasures of the Thermos. And a demitasse cup filled with a blend of warm blackberry liqueur, cognac, and lemon is the most tranquil joy we can imagine before sinking into an unbroken night's sleep.

Hot drinks should be just warm enough so that the flavors seem to float like the soft clouds on an old silk painting, but not so hot that they burn the lips. Heat them in a saucepan or chafing dish to just short of the boiling point; then turn off the flame and let them cool somewhat before pouring.

One of the oldest bar tools for making drinks hot was the loggerhead—a long iron tool with a cup or ball at one end. In colonial days the cup was used, among other purposes, for melting pitch to be poured upon the crews of attacking naval vessels; those were the days when men at loggerheads weren't kidding. It's now remembered as a fireplace device for the much more advanced purpose of heating rum flips. In time the loggerhead was succeeded by the poker, which serves just as well for those who feel like indulging in a bit of showmanship. Find one that's ash-free—old pokers with the soot of ages upon them aren't nearly as practical as clean ones that have never seen a fireplace—and heat it glowing hot in a normal gas flame. For reviving drinks that have become coolish from standing too long, keep the poker in the flame for at least three minutes before plunging it into the waiting mug.

The recipes that follow require no such fiery baptism (though it may win applause, it won't improve the drinks), nor are they intended to be enjoyed only at a bibbing party. Just as they can be served day or night, indoors or out, in fair weather or foul, they'll be the best of drinking companions with a colorful variety of meals: a warm Danish toddy of aquavit and Peter Heering before a smorgasbord or smørrebrød, a buttered bourbon and ginger before a chafing dish of creamed chicken hash, a blackberry demitasse after an urban luau.

Several of the recipes in this chapter depart from the usual one-drink formula. The reason: For some hot potations the nature of the ingredients makes the preparation of a single drink impractical. The blue blazer, for example, should be prepared for two in order to create a decent blaze. The taste of the gin and jerry becomes unpleasantly eggy unless two are made with each egg. The average *café brûlot* set serves eight, so the *café diable* recipe is for that number. And so on; wherever a recipe makes more than a single drink, it's because careful party and taste testing have shown that the number specified is the minimum for best results. But whichever recipes you try, and for however many people, you'll find that all create warm contentment.

APPLE GROG

1½ ozs. applejack
1 tablespoon brown sugar
4 ozs. water
2 whole allspice
1 cinnamon stick
2-inch strip lemon peel
½ oz. 151-proof rum

Pour applejack, sugar, and water into saucepan. Add allspice and cinnamon. Bring to boiling point, but do not boil.

Pour into preheated mug. Twist lemon peel above mug and drop into drink. Float rum on top (pour it over the back of a tablespoon held along inside of mug). Set rum aflame. Let it burn for about a half minute, then stir to stop flaming. Warn guests not to burn lips on mug (take the first sip with a spoon).

APRICOT TOM AND JERRY

1 egg, white and yolk separated
Salt
⅛ teaspoon ground allspice
⅛ teaspoon ground cinnamon
1½ teaspoons sugar
1 oz. apricot-flavored brandy
1 oz. blended whiskey
1 oz. milk
1 oz. heavy cream
Freshly grated nutmeg

Beat egg yolk until light. Add a pinch of salt and the allspice, cinnamon, and sugar, blending well. Beat white separately in a small, narrow bowl until stiff. Slowly fold yolk into white. Put egg mixture into a 10-oz. tom-and-jerry mug. Heat apricot-flavored brandy, whiskey, milk, and cream until bubbles appear around edge of pan. Do not boil. Pour into mug slowly, stirring as liquid mixture is added. Sprinkle with nutmeg.

BLACKBERRY DEMITASSE

1 oz. blackberry liqueur or blackberry-flavored brandy
1 tablespoon blackberry jelly
½ oz. cognac
½ oz. water
½ teaspoon lemon juice
¼ thin slice lemon

Heat blackberry liqueur, jelly, cognac, water, and lemon juice without boiling. Stir well until jelly is completely dissolved. Pour into demitasse cup. Add lemon slice.

BLUE BLAZER
(Serves 2)

6 ozs. Irish whiskey or
    Scotch
2 tablespoons honey

¼ cup boiling water
Lemon peel

Both nightcap and toast, the blue blazer should be served steaming hot and sipped slowly. (And to create a decent blaze, it should always be made for two.) For mixing it, you need two heavy and rather deep mugs, about 12-oz. capacity. Rinse them with hot or boiling water before mixing the drink. Then pour honey and boiling water into one mug and stir until honey is dissolved. Heat whiskey in a saucepan until it's hot but not boiling. Pour into second mug. Light it. Pour the whiskey—carefully—back and forth between the mugs. The flowing blue-flaming stream will be best appreciated in a dimly lit room. Since a few drams of the blazing whiskey may spill, it's best to pour it over a large silver or china platter. When flames subside, pour the blazer into two thick cut-glass goblets. Twist the lemon peel above the blazer and drop it into the drink. Some bartenders wear asbestos gloves when making a blue blazer.

BUTTERED APPLE GROG

1 oz. apple brandy
1 oz. dry vermouth
2 ozs. apple juice
2 whole cloves
¼ baked apple, fresh or
    canned

1 teaspoon syrup from
    canned baked apple, or
    sugar to taste
1 teaspoon sweet butter
1 slice lemon
Sugar

Heat apple brandy, vermouth, apple juice, and cloves until hot but not boiling. Into an old-fashioned glass or coffee cup put baked apple, butter, and lemon slice. Pour apple-brandy mixture into the glass. Add 1 teaspoon syrup if canned baked apple is used, or add sugar to taste. Stir until butter dissolves.

BUTTERED BOURBON AND GINGER

1½ ozs. bourbon	1 cinnamon stick
1 oz. ginger-flavored brandy	6 ozs. apple juice
1 teaspoon sweet butter	Freshly grated nutmeg

Into a 10-oz. mug or silver tankard, pour bourbon and ginger-flavored brandy. Add butter and cinnamon stick to mug. Heat apple juice to boiling point, but do not boil. Pour into mug. Stir until butter dissolves. Sprinkle with nutmeg.

CAFE DIABLE
(8 demitasse cups)

2½ measuring cups extra-strong fresh black coffee	Grated rind of ½ orange
	5 ozs. cognac
2 cinnamon sticks, broken in half	3 ozs. Grand Marnier
	2 ozs. sambuca (anise-flavored Italian liqueur)
8 whole allspice	
4 whole cardamom seeds, removed from shell	2 tablespoons sugar

In a deep chafing dish or *café brûlot* set, simmer ½ cup coffee, cinnamon sticks, allspice, cardamom seeds, and orange rind about 2 or 3 minutes to release spice flavors, stirring constantly. Add cognac, Grand Marnier, and sambuca. When liquors are hot, set ablaze. Stir with a long-handled ladle or spoon until flames subside. Add balance of coffee and sugar. When *café diable* is hot, ladle or spoon it into demitasse cups. A delightful postprandial drink—but you'd best rehearse it before debuting for guests. Once learned, it's an amiably engaging routine.

COFFEE CAUDLE

6 ozs. freshly brewed coffee	1 teaspoon sugar
1½ ozs. coffee liqueur	½ oz. heavy sweet cream
1 egg yolk	Freshly grated nutmeg

Pour coffee into small saucepan. Place over very low flame. In small mixing bowl, using a small wire whip, beat egg yolk and sugar until frothy. Stir in cream. Stir a few tablespoons hot coffee into egg yolk. Slowly pour egg-yolk mixture into saucepan. Heat over a moderate flame 1 minute, stirring constantly. Remove from flame. Stir in coffee liqueur. Pour into mug. Sprinkle with nutmeg.

CRÈME DE CACAO NIGHTCAP
(Serves 4)

¼ cup heavy cream
2 teaspoons sugar
1 tablespoon crème de cacao
10 ozs. milk
4 ozs. crème de cacao
2 ozs. California brandy
3 tablespoons sugar
Cocoa

Beat cream in small, narrow bowl until whipped. Stir 2 teaspoons sugar and 1 tablespoon crème de cacao into whipped cream. Store in refrigerator until needed. Heat milk, 4 ozs. crème de cacao, brandy, and 3 tablespoons sugar until hot but not boiling. Pour hot milk mixture into four footed whiskey-sour glasses or small goblets. Spoon whipped cream on top. Put a small quantity of cocoa into a small fine wire strainer. Shake strainer above each drink, sprinkling lightly with cocoa. Place glass on saucer for serving.

DANISH TODDY

2 whole cloves
2 whole allspice
1 cinnamon stick
1 slice orange
2 ozs. Peter Heering or
    Cherry Karise
1 oz. aquavit
½ oz. kümmel
5 ozs. cranberry juice

Put cloves, allspice, cinnamon stick, and orange slice into a 10-oz. mug. Heat Peter Heering, aquavit, kümmel, and cranberry juice until hot but not boiling. Pour into mug.

GIN AND JERRY
(Serves 2)

4 ozs. gin
1 oz. yellow Chartreuse
3 ozs. orange juice
1 teaspoon sugar
1 egg
Ground cinnamon

Pour gin, Chartreuse, orange juice, and sugar into saucepan. Heat almost to boiling point, but don't boil. Beat egg in narrow bowl with rotary beater until egg is very light and foamy. Slowly, while stirring constantly, pour hot liquid into bowl. Pour into preheated tom-and-jerry mugs or punch cups. Sprinkle lightly with cinnamon.

HOT BUTTERED APPLE

2 ozs. applejack
½ oz. Stone's ginger wine
4 ozs. water
1 cinnamon stick
2 whole cloves
1 teaspoon sugar
1 teaspoon sweet butter
Freshly grated nutmeg

Pour applejack, ginger wine, and water into saucepan. Add cinnamon, cloves, and sugar. Stir until sugar dissolves. Bring to boiling point, but do not boil. Pour into preheated mug. Add butter and stir until butter melts. Sprinkle with nutmeg.

HOT BUTTERED IRISH

1½ ozs. blended Irish whiskey
½ oz. orange juice
½ oz. lemon juice
4 ozs. water
1 teaspoon sugar
2 dashes Angostura bitters
2 whole cloves
1 teaspoon sweet butter
Lemon peel
Freshly grated nutmeg

Pour whiskey, orange juice, lemon juice, water, sugar, and bitters into saucepan. Add cloves. Heat to boiling point, but do not boil. Pour into preheated mug. Add butter and stir until butter melts. Twist lemon peel above drink and drop into mug. Sprinkle with grated nutmeg.

HOT BUTTERED RUM

2 whole cloves
2 whole allspice
1-inch cinnamon stick
1 teaspoon sugar
1½ ozs. hot light rum
½ oz. hot dark Jamaica rum
Boiling water
1 teaspoon sweet butter

Put the cloves, allspice, cinnamon stick, and sugar into a mug with a tablespoon or two of boiling water. Let the mixture stand 5 minutes. Add the hot rum (both kinds), 2 ozs. boiling water, and butter. Stir until butter dissolves. Add more sugar, if desired.

PLAYBOY'S HOT BUTTERED RUM

2 ozs. dark Jamaica rum
½ teaspoon maraschino liqueur
1 oz. lemon juice
1 teaspoon sugar
1 pat butter, equal to 2 teaspoons
Boiling water
1 slice lemon
Freshly grated nutmeg

Pour rum, maraschino liqueur, and lemon juice into 12-oz. mug. Add sugar and butter. Fill with boiling water. Stir to dissolve butter and sugar. Add lemon slice. Grate nutmeg on top.

HOT COCONUT COFFEE

2 ozs. CocoRibe
6 ozs. strong fresh hot coffee
Whipped cream

Pour CocoRibe and coffee into mug. Add dollop of whipped cream. Because of the sweetness of CocoRibe, sugar is usually not necessary in this drink.

HOT COCORIBE ORANGEADE

2 ozs. CocoRibe
4 ozs. orange juice
2 ozs. water
1 cinnamon stick
½ slice orange

Pour orange juice and water into saucepan. Bring up to a boil, but do not boil. Pour into mug. Add CocoRibe. Stir with cinnamon stick, and leave cinnamon stick in mug. Add orange slice.

HOT DRAMBUIE TODDY

2 ozs. Drambuie
½ oz. lemon juice
1 slice lemon
1 slice orange
4 ozs. boiling water
1 cinnamon stick

Pour Drambuie and lemon juice into preheated mug or punch cup. (To preheat mug, fill with boiling water for about a minute; then discard water.) Add lemon slice, orange slice, and 4 ozs. boiling water. Stir with cinnamon stick, and leave it in the mug.

HOT EGGNOG

1 egg
Salt
1 tablespoon sugar
¾ cup (6 ozs.) hot milk
2 ozs. hot cognac
1 teaspoon dark Jamaica rum
Ground nutmeg

Put whole egg and dash of salt into mixing bowl. Beat egg until it is very thick and lemon yellow in color. Add sugar and beat until sugar is blended in. Add hot milk, cognac, and rum. Stir well. Pour into mug. Sprinkle lightly with a dash of ground nutmeg.

HOT GRAPEFRUIT MUG

4 ozs. unsweetened grapefruit juice
2 ozs. orange juice
1½ ozs. gin
½ oz. rock and rye
1 tablespoon honey
2 teaspoons sweet butter
Freshly ground nutmeg

In saucepan, heat grapefruit juice, orange juice, gin, rock and rye, honey, and 1 teaspoon butter. Bring to boiling point, but do not boil. Pour into warm 10-oz. mug. Add remaining teaspoon butter and stir until butter dissolves. Sprinkle lightly with nutmeg.

HOT IRISH AND PORT

1½ ozs. blended Irish whiskey
3 ozs. tawny port
2 ozs. water
1 cinnamon stick
1 slice orange

Pour whiskey, port, and water into saucepan. Heat to boiling point, but do not boil. Pour into mug. Add cinnamon stick and orange slice. Let drink stand about 3 minutes before serving.

HOT LICORICE STICK

1½ ozs. anisette
6 ozs. orange juice
1 teaspoon butter
1 cinnamon stick
Ground coriander

Pour anisette, orange juice, and butter into saucepan. Heat over moderate flame until butter melts. Do not boil. Pour into mug. Add cinnamon stick. Sprinkle with ground coriander.

HOT LINE

1 oz. light rum
1 oz. dark Jamaica rum
3 ozs. water
2 sugar cubes
2 dashes Angostura bitters
1 teaspoon 151-proof rum
1 slice orange
1 slice lemon

Pour light rum, Jamaica rum and water into saucepan. Heat over moderate flame, but do not allow to boil. Place sugar, bitters, and 151-proof rum in 10-oz. mug. Stir until sugar is dissolved. Hold match to mug for brief flame. Pour heated rum mixture into mug. Add orange and lemon slices.

HOT MOCHA CHOCOLATE

½ square bitter chocolate
6 ozs. milk
1 teaspoon sugar
1 tablespoon heavy sweet cream
2 ozs. coffee liqueur

Place chocolate in saucepan over very low heat. When chocolate is completely melted, slowly stir milk, sugar, and cream into saucepan. Increase heat slightly and stir well with wire whip until all ingredients are blended. Bring up to boiling point, stirring frequently, but do not boil. Remove from heat. Stir in coffee liqueur. Pour into mug.

HOT PORT FLIP

3 ozs. port wine
1 oz. cognac
1 teaspoon sugar
¼ teaspoon instant coffee
1 small egg
1 tablespoon heavy sweet cream
Freshly grated nutmeg

Pour wine and cognac into saucepan. Add sugar. Stir well. Heat, but don't boil. Stir in instant coffee. In a narrow bowl, beat egg with rotary beater until very foamy. Stir in cream. Very slowly, while stirring constantly, pour hot liquid into egg mixture. Pour into preheated mug. Sprinkle with nutmeg.

HOT TODDY

1 teaspoon sugar
3 whole cloves
1-inch cinnamon stick
1 thin slice lemon
3 ozs. boiling water
2 ozs. bourbon
Ground nutmeg

Into a heavy mug, put the sugar, cloves, cinnamon stick, and slice of lemon. Add 1 oz. of the boiling water. Stir well. Let the mixture stand about 5 minutes. Add the bourbon and the remaining 2 ozs. boiling water. Stir. Sprinkle lightly with nutmeg.

IRISH COFFEE

5 or 6 ozs. fresh hot black
    coffee
1½ ozs. Irish whiskey
1 teaspoon sugar
Sweetened whipped cream

Warm a thick 8-oz. goblet or Irish-coffee glass by rinsing it in very hot or boiling water. Pour coffee and whiskey into goblet. Add sugar. Stir until sugar is dissolved. Add generous dab of whipped cream.

IRISH TEA

1½ ozs. blended Irish
    whiskey
6 ozs. freshly brewed hot
    Irish black tea
3 whole cloves
3 whole allspice
1 cinnamon stick
1 teaspoon sugar
2 teaspoons honey
1 slice lemon
Freshly grated nutmeg

Put whiskey, tea, cloves, allspice, cinnamon, sugar, and honey into mug. Stir well. Add lemon slice. Sprinkle with grated nutmeg.

JACK AND JERRY
(4 drinks)

2 eggs, separated
2 tablespoons sugar
1 cup milk
1 oz. heavy sweet cream
1 dash salt
¼ teaspoon ground
    cinnamon
⅛ teaspoon ground mace
⅛ teaspoon ground ginger
8 ozs. applejack
1 pint hot milk
Freshly grated nutmeg

Beat egg yolks and sugar in top part of double boiler until well blended. Slowly stir in 1 cup milk, cream, salt, cinnamon, mace, and ginger. Cook over simmering water, stirring constantly with wire whip, until mixture thickens to the consistency of a light sauce. Remove from fire. Beat egg whites until stiff. Slowly stir cooked mixture into beaten egg whites. Divide among four preheated mugs. Pour 2 ozs. applejack into each mug. Fill mugs with hot milk. Stir. Sprinkle with nutmeg.

KIRSCH NIGHTCAP

1 oz. kirschwasser
3 ozs. Stone's ginger wine
4 ozs. water
1 cinnamon stick
2 whole cloves
1 teaspoon sugar
Lemon peel

Slowly heat ginger wine and water to boiling point, but do not boil. Pour into mug. Add kirschwasser, cinnamon, cloves, and sugar. Stir well. Twist lemon peel above drink and drop into mug.

MEXICAN COFFEE

1 oz. Kahlúa coffee liqueur
4 ozs. fresh hot black coffee
Ground cinnamon
Sweetened whipped cream

Pour liqueur and coffee into Irish-coffee glass. Sprinkle with cinnamon. Stir. Top with whipped cream.

MULLED CLARET
(8 drinks)

1 cup boiling water
½ cup sugar
1 lemon, sliced
1 orange, sliced
16 whole allspice
16 whole cloves
4-inch cinnamon stick
1 liter dry red wine

In large saucepan, combine the boiling water, sugar, sliced lemon, sliced orange, allspice, cloves, and cinnamon stick. Bring to a boil. Reduce flame and simmer 5 minutes. Add the wine. Bring to the boiling point. Do not boil, but simmer 10 minutes. Pour the hot mulled wine into thick glasses or mugs. Place a slice of lemon, a slice of orange, and a few whole spices in each glass.

MULLED KÜMMEL

2 ozs. kümmel
1 oz. vodka
½ oz. lemon juice
1 teaspoon sugar
5 ozs. water
2 teaspoons butter
1 cinnamon stick
1 thin slice lemon
½ slice orange
½ oz. aquavit

In saucepan, stir kümmel, vodka, lemon juice, sugar, water, and 1 teaspoon butter. Heat to boiling point, but do not boil. Place cinnamon stick in warm 10-oz. mug. Pour mulled kümmel into mug, and add remaining teaspoon butter. Stir until butter dissolves. Add lemon and orange slices. Float aquavit on top.

MULLED MADEIRA AND BOURBON

2½ ozs. Madeira
1 oz. bourbon
1 oz. Lillet
¼ teaspoon orange bitters
4 ozs. water
1 tablespoon brown sugar
1 cinnamon stick
2 whole cloves
½ slice lemon
Orange peel

Heat Madeira, bourbon, Lillet, orange bitters, water, and brown sugar until hot but not boiling. Put cinnamon stick, cloves, and lemon slice into 10-oz. mug or metal tankard. Fill mug with Madeira mixture. Twist orange peel above drink and drop into mug.

MULLED PORT

4 ozs. ruby port
1 oz. dark Jamaica rum
4 ozs. water
½ oz. lime juice
1 teaspoon sugar
2-inch piece orange peel
1 long cinnamon stick

Pour port, rum, water, lime juice, and sugar into saucepan. Stir. Bring to boiling point, but do not boil. Pour into mug. Twist orange peel above mug and drop into drink. Add cinnamon stick.

MULLED SCOTCH

2 ozs. hot Scotch
1 oz. hot Drambuie
2 dashes bitters
1 oz. boiling water
1 maraschino cherry
Lemon peel

Into an old-fashioned glass, pour the Scotch, Drambuie, bitters, and boiling water. Stir. Add the cherry. Twist lemon peel above the drink and drop into glass.

MULLED SHERRY

4 ozs. amontillado sherry
2 ozs. orange juice
½ oz. brandy
½ oz. lemon juice
1 to 2 teaspoons sugar
1 teaspoon butter
1 cinnamon stick

Heat sherry, orange juice, brandy, and lemon juice in saucepan over low flame until hot. Do not boil. Pour into mug. Add sugar to taste. Add butter. Stir with cinnamon stick until butter melts. Leave cinnamon stick in mug.

RASPBERRY TEA

7 ozs. freshly brewed hot
    black tea
1 slice lemon
1 cinnamon stick
1½ ozs. raspberry liqueur
Sugar

Pour tea into 10-oz. mug. Add lemon slice, cinnamon stick, and raspberry liqueur. Stir well. Add sugar to taste.

ROCK AND RYE TODDY

2 ozs. rock and rye
2 dashes Angostura bitters
1 slice lemon
3 ozs. boiling water
1 cinnamon stick
Grated nutmeg

Pour rock and rye and bitters into old-fashioned glass. Add lemon slice. Add boiling water and cinnamon stick. Stir. Sprinkle with grated nutmeg.

SCIARADA TEA

1 mug hot black tea
1½ ozs. Sciarada
1 slice lemon
1 cinnamon stick

Pour Sciarada into tea. Add lemon slice. Stir with cinnamon stick. An *après-ski* warmer.

SHERRY CAUDLE

6 ozs. freshly brewed black tea
1 egg yolk
2 teaspoons sugar
2½ ozs. cream sherry (oloroso)
Freshly grated nutmeg

Pour tea into small saucepan. Place over very low flame. In small mixing bowl, using a small wire whip, beat egg yolk and sugar until frothy. Stir a few tablespoons of tea into egg yolk. Slowly pour egg-yolk mixture into saucepan. Heat over a moderate flame 1 minute, stirring constantly. Remove from flame. Stir in sherry. Pour into mug. Sprinkle with nutmeg.

SIMMERING PLUM

5 ozs. hot black tea
2 ozs. plum brandy (slivovitz, quetsch, or mirabelle)
1 oz. white crème de menthe
1 teaspoon sugar or more to taste
½ oz. heavy cream
1 cinnamon stick
Ground coriander

Stir tea, plum brandy, crème de menthe, sugar, and cream in saucepan. Heat to boiling point, but do not boil. Pour into warm 10-oz. mug with cinnamon stick. Stir. Sprinkle coriander on top.

SNOWBERRY

1½ ozs. strawberry liqueur
1 oz. vodka
½ oz. rock-candy syrup, or simple syrup
1 oz. lemon juice
5 ozs. water
½ large strawberry, cut in half lengthwise
1 thin slice lemon
½ oz. kirschwasser

In saucepan, heat strawberry liqueur, vodka, rock-candy syrup, lemon juice, and water to boiling point, but do not boil. Pour into warm 10-oz. mug. Dip strawberry into rock-candy syrup. Float lemon slice, strawberry half, and kirschwasser on drink.

SNOWSHOE

1 oz. aquavit
½ oz. blackberry-flavored brandy
1 mug hot black tea
1 cinnamon stick
Sugar
1 slice lemon

Pour aquavit and blackberry-flavored brandy into tea. Stir with cinnamon stick; leave cinnamon in mug. Add sugar to taste. Add lemon slice.

INDEX

Acapulco	163	Applejack Daisy	318
After-Dinner Charade	83	Applejack Manhattan	117
Alabama	122	Applejack Rabbit	118
Alexander's Sister	139	Applejack Sour	118
Alexander with Coffee	139	Apple Knocker	251
Alexander with Gin	139	Apple Lillet	118
Alexander with Prunelle	140	Apple Rum Rickey	335
Alla Salute!	250	Apple Suissesse	118
Allegheny	205	Apricot and Raspberry Sour	122
All-White Frappé	98	Apricot and Tequila Sour	188
Almond Eye	250	Apricot Anise Fizz	325
Aloha	251	Apricot Cobbler	242
Amaretto Cobbler	242	Apricot Lady	163
Amaretto Cream	83	Apricot Pie	164
Americana	135	Apricot Sour	123
Americano	105	Apricot Tom and Jerry	374
Amer Picon Cooler	251	Aquavit Fizz	326
Andalusia	226	Aquavit Rickey	336
Apple and Ginger	116	Aqueduct	197
Apple Blossom	116	Artillerymen's Punch	358
Apple Brandy Cooler	251	Auld Sod	205
Apple Buck	239		
Apple Byrrh	105	Bacardi	164
Applecar	116	Banana Daiquiri	164
Apple Dubonnet	117	Banana Mango	164
Apple Egg Bowl	357	Banana Rum Frappé	99
Apple Ginger Fix	321	B & B Collins	246
Apple Ginger Punch	358	Banshee	84
Apple Ginger Sangaree	339	Barbados Bowl	358
Apple Grand Marnier	117	Barbados Planter's Punch	252
Apple Grog	373	Bases Filled	222
Applehawk	117	Bastardo	106
Applejack Collins	246	Battering Ram	252

INDEX

Bayard Fizz	326	Bourbonnaise	206
Bayou	123	Bourbon Rumbo	256
Beachcomber	165	Bourbon Sloe-Gin Fix	322
Beachcomber's Gold	165	Brandied Apricot	123
Beaujolais Cup	252	Brandied Apricot Flip	345
Beer Buster	252	Brandied Banana Collins	247
Bee's Knees	165	Brandied Cordial Médoc	124
Belfry Bat	253	Brandied Ginger	124
Bennett	140	Brandied Madeira	226
Berliner	140	Brandied Peach Fizz	327
Bermuda Blanc	222	Brandied Peach Sling	257
Bermuda Bourbon Punch	359	Brandied Port	227
Berries and Cream	84	Brandtini	124
Between the Sheets	165	Brandy Alexander	124
Biscayne	140	Brandy and Amer Picon	125
Bishop's Cocktail	141	Brandy Apricot Frappé	99
Bitter Apple	119	Brandy Berry Fix	322
Bitter Banana Cooler	253	Brandy Buck	240
Bitter Bourbon	314	Brandy Cassis	125
Bitter Bourbon Lemonade	253	Brandy Cobbler	243
Bitter Brandy and Sherry	254	Brandy Crusta	125
Bitter-Lemon Bracer	254	Brandy Eggnog Bowl	360
Bitter-Lemon Cooler	254	Brandy Fino	125
Bitter-Orange Cooler	254	Brandy Gump	126
Bitter Pernod	255	Brandy Manhattan	126
Bitter Planter's Punch	255	Brandy Melba	126
Bittersweet	106	Brandy Mint Fizz	327
Blackberry Demitasse	374	Brandy Mist	349
Black-Cherry Rum Punch	360	Brandy Sangaree	339
Black Currant Cooler	314	Brandy Sour	126
Black Devil	166	Brass Hat	167
Black Hawk	206	Brave Bull	84
Black Russian	197	Bright Berry	222
Blended Comfort	255	Brighton Punch	257
Blended U.S. Whiskey Mist	350	Brittany	141
Blenheim	119	Bronx	142
Blenton	158	Buckeye Martini	198
Bloodhound	158	Buenas Tardes	257
Bloody Maria	188	Bullshot	198
Bloody Mary	198	Bunny Bonanza	189
Bloody Sake	226	Bunny Mother	258
Blue Angel	84	Bushranger	167
Blueberry Rum Fizz	326	Buttered Apple Grog	375
Blue Blazer	375	Buttered Bourbon and Ginger	376
Blue Devil	141	Butterfly	106
Bolero	166	Byrrh Brandy	106
Bolo	166	Byrrh Cassis	107
Bombay	123	Byrrh Cassis Cooler	258
Bonnie Prince	141	Byrrh Cocktail	107
Border Crossing	256		
Borinquen	166		
Bourbon and Madeira Julep	256	Caballo	258
Bourbon Collins	247	Cadiz	85
Bourbon Cream	84	Café Diable	376
Bourbon Daisy	319	Californian	107
Bourbon Manhattan	220	Calm Voyage	85
Bourbon Milk Punch	256	Calvados Fizz	327
Bourbon Mist	350	Calypso Cooler	258

INDEX 393

Canadian and Campari	107	Cherry Vodka	198
Canadian Apple	206	Chico	261
Canadian Blackberry Fix	322	China	168
Canadian Cherry	206	Chiquita	198
Canadian Cocktail	207	Chiquita Punch	86
Canadian Daisy	319	Chocolate Black Russian	86
Canadian Manhattan	220	Chocolate Éclair	86
Canadian Mist	350	Chocolate Mint	87
Canadian Old-fashioned	207	Chocolate Orange Frappé	99
Canadian Pineapple	207	Chocolate Rum	87
Canadian Stave	352	Chocolatier	87
Cape Cod Cranberry Punch	360	Clam Juice Cocktail	352
Caramel Cow	85	Claret Cobbler	244
Cara Sposa	85	Claret Cocktail	227
Caraway Flip	346	Claret Cooler	261
Cardinal I	108	Claret Rum Cooler	262
Cardinal Cocktail II	167	Classic	127
Carib	167	Classic Champagne Cocktail	138
Caribbean Champagne	135	Cloister	142
Caribbean Coffee	259	Clover Club	143
Caribbean Mule	259	Clover Club Royal	143
Caribbean Sling	259	Coco Amor	87
Carthusian Cooler	260	Coco Banana	88
Carthusian Cup	315	Coconut Cooler	262
Casablanca	168	Coconut Cooler in Shell	262
Celtic Cup	315	Coconut Fizz	263
Chablis Cooler	260	Coconut Gin	143
Champagne Blues	361	Coconut Grove	263
Champagne Fraise	136	Coconut Mint	88
Champagne Manhattan	136	Coconut Tequila	189
Champagne Normande	136	Cocoribe Milk Punch	263
Champagne Noyaux	136	Coexistence Collins	247
Champagne Old-fashioned	137	Coffee Caudle	376
Champagne Polonaise	137	Coffee Cooler	264
Champagne Punch with Kirsch	361	Coffee Cream	88
Champagne Punch with Maraschino	361	Coffee Eggnog	264
		Coffee Flip	346
Champagne Sherbet Punch	362	Coffee Grand Marnier	100
Champs-Élysées	127	Coffee Grasshopper	88
Chapala	189	Coffee Milk Punch	264
Chapel Hill	207	Coffee Roiano	88
Chartreuse Champagne	137	Coffee Rum Cooler	264
Chartreuse Cognac Frappé	99	Cognac Coupling	352
Chartreuse Cooler	260	Cognac Menthe Frappé	100
Chatham	142	Cold Gin Toddy	143
Cherry Blossom	127	Cold Irish	265
Cherry Champagne	137	Cold Turkey	265
Cherry Cobbler	243	Columbia	168
Cherry Daiquiri	168	Combo	108
Cherry Ginger Frappé	99	Commodore	208
Cherry Isle	260	Commonwealth	208
Cherry Planter's Punch	261	Conch Shell	169
Cherry Rum	86	Continental	169
Cherry Rum Cobbler	243	Cool Colonel	265
Cherry Rum Cola	261	Cool Guanabana	266
Cherry Rum Fix	323	Cool Jazz	222
Cherry Sling	142	Copenhagen	144
		Cordial Martini	159

394 INDEX

Cordial Médoc	144	8-to-1 Martini	158
Cordial Médoc Cup	266	Elephant's Eye	271
Cordial Médoc Sour	144	El Presidente	171
Corkscrew	169	Emerald Bowl	362
Cranberry Cooler	266	English Mule	271
Cranberry Eye	222	Erin and Sherry	209
Cranberry Fizz	328	Eureka	228
Cranberry Flip	346		
Cranberry Frappé	100		
Cranberry Rum Punch	266	Femina	128
Cranberry Sangaree	340	Fern Gully	171
Cranbourbon	267	Fern Gully Fizz	329
Creamy Charade	89	Finlandia	272
Creamy Irish Screwdriver	208	Fino	109
Creamy Orange	227	Fino Martini	159
Creamy Screwdriver	267	Fino Rickey	336
Crème de Cacao Nightcap	377	Fiord	228
Creole	169	Fish House Punch I	362
Croton	208	Fish House Punch II	363
Cuba Libre	267	Florentine Punch	363
Cuba Libre Cocktail	169	Florida	228
Cucumber Champagne	268	Floridian	109
Cuernavaca Collins	248	Flying Dutchman	159
Culross	170	Flying Grasshopper	199
Curaçao Cooler	268	Foggy Day	144
Currier	209	Fort Lauderdale	171
Cynar Calypso	268	4-to-1 Martini	158
Cynar Screwdriver	268	Foxhound	128
Cynar Sour	108	Fraise Fizz	329
		Framboise Sour	129
Daiquiri	170	French Colonial	272
Dame Melba	127	French Curve	223
Danish Gin Fizz	328	French Foam	272
Danish Toddy	377	French Pick-Me-Up	352
Deauville	128	French 75	272
Deep End	269	Frosty Dawn Cocktail	172
Delta	209	Froupe	129
Derby Daiquiri	170	Frozen Apple	119, 199
Derby Rum Fix	323	Frozen Apple and Banana	119
Devil's Tail	170	Frozen Applecart	120
Diabolo	108	Frozen Apple Daiquiri	172
Double Derby	269	Frozen Aquavit	228
Down Yonder	269	Frozen Banana Daiquiri	172
Dracula	270	Frozen Banana Mint	89
Dry Cold Deck	128	Frozen Berkeley	172
Dry Manhattan	220	Frozen Blackberry Tequila	189
Dry Manhattan Cooler	270	Frozen Black Currant	89
Dry Sherry Collins	248	Frozen Brandy and Port	129
Dubonnet Cocktail	109	Frozen Brandy and Rum	129
Dubonnet Fizz	328	Frozen Coco Banana	90
Dulcet	89	Frozen Daiquiri	173
Dundee	144	Frozen Guava Daiquiri	173
Dutch Pear Frappé	100	Frozen Guava-Orange	
Dutch Treat	227	Daiquiri	173
		Frozen Matador	190
East-West	270	Frozen Mint Daiquiri	173
Eau de Vie Campari	270	Frozen Passion-Fruit	
Eggnog Framboise	271	Daiquiri	174

INDEX 395

Frozen Peach Daiquiri	174	Guava Cooler	276
Frozen Pineapple Daiquiri	174	Guava Milk Punch	363
Frozen Sesame Daiquiri	174	Gypsy	199
Frozen Sherry Daiquiri	229		
Frozen Soursop Daiquiri	175	Habitant Cocktail	210
Frozen Sunset	190	Harvard	130
		Harvey Wallbanger	276
Gaelic Glee	90	Hawaiian Daisy	319
Gaspé	273	High Pocket	276
Gator Alley	209	Hillsborough	130
Gauguin	175	Honeydew Cooler	277
Genever Cocktail	229	Honky Tonic	277
Genoa	145	Horse's Neck with Gin	277
Georgia Rum Cooler	273	Hot Buttered Apple	378
Gibson	158	Hot Buttered Irish	378
Gimlet	145	Hot Buttered Rum	379
Gin and Campari	109	Hot Coconut Coffee	379
Gin and Ginger Cooler	273	Hot Cocoribe Orangeade	380
Gin and It	159	Hot Drambuie Toddy	380
Gin and Jerry	378	Hot Eggnog	380
Gin and Lime	145	Hot Grapefruit Mug	380
Gin Aquavit	146	Hot Irish and Port	381
Gin Bracer	353	Hot Licorice Stick	381
Gin Buck	240	Hot Line	381
Gin Cassis	146	Hot Mocha Chocolate	382
Gin Daiquiri	146	Hot Port Flip	382
Gin Daisy	319	Hot Toddy	382
Gin Fizz	329	Hudson Bay	148
Gingerman	90	Hurricane	176
Gin Mint Fix	323		
Gin Mist	350	Iced Coffee Oporto	315
Gin Old-fashioned	146	Iced Rum Coffee	278
Gin Rickey	336	Iced Rum Tea	278
Gin Sidecar	147	Il Magnifico	91
Gin Sour	147	Independence Swizzle	278
Gin Southern	147	Indian River	210
Gin Swizzle	274	Interplanetary Punch	364
Glasgow	210	Irish Alexander on the	
Gold Cadillac	90	Rocks	91
Gold Coaster	274	Irish Almond	210
Golden Frog	91	Irish Apple Bowl	364
Golden Gate	175	Irish Canadian Sangaree	340
Golden Gin Fizz	330	Irish Coffee	383
Golden Hornet	147	Irish Eggnog	279
Granada	274	Irish Fix	324
Grand Marnier Quetsch	101	Irish Milk-and-Maple	
Granville	148	Punch	279
Grapefruit Cooler	275	Irish Tea	383
Grapefruit Nog	275	Isle of the Blessed Coconut	176
Grappa Strega	229	Italian Perfume	223
Grasshopper	91		
Grass Skirt	91	Jack and Jerry	383
Great Dane	229	Jack Rose	120
Greek Buck	240	Jackson Square	211
Green Devil	148	Jade	176
Gringo	275	Jamaica Elegance	279
Guanabana	176	Jamaica Ginger	279
Guanabana Cooler	276	Jamaica Glow	148

396 INDEX

Japanese	130	Mexico Pacifico	191
Japanese Fizz	330	Mia Vida	191
Jocose Julep	280	Midnight Sun	230
John Collins	249	Mint Collins	248
Joulouville	149	Minted Gin	149
		Mint Julep	283
Kalani Wai	92	Mint Julep, Dry, Party Style	283
Kentucky	211	Mint Spritzer	283
Kentucky Cobbler	244	Mint Tequila	191
Kerry Cooler	280	Misty Irish	284
Key Cocktail	149	Mixed Mocha Frappé	101
Kir	229	Mobile Mule	284
Kirsch Cuba Libre	280	Mocha Cobbler	244
Kirsch Nightcap	384	Mocha Cooler	284
Kirsch Rickey	336	Mocha Mint	92
Kirschwasser Mist	349	Moldau	150
Knickerbocker	160	Molokai	284
Kremlin Colonel	199	Mon Dieu	110
Kretchma	200	Monk's Wine	223
Kümmel Blackberry Frappé	101	Morning Fizz	353
		Morning-Glory Fizz	330
Lady in Green	92	Morro	150
Lait de Vie	280	Moscow Mule	285
La Jolla	130	Moselle Bowl	364
Latin Dog	281	Mountain Red Punch	365
Lawhill	211	Mulled Claret	384
Leeward	177	Mulled Kümmel	385
Lemon Rum Cooler	281	Mulled Madeira and	
Lillet Cocktail	110	Bourbon	385
Lillet Noyaux	110	Mulled Port	385
Long Suit	281	Mulled Scotch	386
Lorenzo	200	Mulled Sherry	386
		Muscari Cooler	285
Madama Rosa	281	Muscari Manhattan	220
Madeira Mint Flip	346	Muskmelon	178
Mai Tai	177		
Mandeville	177	Navy Grog	178
Mango Cooler	282	Nectarine Cooler	285
Manhasset	212	Negroni	111
Manhattan	220	Nevins	212
Manhattan Milano	110	New Orleans Buck	240
Margarita	190	New Orleans Gin Fizz	330
Marsala Martini	160	New World	212
Martinez	160	New Yorker	213
Martini	157	New York Sour	213
Martini, Holland Style	160	Night Shade	213
Mary Kümmel	230	Norteamericano	192
Matinée	149	Northern Lights	230
Maui	92	Numero Uno	92
May Cocktail	212		
McBrandy	130	Oahu Gin Sling	286
Melba Champagne	138	Ocho Rios	178
Melba Tonic	282	Old-fashioned	214
Mexican Clover Club	190	Old-fashioned Artichoke	286
Mexican Coffee	384	Old-fashioned Rum and	
Mexican Connection	191	Muscari	286
Mexican Milk Punch	282	Ophelia	231
Mexican Mule	282	Oracabessa	93

INDEX 397

Orangeade with Peppermint Schnapps	286	Pink Squirrel	95
Orange Almond Bowl	365	Pink Veranda	179
Orange Blossom	150	Pinky	290
Orange Blossom, Frozen	151	Pirouetter	151
Orange Buck	241	Pisco Sour	231
Orange Champagne	138	Pistachio Cream	95
Orange Comfort	93	Pistachio Lime Collins	248
Orange Cooler in Shell	287	Planter's Punch	290
Orange Fizz	331	Planter's Punch with Falernum	291
Orange Flower	93	Playboy Cooler	291
Orange Oasis	287	Playboy's Hot Buttered Rum	379
Orange Wake-up	353	Plum and Tonic	291
Ostend Fizz	331	Plum Aperitif	111
Ouzo Cognac Rickey	337	Plum Rickey	337
Pago Pago	179	Polish Sidecar	152
Paisley Martini	161	Polonaise	131
Palmetto Cooler	287	Polynesia	180
Panama Cooler	288	Polynesian Apple	120
Parson Weems	94	Polynesian Paradise	180
Passion Fruit Cooler	288	Polynesian Pick-Me-Up	353
Payoff	94	Polynesian Punch Bowl	366
Peace Feeler	200	Pompano	152
Peachblow Fizz	331	Ponce de León	180
Peach Buck	241	Portamento	292
Peach Cup with Chablis	316	Port and Cognac Milk Punch	292
Pear Rickey	337	Port Antonio	180
Pensacola	179	Port Arms	292
Peppermint Schnapps Fizz	332	Port Cassis	292
Perfect	161	Port Charlotte	181
Pernod and Peppermint	288	Port Cobbler	244
Pernod Curaçao Frappé	101	Port Collins	249
Pernod Drip	231	Portcullis	293
Pernod Flip	347	Port Maria	181
Pernod Martini	161	Pousse-Café	103
Petroleo	192	Prado	192
Phi Beta Blueberry	366	Prairie Oyster	354
Phoebe Snow	131	Prince Edward	214
Picasso	131	Princeton	152
Picon on the Rocks	111	Puerto Apple	120
Picon Punch	111	Puerto Rican Pink Lady	181
Pike's Picon	223	Punta Gorda	293
Pile Driver	289	Punt e Lemon	293
Pimm's Cup	289	Punt e Mes Negroni	112
Piña Colada	289		
Pineapple Mint Cooler	289	Quadruple Pineapple	294
Pink Almond	94	Quaker	131
Pink Carnation	94	Quebec	214
Pink Coconut	95		
Pink Creole	179	Rabbit's Foot	121
Pink Gin	151	Racquet Club	161
Pink Lady	151	Ramos Gin Fizz	332
Pink Lemonade à la Playboy	290	Rancho Contento	294
Pink Margarita	192	Raspberry Claret Cup	295
Pink Ribbon	95	Raspberry Rickey	338
Pink Rum and Tonic	290	Raspberry Tea	386

INDEX

Red Apple	200
Red Bait	295
Red Carpet	224
Red Cloud	152
Red Dane	295
Red Kir	224
Red Light	153, 224
Red Manhattan	224
Red Peril	295
Renaissance	153
Rendezvous	153
Rhenish Raspberry	296
Right On	153
Robber Baron	215
Rob Roy	215
Rob Roy, Holiday Style	215
Rock and Rye Cooler	296
Rock and Rye Toddy	386
Rocky Dane	154
Rocky Green Dragon	231
Roman Cooler	296
Roman Frullati	296
Rose	154
Rose Hall	181
Rosé Punch	367
Royal Gin Fizz	332
Ruby	225
Ruddy Mary	354
Rum and Coconut Cooler	297
Rum and Pineapple Cooler	297
Rum and Sherry	182
Rum and Soursop	316
Rum Aperitif	112
Rumbo	316
Rum Buck	241
Rum Cassis	182
Rum Citrus Cooler	297
Rum Coconut Fizz	332
Rum Cup with White Wine	367
Rum Curaçao Cooler	298
Rum Dubonnet	182
Rum Mist	350
Rum Old-fashioned	182
Rum Pineapple Fizz	333
Rum Royale	298
Rum Screwdriver	183
Rum Sidecar	183
Rum Sour	183
Russian Bear	201
Russian Caramel	95
Russian Coffee	96
Russian Espresso	201
Rusty Nail	215
Rye Mist	350
Saguenay	183
St. Augustine	184
St.-Croix Cooler	298
St.-Lô	154
Sake Cassis	299
Sake Sour	232
Sake Stinger	232
Sake Sunrise	299
Saketini	162
Salty Dog	201
Sambuca Coffee Frappé	102
Sanctuary	112
Sangaree Comfort	340
Sangria	367
Sangrita	193
San Juan	184
San Juan Sling	299
San Sebastian	154
Santa Fe	132
Sarasota	299
Saratoga	132
Sazerac	216
Sazerac à la Playboy	216
Sciarada Tea	387
Scorpion	184
Scotch Apple	300
Scotch Buck	241
Scotch Holiday Sour	216
Scotch Horse's Neck	300
Scotch Mist	349
Scotch Orange Fix	324
Scotch Sangaree	341
Scotch Solace	300
Screwdriver	201
Screwdriver with Sherry	300
Seaboard	217
Sea Rover	232
Señor Stinger	193
September Morn	184
Sesame	185
Seville	155
Shark's Tooth	185
Shaw Park	185
Sherried Coffee	96
Sherried Cordial Médoc Frappé	102
Sherry Caudle	387
Sherry Cobbler	245
Sherry Gimlet	232
Sherry Sour	233
Sherry Spider	233
Shinto	233
Shoo-in	301
Shoot, The	217
Shore Leave	301
Sidecar	132
Silver Kirsch	112
Simmering Plum	387
Simpatico	301
Simple Syrup	38
Singapore	217

INDEX

Singapore Gin Sling	302	Sweet Talk	97
Ski Jumper	302	Sweet William	97
Sloe and Bitter	302		
Sloe Brandy	132	Tahiti Club	186
Sloe Cranberry Cooler	302	Tall Annie	306
Sloe Dog	303	Tall Blonde	306
Sloe Down	303	Tall Dutch Eggnog	307
Sloe Gin Fizz	333	Tall French Gimlet	317
Sloe Lime Frappé	102	Tall Haole	307
Sloe Swede	303	Tall Islander	307
Sloe Tequila	193	Tall Limone	308
Sloe Vermouth	113	Tall Margarita	308
Snifter	96	Tall Midori	308
Snowberry	388	Tall Muscari	308
Snowshoe	388	Tall Order	309
Soft Landing	96	Tall Sack	309
Soft Rock	113	Tall Sardinian	309
Soft Touch	225	Tall Sunrise	309
Southern Banana Comfort	185	Tall Tawny	310
Southern Comfort Strawberry Frappé	102	Tamarind Cooler	310
		Tee Off	310
Southern Ginger	217	Tequila Colada	310
Southern Peach	96	Tequila Cooler	311
Southern Raspberry	303	Tequila Dubonnet	194
South Pacific	133	Tequila Fizz	333
South Side	155	Tequila Fresa	194
Southwest One	113	Tequila Frozen Screwdriver	194
Soviet	202	Tequila Guayaba	195
Sparkling Galliano	138	Tequila Miel	311
Spiced Apple Flip	347	Tequila Old-fashioned	195
Spiced Walnuts	359	Tequila Rickey	338
Splashdown	133	Tequila Sour	195
Steeplejack	304	Tequini	196
Stinger	133	Thumper	133
Stone Fence	304	Tiger Tail	311
Stonybrook	218	Tobacco Road	234
Stratosphere	186	Tobago	186
Strawberry Blonde	304	Tokay Flip	348
Strawberry Cream Cooler	304	Tom Collins	249
Strawberry Frozen Daiquiri	186	Torridora Cocktail	187
Strawberry Kiss	97	Tovarich	202
Strawberry Rum Flip	347	Trade Winds	187
Strawberry Swig	155	Trio	113
Strawberry Vermouth Cooler	305	Trois Rivières	218
		Turf	156
Strawberry Vin Blanc	305	12-to-1 Martini	158
Strawberry White Port	305	Twin Hills	218
Strega Flip	347		
Strega Sour	155	Ultra Suede	98
Suissesse	233	Unisphere	187
Summer Light	306		
Sunrise	193	Vampiro	311
Sunrise Anise	194	Verboten	156
Surf Rider	306	Vermouth and Ginger	312
Svetlana	202	Vermouth Cassis	114
Swedish Sidecar	234	Vermouth Cooler	312
Sweet Martini	162	Vermouth Maraschino	114
Sweet Offering	97	Vermouth Sciarada	114

400 INDEX

Vermouth Triple Sec	114	Whiskey Curaçao Fizz	334
Vesuvio	225	Whiskey Daisy	320
Via Veneto	134	Whiskey Mac	219
Villa Nova	312	Whiskey Ouzo Fix	324
Vodka Fraise	202	Whiskey Punch	368
Vodka Gimlet	203	Whiskey Sour	219
Vodka Grand Marnier	203	Whiskey Toddy, Cold	219
Vodka Martini	203	White Rose	156
Vodka Mist	349	White Sangria	368
Vodka Old-fashioned	203	White Wine Cooler	313
Vodka Sour	203	White Wine Punch	369
Vodka Stinger	204	Wine and Bitters	225
Voluptuoso	312	Woodstock	156
Ward Eight	218	Yellow Fingers	98
Warsaw	204	Yellow Plum	234
Waterbury	134	Yucatán Tonic	314
Watermelon Cassis	313		
Watermelon Cooler	313	Zaza	115
Whiskey Cobbler	245		